D1759669

Consumerism, Romance and the Wedding Experience

Consumerism, Romance and the Wedding Experience

Sharon Boden
Department of Sociology
University of Warwick

First published 2003 by
PALGRAVE MACMILLAN
Houndmills, Basingstoke, Hampshire RG21 6XS and
175 Fifth Avenue, New York, N.Y. 10010
Companies and representatives throughout the world.

PALGRAVE MACMILLAN is the global academic imprint of the Palgrave
Macmillan division of St Martin's Press, LLC and of Palgrave Macmillan Ltd.
Macmillan® is a registered trademark in the United States, United Kingdom
and other countries. Palgrave is a registered trademark in the European
Union and other countries.

ISBN 1–4039–0431–6 hardback

This book is printed on paper suitable for recycling and
made from fully managed and sustained forest sources.

A catalogue record for this book is available
from the British Library.

Library of Congress Cataloging-in-Publication Data

Boden, Sharon, 1974–
    Consumerism, romance, and the wedding experience / Sharon Boden.
        p. cm.
    Includes bibliographical references and index.
    ISBN 1–4039–0431–6
    1. Weddings–Economic aspects–United States. 2. Weddings–United
States–Equipment and supplies. 3. Marriage in popular culture–United States.
4. Consumption (Economics)–United States. 5. United States–Social life and
customs. I. Title.

HQ754.B63 2003
395.2'2–dc21

                                                        2003042912

10 9 8 7 6 5 4 3 2 1
12 11 10 09 08 07 06 05 04 03

Printed and bound in Great Britain by
Antony Rowe Ltd, Chippenham and Eastbourne

For my parents,
Anthony and Barbara

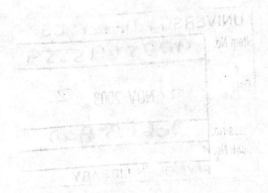

Contents

List of Figures and Tables

Figures

Tables

Acknowledgements

I would like to thank those people who have helped during the writing of this book. Carol Wolkowitz has not only sustained and encouraged me throughout the project, but also has constantly provided stimulating advice and enthusiastic suggestions – thank you. The support of Simon Williams should equally be acknowledged in this respect. Several other individuals at various universities have provided valuable suggestions and encouragement at different stages in this study, in particular Elizabeth Dowler, Simon Bainbridge, James A. Beckford, Richard Lampard, Rebecca Leach, Celia Lury, Ian Procter, Deborah Lynn Steinberg, Dale Southerton and Pnina Werbner. Joan Haran, Sally-Anne Barnes and James Mittra have been invaluable friends throughout and I am grateful to them, along with many other postgraduates in the Department of Sociology, University of Warwick. I am, of course, also heavily indebted to and appreciative of the fifteen couples who participated in this research for their interest in and commitment to the project. Some of this book is based on doctoral research funded by the Economic and Social Research Council (ESRC). Their financial assistance is gratefully acknowledged. I also appreciate the help of Heather Gibson and Jennifer Nelson at Palgrave Macmillan for their assistance in producing this book.

Most importantly, a big thank you to my parents, Barbara and Anthony, to Duncan Adam and to my whole family for their continuing love and support.

Wedding and Home / IPC Media for an extract from their June/July 1999 issue.

Wedding Day / Crimson Publishing for the cover image and extracts from their November 1999 issue.

You and Your Wedding / The National Magazine Company for extracts from their May/June 1999 issue.

Some of the arguments presented in Chapters 2 and 3 have been published elsewhere. Extracts from S. Boden, '"Superbrides": Wedding Consumer Culture and the Construction of Bridal Identity', in *Sociological Research Online*, 6 (1) (2001) http://www.socresonline.org.uk/6/1/boden. html have been reprinted by permission of Sage Publications Ltd (© BSA Publications Ltd, 2002).

Similarly, extracts from S. Boden and S. J. Williams, 'Consumption and Emotion: The *Romantic Ethic* Revisited', in *Sociology*, 36 (3) (2002) 493–512 have been reprinted by permission of Sage Publications Ltd (© BSA Publications Ltd, 2002).

Since the research for this book was undertaken, Inline Publishing Ltd, which produced *Bliss for Brides*, has ceased trading. Also, *Bride and Groom* has not been published for nearly two years and has been reinvented as *Cosmopolitan Bride*. These developments mean that there is no direct copyright holder for the issues used in this book. Every effort has been made to trace all the copyright holders but, if any have been inadvertently overlooked, the publishers will be pleased to make the necessary arrangements at the first opportunity.

1
Introduction: Consumerism, Romance and the Wedding Experience

> You may have noticed, Madam Deputy Speaker, that today every national newspaper is carrying a delightful picture of yesterday's royal wedding. I hope that you have also seen a wonderful British film called 'Four Weddings and a Funeral', which is a considerable box office hit – one of the most successful British films ever made. It is playing to marvellous business throughout this country and on five continents. It seems that the whole world loves an English wedding ...
>
> (Mr Gyles Brandreth, Third Reading of the 1994 Marriage Bill, House of Commons, 15 July 1994)[1]

Weddings are big news and big business. They were changed forever by the 1994 Marriage Act, which licensed approved premises for civil ceremonies in England and Wales. This Act was both a symptom and a source of wider underlying changes in society and in intimate relationships. The basic legal requirements necessary for a marriage to take place are certainly far removed from the catalogue of artifacts and rituals that now constitute the contemporary wedding experience.

This book is concerned with the consumption *of* a wedding. The terminology I use is indicative of a new way of looking at the wedding which has been made possible through continual advancements in the study of consumption and the consequent opening up of new areas of exploration, such as the commodification and consumption of life and calendar events. As I will go on to demonstrate later in this book, most earlier wedding research touched only occasionally on the commercial consumption involved *in* the wedding, or *for* the wedding, or *at* the wedding, rather than conceptualizing 'the wedding' as something which is produced and consumed as a whole. However, borrowing ideas developed from consumer ethnographies of tourism (Urry, 1991, 1995) and Christmas (Miller, 1993), for example, it is now possible to speak of the wedding itself as a commodity and analyse it in relation to a consumer industry that produces the bridal role in particular as a consumer identity.

Given its ubiquity and social importance though, the wedding remains relatively unexplored by academics. This book is a new study which integrates the phenomenon of the new commercial wedding more fully into sociological theory, addressing some central issues in the consumer culture literature along the way. It provides data on the beliefs and actions of English brides and grooms during their whole wedding experience. The context of their consumption is analysed in terms of the commonsenses constructed and circulated in popular culture that give meaning to the occasion. I investigate wedding consumption in the light of changes initiated in 1994 – changes which are also occurring or are likely to occur in other Westernized countries – and also consider the ideological output of the wedding industry and the depiction of weddings in the popular media. In particular, using Colin Campbell's (1987) concept of a 'Romantic ethic' as a point of departure, this book highlights the emotional and imaginative dimensions of wedding consumption, and explores the legacies of Romanticism, the practice of self-illusory hedonism, and the conceptualization (as well as the *experiencing* and *gendering*) of reason/emotion relations in contemporary consumer culture. At the same time though, broader connections are demonstrated between these themes and the interpersonal and social structural relations in which wedding consumption takes place.

This chapter introduces the study by contextualizing current sociological understandings of consumption and Romanticism, before moving on to consider the changing nature of the wedding and its relationship to wider family, kin and community structures and processes, including contemporary understandings of marriage, romantic love and gender. I conclude with an outline of the book's structure and content.

The assumptions of consumption

... there can be few topics in which most of the population and most academics share a set of ideological assumptions which bear so little resemblance to any scholarly information we have on a particular subject. Without an explicit repudiation of the clichés, it will remain very difficult to embark on any considered attempt to characterise the actual imperatives behind consumption. (Miller, 1995, p. 20)

As a concluding remark to a section entitled 'What is Consumption?' Miller's (1995, p. 34) assertion that 'consumption as a topic cannot therefore be usefully defined' appears to have gone unnoticed by many academic writers in this area. Not only is usage of the term 'consumption' continually being redefined, as a target of academic analysis 'consumption' has expanded from a mere 'topic' into a concept, an ideology, a symbol, a process and a way of life – in short, 'consumption' is now an all-embracing, generalized phenomenon. Although Bocock (1993, p. 120) may be correct in emphasizing that 'Literally, "consumption" means the use of commodities for the satisfaction of needs and desires', the literal meanings of the term are usually disregarded in favour of more cultural, social and political significations. A brief perusal of the relevant literature reveals the meanings of consumption being employed in anything but their literal senses. Appleby (1993, p. 171), for instance, states that 'consumption registers the range of human satisfactions'. Nava (1992, p. 185) claims it to be a 'powerful and evocative symbol of contemporary capitalism'. Lee (1993, p. xiii, original emphasis) describes consumption as '*the* social activity which, above all others, unites economy and culture', whilst Tomlinson (1991, p. 31) argues, nevertheless, that consumer culture 'remains a social and economic construction'.

Yet, interestingly, what does not follow from this conceptual ambiguity is an implosion of meaning, stunting or making void the application of such frameworks by consumption theorists. Rather, there has developed a wide range of terms for deconstructing consumption at different levels. This 'language of consumption', as Campbell (1995, p. 101) puts it, has become rich in descriptive detail and theoretical understanding. We may speak with knowledge of vertical and horizontal consumption (Fine and Leopold, 1993), distinguish the functions and values of consumption (Warde, 1992), compare consumer ethics, logics and spirits (Campbell, 1987), discuss consumerism and consumerist individuals (Abercrombie, 1994), debate consumer politics (Corner, 1994), and consider the commodification of consumption (Giddens, 1991). It has become useful and imperative not just to *define* consumption, but to understand how the ramifications of this concept, and the terminology that surrounds it, can help sociologists more accurately describe, predict and analyse contemporary human activity.

Above all, consumption tells us about human relations. Relations with material objects, that is, between shoppers and the products they buy; relations between the individual and society, the consumer and the market; personal and cultural engagements with the imagination, the body and identity; and the relations of gender, age, class and 'race'. Consumption is itself an experience, one that is both 'materialistic' and 'mentalistic' in nature, and one that is shaped by what goods and services are available in the marketplace and how they are appropriated into existing social practices. It is, of course, a socially embedded and embodied phenomenon, put to use throughout centuries for the purposes of social emulation and imitation, as a means of social display and communication, and as a strategy in the power games of competing social groups. Campbell's (1995) definition of consumption in fact seems most sensitive to the broad scope of the phenomenon, taking into account as it does these multiple related issues. Consumption, for him, constitutes any activity 'involving the selection, purchase, use, maintenance, repair and disposal of any product or service' (Campbell, 1995, p. 102). In addition to this emphasis upon the wide-ranging dynamics of consumption, there must be a continual appreciation of how understandings of consumption develop through time. Any baggage that the concept of consumption carries with it into contemporary sociological debate needs to be seen in part through a historical perspective.

As I have already mentioned, this book is informed by Colin Campbell's (1987) work on the Romantic dimensions of consumption. Yet whilst it engages with the Romantic ethic thesis, it also departs from it to a certain extent to consider wedding consumption within a broader framework – a framework which not only acknowledges alternative approaches to consumption and consumerism, but one that remains sensitive to the significance of changing social structures and processes. At this juncture then, I will briefly outline several other perspectives on consumption that have influenced the content of this book. For the sake of clarity and simplicity, I identify these as 'Veblenesque', 'manipulationist', 'postmodern', 'social relations' and 'feminist'.

A Veblenesque perspective concentrates on the signs and symbols communicated through the consumption of material goods. Veblen's (1925) original thesis identified the practice of 'conspicuous consumption' by the *noveaux riches* of the late nineteenth century. Consumption was, for them, a purposive activity of social display, undertaken strategically to impress onlookers and to exude wealth and status. As an index of one's location in the social structure, consumer goods were either appropriated or rejected in relation to class fashions. Above all, consumption was characterized by the imitative and emulative behavioural motivations of its participants. As Campbell (1987, p. 49) has rightly acknowledged, both Veblen's writing and more recent developments of his ideas, although limited in their considerations of the functions and outcomes of consumption, endorse it as an activity of 'profound socio-cultural significance'.

Manipulationist approaches to the study of consumption are most often associated with the neo-Marxist writers of the Frankfurt School, in particular Adorno and Horkheimer (1977) and Marcuse (1964). Such critics of mass consumerism argued that advertising and other ideological institutions in consumer culture transmitted discursive meanings that were generated by those in hegemonic positions of power. Marcuse (1964, p. 8) specifically attacked mass media as 'agents of manipulation and indoctrination' which served the interests of the ruling classes by creating 'false needs'. The satisfaction of such 'false needs' through consumption was ultimately dependent upon the economic resources of the consumer, causing Marcuse to interpret the indirect consequences of advertising as tying the individual into the capitalist system. Consumerism, in effect, was a capitalist tool. Not only did the culture industry's generation of 'false needs' and subsequent promises of liberation in the marketplace exploit consumers, it prevented the genuine repression of the subordinate classes from ever being consciously realized.

Several other writers have also strengthened this theorization of consumer culture. Packard (1957) has written from the extreme end of perspectives which stress the manipulative side of consumption temptations. From this standpoint, advertising is the product of a conspiracy attempting to control the thought processes of potential purchasers. Creating consumer anxieties, hopes and fears, advertisers, he argues, have begun to add new psychological depth to their images which 'channel our unthinking habits, our purchasing decisions' (Packard, 1957, p. 11). Similarly, Ewen (1976) suggests that the ideological control superimposed by the advertising industry is a disturbing example of the extension of bureaucratic, corporate surveillance over individual, creative autonomy. As a generalization, then, the manipulationist model of consumption assumes that consumers are *acted upon* by the commercial culture industry. Often appearing pessimistic and moralistic in tone, such theories have been widely critiqued for constructing an over-simplistic and deterministic relationship between the homogenizing powers of mass culture and the supposed passive response of duped consumers (Robins, 1994).

Whilst Veblenesque and manipulationist approaches remain significant undercurrents in present-day debates on consumption, there has been a very definite attention shift by sociologists towards examining the practices of consumption in a supposedly 'postmodern' climate. One of the most prominent writers on the logics of postmodern consumption is the French social theorist Jean Baudrillard (1998). According to Baudrillard, in postmodern, media-saturated societies the sign-value and use-value of material goods have become divorced. The disconnection of the symbolic and the real generates a simulational culture in which commodities are purchased primarily for their sign-value. It is this material obsession with the symbolic that supplies the momentum of a postmodern consumer culture. The inscription of meaning onto commodities promotes a type of dialogue through material objects, enabling them to exist as creative tools that aid the expressive performance of self-identity. Consumption, in this sense, becomes a site of play, performance, spectacle and symbolic creativity. Consumers become composers of their worlds rather than mere representers – the implication being that consumption is an active, symbolic form of identity construction. Giddens (1991, p. 100), for instance, argues that the increasingly significant relationship between consumption and individuality, the 'project of the self', is an example of the reflexive attention paid to the body in conditions of high or postmodernity.

Theorists following a postmodernist approach to reconceptualizing consumption have certainly provided some original and stimulating, if sometimes contentious, interpretations. Many continue to explore the theoretical links between consumer culture, consumption and the core conditions of postmodernity. Critical postmodernists, however, are somewhat sceptical about the benign consequences of these sorts of developments. Jameson (1985), for example, drawing from Baudrillard's system of signs thesis, argues that the disconnections and uncertainties that overwhelm us in postmodernity have serious consequences for human society. Postmodern culture is described as 'schizophrenic', where life is lived under ceaseless disorienting and panic-like conditions (Jameson, 1985). The explosion of symbolic capital creates a depthless culture devoid of any 'real' personality or individuality. Whilst material objects may communicate social and individual differentiation, consumers are left as mere empty vehicles for expressing these differences (Lury, 1996). In other words, the somewhat superficial consumption of styles, images and signs is prioritized at the expense of 'real' substance and content (Lash and Urry, 1994; Strinati, 1994). Featherstone (1991, p. 60), furthermore, warns that a postmodern approach to the study of consumption tends to involve more 'abstracted' and 'hypostatized' discussions, leaving many of the fundamental 'who, when, why and how many' questions unanswered.

Researching from what I will term the 'social relations' perspective on consumption seems to be the emergent theme of a new era in the study of consumer culture, in part because it deals with precisely these sorts of questions. Here one can identify a subtle shift away from the social dislocations of (some) postmodern consumer culture theory. On the whole, though, the general impression given by such writings is not to deny the claims of postmodernists about the highly symbolic and stylistic nature of much consuming, but rather to throw into critical relief some of their assumptions and to supplement their theoretical work with more grounded, balanced and maybe more realistic accounts of the consuming experience. Sociologists are (as always) keen to identify the social context of consumption which underwrites individual expression, whether conceptualized as postmodern or otherwise. Edgell and Hetherington (1996, p. 5), for example, critique the 'underlying individualism' they believe currently pervades consumption studies, insisting instead that 'social relations shape the experience of consuming'.

The ideas of French social theorist Pierre Bourdieu (1984, 1993) seem to provide the launchpad for many studies of consumption which aim to avoid the postmodern downplaying of structural determinants. In particular, via his concept of habitus, 'a set of dispositions which generates practices and perception' (1993, p. 5), and the very embodiment of taste, Bourdieu provides a socially embedded account of consumption and the struggle for social distinction. Reverberations, explicit or implicit, of Bourdieu's ideas abound in consumer culture literature. Lury (1996, p. 83), for example, describes how taste is 'socially patterned', and alludes to the ways consumption is implicated as a mechanism of social reproduction. Warde (1992, 1994a, 1994b), too, in a number of articles often pitched against the one-sided individualistic models of consumption proposed by Giddens (1991), Beck (1992), and especially Bauman (1992), argues that current theorizing on consumption portrays the consumer as an under-socialized agent. In Warde's opinion, such writers emphasize the supposed symbolic struggles each consumer experiences at an individual level without fully acknowledging the simultaneous social, and by extension, material hierarchies in which they are located.

'The practices of the poor,' Warde reminds us, 'are a foil to accounts that see the contemporary world revolving around the play of signs and images' (1992, p. 26). Rather, consumption is put to use for a number of other purposes, each being equally as relevant as the much cited self-identity quest: 'People also use commodities to exercise power, to express indifferences to others and to manipulate social situations in accordance with personal ambition' (Warde, 1994b, p. 66). The appropriation or rejection of signs and images may to a certain extent characterize contemporary consumption, but, it is argued, this practice can never achieve total autonomy from external, structural determinants – as Warde puts it, *'people play with the signs they can afford'* (1992, p. 26, original emphasis). From this perspective, as I argued earlier in this chapter, consumption is, as it always has been, a socially embedded and embodied phenomenon, a fact that current and future research agendas must remain alive to.

Feminist literature on consumption is wide-ranging and extensive. Yet for the purposes of this brief tour of consumption perspectives, I prioritize two issues – the identities of women as consumers and the feminist deconstruction of media texts, with particular reference to the relationship between advertising and gender. These issues, plus many more raised by feminist research, have already significantly shaped the agenda of consumption studies and will no doubt continue to do so for years to come. Consumption is, of course, heavily implicated in the construction of gender identity. This fact is linked to the now well-established notion of 'gender' (as the behaviour, roles, temperament, expectations and so on associated with the social construction of femininity) as something separate and distinct from 'sex' (as biological and inherent natural difference). Consumption, that is to say, is heavily implicated in the production and exaggeration of gender identity (Costa, 1994). For some feminists, at least, the sphere of consumption exists as another site in which women are exploited and subordinated; assumed to be 'cultural dopes' within a consumer culture manipulated by male power.

To this classic feminist argument we can add the more recent insights of postmodern feminists who suggest that consumer culture offers us a world of possibilities in which 'gender' identity can be put on or taken off at will in playful or ironic imitation of ideals or norms of appearance. Following Butler (1990), 'gender' becomes (re)presented and (re)invented in a continual circuit of identity construction and performance. Performing gender through consumption is interpreted by postmodern feminists as 'the refusal to embody *any* positioned subjectivity at all; what is celebrated is continued creative escape from location, containment and definition' (Bordo, 1993, p. 281). A liberation or emancipation, then, to a certain extent – of which 'Madonna' is to some the most celebrated example (Schwichtenberg, 1993) – from the binds of fixed gender scripts.

Feminist research has been invaluable for illuminating the historical processes which led to consumption being socially perceived as a feminine task. Firat (1994), among many others, argues that modernity ordered society along strict gendered lines through the separation of spheres. Processes of production and of consumption were not only gendered by modernity but attributed differential prestige, worth, value and overall importance in the social world – the former forming part of the masculine, public sphere, the latter located in the feminine, private sphere. Furthermore, as part of this dichotomization of the significations of gender, women were characterized as passive, emotional subjects (as opposed to their counterparts – the active, rational male actor) within whom desire can be induced and control can be exercised over perception, behaviour and, ultimately, over their motivations to consume.

Feminists have therefore argued that since the early nineteenth century the identities of 'woman', 'housewife' and 'consumer' were, effectively, one and the same (Loeb, 1994; see also Miller, 1995); consuming was regarded as an extension of the domestic labour primarily undertaken by women. Loeb, in fact, notes an important development in the relationship women had to consumption occurring in the Victorian period – the ramifications of this, as we shall see, still being apparent today. With freer leisure time and an increased propensity to consume, the Victorian middle-class housewife herself became the object of advertising texts. Women, it is argued, were encouraged to invest the same amounts of time, effort and money traditionally reserved for domestic and familial consumption in their own quests for beauty. There was, for instance, a great explosion in advertisements for the latest fashions, hair products, perfumes and skin creams. Advertisements such as these constructed a commercially defined femininity in which women, through consumption, were prompted to cultivate a refined, ornamental appearance to display to others (Loeb, 1994).

Aspects of Victorian domestic ideology, then, in particular what was considered appropriate feminine behaviour and what activity women should invest their labours in, found clear material and commercial expression. Winship (1987) has further argued that this idea of the 'work' of consumption being an exclusively feminine enterprise is still an assumption of late modern consumer culture. The continuing role of the media, and advertising texts especially, in the marketing and deployment of cultural commonsenses therefore remains an important feminist research interest. Such research has often tried to expose the strategies employed by advertisers, journalists and other media producers to mobilize positive consumer action through explicit or implicit gendered significations (Winship, 1987; McCracken, 1993; Williamson, 1993; Van Zoonen, 1994). Advertisements, as well as the media texts in which they are often located, are argued to exist as discursive sites for the reproduction of and challenge against conventional relations of gender and sexuality (and also a range of other social divisions and inequalities).

Winship (1981), for instance, has suggested that advertising 'genders' products and, as such, can be said to be selling a form of gender ideology. It is 'not just commodities' that are available to be marketed and consumed 'but also our personal relationships in which we are *feminine*' (Winship, 1981 p. 218, original emphasis). Certainly, as advertisements get more sophisticated it becomes increasingly difficult to disentangle the ideological package from the product itself. Women consumers may be encouraged to buy this or that product through an implied identification with the 'subject position' of 'mother', 'housewife', 'sexually attractive woman' signalled by the model in the advertisement (Winship, 1981, p. 218). This process of gender signification is so advanced that it extends well beyond the visual and discursive frame of the advertisement itself to one's sense of self as a female consumer.

Disparities and dualities in consumption studies

So far, this brief sketch of a number of consumption perspectives has made clear that the subject is riddled with differing assumptions, some of which can be traced as continuities through certain perspectives whilst some can be identified as competing explanations. According to Miller (1995, p. 20), it is this 'dead wood' which surrounds consumption, in particular its moral implications and social consequences, that needs to be removed or at least explicitly recognized before consumption studies can advance into a 'more mature phase'. Consumption studies, it seems, has continually defined its object of inquiry through an expanding series of dualities. These pairings range from the simplistic notion of consumption being either 'good' or 'bad' for us (Miller, 1995, pp. 28–30; Bocock, 1993, p. 110), a practice that one should be clearly 'for' or 'against' (Featherstone, 1991, p. 34), to a number of other paired assumptions. Dichotomies such as agency/structure, active/passive, autonomy/manipulation, masculine/feminine, empowerment/ repression, creativity/constraint, commodification/authenticity, public/private have long been put to use to classify the consumption experience and to construct a profile of 'the consumer' in academic writing. In fact, a key theoretical concern of this book – the consequences of dualistic conceptions of reason/emotion, mind/body relations for contemporary notions of the Romantic consumer – is but one example of how dualistic thinking has shaped consumer research for many years.

Several suggestions have been put forward to explain the seeming disparities and dualities in accounts of consuming and of the consumer. Robins (1994), for example, implicates the generational development of consumption studies as a major shaping force in the literature – that is, each generation of consumption theorists shifts its focus of attention and which aspects of consumption they privilege, downplay or regard as commonplace, often celebrating what the previous generation deplored; a type of academic 'oedipal struggle', he argues, for better or worse (Robins, 1994, p. 451).

In a similar vein, Warde (1996, p. 311) highlights the 'continuing stand-off' between the various social science disciplines, especially cultural studies and political economy, in the sociological approach to consumption. For example, the current 'cultural turn' of much sociological work has undoubtedly influenced the way consumption is theorized and researched. Consumption has, by the late twentieth century, become a sphere of interest in the circuit of capital. It is now regarded by most sociologists as a fluid, ongoing, complicated process with its own internal logics and structures that are influenced but not determined by traditional social-structural factors. The field of consumption, however, remains in Warde's (1996, pp. 302, 311) view 'widely dispersed and highly fragmented', with a series of 'partial, competing perspectives' jostling with each other for pre-eminence.

Greater dialogue, to be sure, must take place between the many sub-fields and strands of thought and research in consumption studies as elsewhere. This leads me to a final point in this section. Whilst my book prioritizes the relationship between consumption and emotion (using Campbell's Romantic ethic thesis as a starting point – see next section), many issues I raise nonetheless anticipate and echo broader debates within consumer culture and beyond. These, for example, following the sequence of perspectives outlined above, include: the extent to which wedding consumption may be conspicuous, that is, put to use for the purposes of social (and celebrity) emulation and display; the role of the wedding industry and wedding imagery in the popular media in mobilizing and manipulating consumer desire and (false) needs; the possible existence of a 'postmodern' wedding, its characteristics and meanings; the way social context, structured as it is by class, gender, age and 'race', influences consumption; the differential effects and affects of wedding consumption and the rhetoric of the wedding industry (especially its deployment of romantic ideology) for the bride and groom. In doing so, and in the context of consuming for a wedding, this book will not only explore the relevance of these competing perspectives but also further develop their connection to understandings of emotion, romance and Romanticism in the consumption experience.

Researching the Romantic ethic

> The riddle of the modern consumer and the whole consumer society inevitably confronts us with questions concerning a) the *constitution of desire* exceeding the '*necessary*', b) the *limitlessness* of the desire and c) the endless longing for the *new*. (Falk, 1994, p. 94, original emphasis)

Thinking through what has become commonplace in consumption studies brings us sooner or later to the issue of *consumer desire* – the deeply embodied and socially embedded emotional and imaginative impulses that underpin much consuming behaviour. Campbell's contribution to the consumer culture literature revolves around just this particular issue, attempting to explain the origin and nature of the compulsion to consume as largely independent from the manipulations of the market and socio-cultural influences in general. As such, Campbell is fairly dismissive of 'manipulation' or 'emulation' theories of consumption since he disconnects consumption from the shifting relationship between individual and society in which other theorists (such as Bourdieu or Baudrillard) see it emerging. Desire, according to Campbell's Romantic ethic, results instead from autonomous mentalistic activity (that is, the conscious monitoring and manipulation of emotion and motivation), thus 'pre-existing' the machinations of the commercial sector.

Although the following chapter provides a substantial analysis and critique of Romantic consumption, two points deserve making at this stage. First, whilst Campbell's perspective, along with those who have engaged with his work, provides important insights into how individuals imaginatively experience the act of consumption and how they deal with, or manage, its associated emotions, the central assumptions of the Romantic ethic are long overdue for thorough empirical investigation. In particular, what has not received much critical sociological attention is Campbell's conceptual model of the 'rational passion' involved in consumption – one which facilitates an interesting exploration of the persistence of reason/emotion and other pairings as oppositional categories in the consumption litera-ture. Nor have there been many attempts to explore the relevance of a Romantic ethic within the social and interpersonal relations of consumers.

Second, concerning Campbell's use of 'Romanticism', one can make reference to ongoing debates about this term in consumption studies, as elsewhere (Fay, 1998). Certainly, a feature of twentieth-century sociological debate has been the confusion and hostility with which Romanticism and other derived ideas from the Romantic period are treated, resulting in these ideas bearing 'heavily unfavourable' connotations (Williams, 1976, p. 231). Similarly, one could also argue that mass consumption too has come to occupy an equally equivocal position in social theory, as few commentators are willing to fully endorse the possibilities offered by consumer culture without some reference to its uncertain or dubious effect on society. Indeed, it would not be unfair to suggest that the negativity associated with both Romanticism and consumption is doubled when they are theorized as integrated phenomenon. For example, whilst Tomlinson concedes that consumption can be 'a passionate ex-perience, an expressive act', this celebratory tone is quickly kept in check by a cautionary warning that could have easily been taken from a critique of Romantic idealism – 'It can also appear vulgar, selfishly indulgent and sadly bathetic' (Tomlinson, 1991, p. 17).[2]

However, some sociologists see affinity rather than antagonism between sociology and the Romantic vision. If indeed there exists a 'Romantic ingredient' in modern consumer behaviour, there is no shortage of texts which identify the major themes of the original Romantic movement. Sociological discussions identify both Romanticism and realism as influential concepts within the disci-pline (Gouldner, 1973; Silverman, 1989; Strong and Dingwall, 1989; Wolfe, 1995). Nisbet's (1977) work in particular stands out as the most insightful recognition of the close affinity between sociological inquiry and the compulsions of Romanticism. As he puts it:

> I have also been struck repeatedly by the number of instances in which visions, insights and principles native to sociology in its classical period were anticipated, were set forth in almost identical shape and intensity, by artists, chiefly Romantic, in the nineteenth century. We cannot take away from Tocqueville, Marx, Weber and the other sociologists the visions for which they are famous: visions of mass society, industrialism, bureaucracy, and the like. But we live in ignorance if we do not see clearly these same visions, albeit stated differently, in the earlier writing of such minds as Burke, Blake, Carlyle, Balzac and a score of others whose reactions to the democratic and industrial revolutions created a pattern of consciousness that the sociologists and others in philosophy and the sciences fell into later. (Nisbet, 1977, p. 8)

Literary theory examines the history and ideas of the Romantic movement (Schenk, 1966; Furst, 1972; Lockridge, 1989), tracing 'what has come down to us as Romanticism' and how its legacies have 'shaped our thought and experience in manifold ways' (Larmore, 1996, p. xv). The major strands of Romanticism can therefore be separated out analytically – the supplantation of imagination over rationality as the superior human faculty; a critique of formalism, constructed artificiality, and conformity of all kinds; the reorientation towards nature as an animate and awesome being, which extends to include the supernatural; a questioning of the relationship between the self and the external environment, often leading to a melancholic world sadness, or *Weltschmerz*; the idealization of love as a synthesis of romantic passion, spiritual regeneration and (hetero)sexual union; and an emphasis on personal creativity as autonomous, individualistic and expressive.

Recently, Romanticism or the persistence of a Romantic spirit or ethic has been used to provide fresh insights for issues as diverse as environmental protest (Veldman, 1994); film theory and film makers (McConnel, 1975); vegetarianism (Adams, 1990); science fiction (Kroeber, 1988); the formation and stabilization of self and group identity (Wilson, 1986); authorship (Woodmansee and Jaszi, 1994); and tourism (Urry, 1991, 1995). Yet despite Campbell's observations, made over a decade ago, concerning the lack of sociological interest in Romanticism, and his own impressive attempts to redress this neglect within consumer culture theory, until this present study little empirical research has been undertaken on the possible persistence of a Romantic spirit animating the motivations of contemporary consumers.

The changing social and cultural significance of the wedding

Engaging with the idea of 'Romantic consumption' then, this book takes the 'new' commercial wedding in Britain as a case study to add fresh insight to sociological debates on the motivations that underpin consumer behaviour. Whereas before 1994 the law recognized only civil marriages in a registry office, the 1994 Marriage Act in England and Wales enabled couples to marry by civil ceremony outside their district of residence and introduced the ability to marry in 'approved premises'.[3] Licensing more unconventional premises for civil marriages (for example, castles, football clubs, stately homes) was indeed a significant step in bringing the wedding occasion into closer alignment with the issues of consumer choice and the aesthetization and individualization of the life-course. This leads me at this point to recognize that the changing social and cultural significance of the wedding does not just implicate commercialism and consumerism as important contributing factors, but also its relationship to wider family, kin and community structures and processes, including contemporary understandings of marriage, romantic love and gender.

Tracing the effects of social, legal and economic processes upon marriage and the wedding occasion certainly highlights these additional issues, a number of which stem from changes in the nature of relationships between men and women. Rituals of courtship and marriage have of course developed over centuries. The British marriage practice, from the early Middle Ages onwards, was always a public ceremony – whether religious or secular – which not only united husband and wife but also involved the joining of families, peers and neighbours in a collective process (Gillis, 1985). Courtship, moreover, was characterized by a series of negotiations between the groom, his family and the bride's kinsmen to agree the formal transfer of the bride from one male to another. Common law arrangements until the nineteenth century in turn reflected the disparate status of men and women within marriage through incorporating the legal existence of the woman into that of her husband's, and by sanctioning that a woman's property (and the woman herself *as* property) be passed into the hands of the man she was to marry.

Yet, from the 1850s onwards, an increase in the number of wage-earning wives combined with a growing feminist consciousness among some women led to transformations in the legal status of women and the acknowledgement of married women's property rights.[4] Pahl's (1989) work is insightful here in showing how historical and legal changes in the relations (especially the economic relations) of husbands and wives have impacted on contemporary marriage. In particular, Pahl notes how the traditional assumption of the husband as 'breadwinner' and of the wife as 'dependant' has gradually been eroded and been replaced, she proposes, by a number of different systems of money allocation within marriage – the most prevalent of which (within more or less stable or happy couples) being the *pooling system* or *shared management* system of money whereby couples have a joint account into which both incomes are paid, have equal access to this account and have shared responsibility for expenditure (Pahl, 1989, p. 71).[5]

These issues, in turn, feed into a broader set of changes in the reasons people marry and in the roles and responsibilities men and women expect to have once married. To a certain extent, as Giddens (1992) and Beck and Beck-Gernsheim (1995) discuss, important transformations have taken place in the character of intimate relationships. Contemporary sociological accounts of changes in romantic love like these provide a useful context for the emergence of the wedding as a union of two individuals who *choose* to commit to each other.

We are living, according to such writers, in an era of late or high modernity where *reflexivity* permeates every facet of our lives. One of Beck's (1992) arguments, for instance, forming part of his observations on the 'risk society' and 'reflexive modernity', is the freeing of the individual from the bonds of social structural relations, including religious and family ties, hence a corresponding erosion of 'traditional' values and assumptions of the 'proper' or 'standard' way things should be done. Whilst, in this sense, self-identity is said to have been liberated, to a certain extent, through a lack of traditional authority brought about in the absence of clear rituals or guidelines, such newfound freedoms bring with them an ever-expanding array of choices and decisions. In the case of the contemporary British wedding, the choices one may face as a 'consumer' of this occasion seem endless – not simply whether or not to marry, but where to do it, what theme to choose, what budget to set, who to turn to for advice, what insurance policy to take out, which exhibition to visit and so on.

Individuality then, we are told, along with reflexivity, is equally a major structuring factor in our interpersonal relationships. According to Beck and Beck-Gernsheim (1995, p. 6), the processes of individualization – that is, the freeing of men and women from the gender roles prescribed by industrial society for life in the nuclear family – have led to a situation where the family is no longer the central or exclusive referent for identity construction, but has been replaced by the labour market and its demand for a functional, committed, ambitious, mobile and altogether independent workforce of 'individuals'. Intimate relationships may still involve 'sex, affection, marriage, parenthood', but they can no longer remain isolated from the influences of 'work, profession, inequality, politics and economics' (1995, p. 13). Issues of emancipation and equal rights, in particular, are now infused into the private sphere and consequently shape everyday relationships between men and women.

Yet the growth of the (reflexive) individual has not necessarily signalled the demise of romantic love, intimate companionship or, indeed, the family. In fact, Beck and Beck-Gernsheim argue quite the opposite. The more individual we become, the more we need a 'significant other' with whom to share the hopes and fears, gains and losses experienced through release from traditional norms. Love therefore, in this context, becomes more important than ever – an antidote to modern living, representing 'a sort of refuge in the chilly environment of our affluent, impersonal, uncertain society, stripped of its traditions and scarred by all kinds of risk' (Beck and Beck-Gernsheim, 1995, p. 2).

Given that 'love' and loving relationships, especially romantic and sexual ones, are the new centre around which our now detraditionalized lives revolve, different types of intimate unions are developing – 'informal' marriage or cohabitation, 'contractual' or 'companiate' marriage, Giddens' democratic 'pure relationship'[6] – permutations of which emphasize a relationship of sexual, emotional and economic equality between partners and in turn signify a marked transition from the idea of marriage as an *institution* to marriage as a *relationship* (Finch and Summerfield, 1991). Set in the context of these wider social and interpersonal transformations, then, the contemporary wedding has become increasingly significant as an occasion *chosen* by brides and grooms, prepared and performed by and for *each other*, and, increasingly, as a forum for decision-making and the negotiation of roles and responsibilities within the relationship, especially the thorny question of 'who pays for what?'

The above discussions certainly lead us to conclude that the 1994 Marriage Act was in part a symptom of wider underlying changes in contemporary understandings of marriage and intimate relationships. If the Parliamentary debates detailing the rationale for the introduction of the Act are examined,[7] it becomes evident that, in response to feedback in the consultation process from various professional societies, corporate bodies and voluntary organizations as well as the views of the general public, Parliament wished to modernize and reform the registration service to give Local Authorities greater scope and flexibility to deliver a service geared to the needs of the local population. The existing laws on marriage, enacted in 1949, were deemed to be out of date, restrictive and unsuitable as they did not give couples who wanted to get married the same rights and choices as those in other countries. In fact, at that time, as MPs correctly noted, marrying couples were beginning to 'vote with their feet' and marry abroad in the search of a romantic day – the typical British registry office being described in this debate as 'not sufficiently stylish or large' (*Hansard* 1994, column 1327).

Plans are also afoot, at the time of writing, for further modernizing the civil wedding. These plans, proposed in a Government White Paper (January 2002) and likely to be implemented by 2004, concern the licensing of 'celebrants' – that is, civil registrars or certified clerics from recognized faiths – who will be able to declare marriages legal under British law. Approximately 15,000 celebrants will be responsible for ensuring the chosen venue for the wedding ceremony is safe and appropriate, with public access, and that the solemnity and dignity of the occasion will be preserved.[8]

Therefore, with the licensing of new approved premises for civil marriages and the anticipated licensing of celebrants, combined with the historical secularization of society, it is true to say that contemporary weddings do not have a fixed, 'traditional' nature or meaning. The wedding nowadays, for example, no longer marks the 'birth' of a couple, since more first marriages are preceded with pre-marital cohabitation than not.[9] There is also often a transparent reordering of the sequence of marriage then parenthood as it is now not uncommon for couples to celebrate weddings accompanied by their children. To these points we may add the reality of current divorce statistics[10] as well as the remarriage rate[11] – further evidence to challenge the assumption that a bride's own 'big day' will be a once in a lifetime event and that the relationship it celebrates will last forever. Of course, one of the key implications of all this is an erosion of the 'traditional' bridal identity and the ideals of innocence, virginity and purity it signified.

Following from these legislative and demographic changes, the subject matter of this book seems to be tapping into a growing public consciousness of changes in the ways couples choose to marry, and interest in the possible reasons for such changes over and above the legal opportunity that now exists.[12] A recent article in *She* magazine

(July 1999, pp. 27–30), for instance, typifies the resurgence of popular interest in the significance of the wedding as an irreplaceable, emotional experience. It reads:

> This need for intense emotions is just one more example of the dramatic shift in the *Zeitgeist*. Since the Middle Ages, logic, rationalism and academic learning have been consistently top dog in our evaluation of human qualities – but not so anymore ... There are some moments in life where we don't have to try too hard to feel a lot. Now we'll be putting even more effort into ensuring that these experiences more than live up to our expectations. Compare the pragmatic weddings of the 70s with today's lavish spectacles. The emotional significance is underlined with romantic symbols at every juncture, from hand-made invitations (Posh and Beckham even had a 'home-made' coat of arms) to rose petals fluttering down on the happy couple.

Having a wedding today, particularly when there are so many apparent reasons not to, becomes celebrated for the heady, romantic pleasures of the day itself, thereby disassociating the image of the wedding somewhat from that of the marriage and, especially, the married life it presages.

In light of these changes to the role of the wedding and, by implication, its leading lady, one might argue that current emphasis upon the wedding as a *cultural* event or performance which generates its meaning primarily through consumerism and romance (rather than, say, religion) counterbalances any wavering belief or confidence in the wedding as a necessary social rite of passage. The wedding may no longer always be a genuinely religious celebration (even if it takes place in a religious setting), but rather exists as a cultural performance which, ideally, should express and display the romantic commitment of two people. Similarly, one could further suggest here that the additional emphasis upon training women as successful wedding consumers (that is, as 'superbrides'; see Chapter 3) is a strategy of the wedding industry to deflect attention from the 'institution' of marriage and its apparent crisis. In fact, as we shall see later in this book, in negotiating her own complex and demanding identity, the 'superbride' is required to focus exclusively upon the wedding and not the marriage she is entering into.

An additional reason for choosing the contemporary commercial wedding as the focus of this present book is to trace the workings of a

Romantic ethic within contemporary consumer behaviour. As I shall go on to discuss in the following chapter, the longstanding historical thematic and conceptual connections between literary Romanticism, romance and romantic emotion suggest, at least theoretically, that consumers are more likely to be involved in Romantic, hedonistic acts of consumption if they are linked to a romantic event, place or relationship. Weddings, because of their traditional romantic con-notations, combined with their potential for aesthetic and phenome-nological impact, are therefore an excellent example to investigate in what sense the experience of consuming in an overtly romantic context might be underpinned by a Romantic ethic. They also allow us to think through the relationship of Romantic consumption to popular, commodified expressions of romance as they exist within inti-mate, heterosexual partnerships.

At the beginning of the twenty-first century, then, the romantic, imaginary quality of the wedding seems to have utmost importance, along with the consumption practices that transform the wedding from a standardized life-course event into a new kind of cultural site that evolves around the style and taste of its organizers.

The nature of this book

In brief, two objectives guide this book: first, to understand the wedding as an expanding, commercial phenomenon, and, second, to offer an empirically grounded exploration of Campbell's Romantic ethic, supplementing and revising it in the light of recent sociological advances in theorizing consumption, emotion, embodiment, romance and gender. Data on these topics were produced through qualitative interviews with fifteen marrying couples, conducted both before and after their own 'big day'. Depictions of weddings in the popular media and in a particular fraction of the wedding industry (the bridal maga-zine) also form part of this study. I refer the reader to Appendix A for a more substantial account of how the research was conducted.

Following on from this introduction, Chapter 2 will examine several key debates in the sociology of consumption. I begin by outlining the theoretical and conceptual features of Campbell's Romantic ethic thesis, focusing upon his interpretation of emotions and their connec-tion to Romanticism and its legacies. A critical appraisal of Romantic consumption then follows, one which not only recalls and draws together existing critiques, but develops new arguments and engages with more broader and recent scholarship in this area. This leads me to suggest alternative ways of thinking about the legacies of Romanticism as well as contemporary, commodified expressions of romance – that is to say, the imbrication of 'Romantic' and 'romantic' influences – upon the emotional and imaginative dimensions of consuming.

Next, Chapter 3 examines the role of the media in articulating and sustaining the tension between Romanticism, fantasy and rationality as key dimensions of wedding consumption. As a context setting exercise, I begin by highlighting the scale and scope of commercial weddings in an international context. Two types of British media – the coverage of celebrity and unconventional weddings in the popular presses and a selection of bridal magazines – are then analysed further to discuss the contemporary emphasis upon the wedding as a spectacular, within-reach consumer fantasy. In doing so, I deconstruct the recently formed consumer identity of what I term the 'superbride' – a heroic consumer identity constructed by bridal magazines and promoted as an 'ideal' model for ordinary brides to emulate – to reveal two underpinning aspects of her personality: the rational 'project manager' existing alongside the emotional 'childish fantasizer'. Indeed, theorizing the bridal identity as such a split personality leads me later in this chapter into a more general discussion about the operation of a reason/emotion duality in media representations of wedding consumption.

Chapter 4 marks the first of three, interview-based chapters to consider the experiences of marrying couples. It sets out the general criteria which brides and grooms take into account in their initial stages of wedding planning and demonstrates the relationship of consequent consumption choices to a number of factors. Such criteria, I shall argue (indeed developing the arguments made by brides and grooms themselves), are directly related to the wedding's 'new' status as a highly commodified and commercial event in which notions of consumer choice are paramount. I then focus upon the gendered dimensions of Romantic, hedonistic consumption and the embodied activities in which a Romantic ethic might be enacted and negotiated. We shall see throughout how stylistic choices (or *non*-choices) as well as structural constraints are implicated in the decision-making processes of the sampled couples.

Taking as its focus the immediate pre-wedding build-up through to and including the big day itself, Chapter 5 investigates how far brides and grooms negotiate 'the perfect marriage' between rationality and emotion to secure a successfully romantic experience (if they so desired it). To begin, following the chronology of events related to me by brides and grooms, I briefly sketch what I take to be the typical wedding narrative. Formative stages here, as we shall see, include the last few days of preparation, the wedding morning, the final transformation into the bride, the ceremony and the reception. Having done so, I then move to consider these events in relation to three key issues. First, I ask what the experiences of marrying couples, as 'emotional consumers' of their wedding day, can tell us about the relationship between consumption and emotion in this context? Second, I explore how the wedding is constructed and experienced as a fantasy, fairy-tale occasion. In particular here, I chart how some women are transformed, objectified and finally 're-enchanted' through their embodiment of the bridal identity. Third, I discuss the surrounding romanticism of the wedding day and explore in what sense a traditional romantic narrative continues to structure the occasion.

Then, in Chapter 6, I focus on the aftermath of wedding consumption. By and large, the later ramifications of any consumer behaviour remain an oversight in the literature, as few sociologists dare to boldly go beyond the actual moment of consumption and few marketeers care about the consumer once she or he has consumed. And yet the effects and affects of consuming for a wedding exert a strong, continuing influence over the bride and groom long after the curtain has drawn on their own big day. This chapter therefore explores how the wedding and its associated consumption are evaluated in hindsight. In doing so, I argue that the wedding aftermath is a period of highly reflexive, mentalistic exercise. The arguments and evidence presented in this chapter in turn build a case for extending and developing theories of Romantic consumers to include their post-consumption activity.

Chapter 7 concludes the book by summarizing the key themes, issues and arguments presented, reflecting on the insights and limitations of this current undertaking and raising additional points for future discussion.

2
Romancing the Consumer: Campbell's *Romantic Ethic* and Beyond

In the introduction to this book I alluded to a seminal text on consumption, Colin Campbell's *The Romantic Ethic and the Spirit of Modern Consumerism* (1987), for firmly placing the issue of consumer desire on the consumption research agenda. His text throws the nature of consumer desire and its elusive satisfaction into critical relief, alongside the pre-acquisition phase of consuming and its aftermath. In its emphasis on the mentalistic dimensions of modern consumption it has also sought to understand consumer behaviour in relation to an underlying cultural logic – one, it is claimed, stemming from a commitment to Romanticism and its associated values. Throughout the text, consumption is emphasized as a creative, hedonistic activity in which imagination and emotions play pivotal roles.

Whilst Campbell's work has been well received in the sphere of consumption studies, recent developments in related areas such as the sociology of emotion and embodiment (Barbarlet, 1998; Lupton, 1998; Williams and Bendelow, 1998; Williams, 2001) demand a critical review of the *Romantic Ethic*'s legacies. This chapter therefore seeks to problematize Campbell's view of consumption, emotions and Romanticism alike. It is not my intention in doing so, however, to downplay Campbell's contribution to the consumption literature. The extent to which Campbell's ideas still provide a key resource for consumer researchers certainly reinforces the relevance of my own current undertaking – this study in so many ways indeed stands as a testament to the scope and breadth of his theory in both its applicability and its continued presence as a site for further critical discussion and debate. Nor is it my intention to formulate a theory to replace it. Instead, I suggest ways of capturing a more complete picture of the emotional dimensions of consumption, ones which both anticipate and inform my own later arguments in the light of the wedding research.

I begin by detailing the key arguments of Campbell's theory, focusing upon his interpretation of emotions and their connection to Romanticism and its legacies. In addressing these issues, I also show how the *Romantic Ethic* has influenced subsequent theorizing on consumption, as well as referring to research evidence in support of its claims. I then offer a critical appraisal of the Romantic ethic thesis, recalling and drawing together existing critiques and developing new arguments. This discussion problematizes Campbell's assertion that the rationally controlled (de)control of emotion when consuming is ever fully autonomous. Instead, I point to external factors which mediate the consumption experience. The last section of this chapter narrows in focus to explore a single point of critique – Campbell's partial view of romance and romantic emotion in his considerations of Romanticism, consumption and interpersonal relationships. Incorporating the ideas of several other writers, I then suggest ways of thinking about the relationship between 'Romantic' (that is, having explicit or implicit connection to the original Romantic movement) and 'romantic' (referring to its general usage to describe a quality of interpersonal relationships) influences upon, and dimensions of, consumer desire.

Modern consumerism and its Romantic ethic

> ... *while it may not explain everything*, Campbell's Romantic ethic helps us comprehend why consumers are consumed with consumption, take pleasure from pleasure, desire to desire and want to want. (Brown *et al.*, 1998, p. 8, my emphasis)

Campbell's *The Romantic Ethic and the Spirit of Modern Consumerism* (1987) has a decidedly different focus of attention from much theorizing on consumption. Modelling itself upon Weber's (1974 [1930]) classic theory of an ethic of Protestant asceticism fostering the spirit of capitalism, Campbell's book sets out to identify and describe the corresponding ethic that drove, and continues to drive, consumerism. As such, Campbell is often credited with pursuing the 'intellectual origins' (Gronow, 1997, p. 78), the 'mental basis' (Falk, 1994, p. 38), and the 'psychic structuring' (Nava *et al.*, 1997, p. 3) of modern consumption. The parameters of Campbell's own research objectives do therefore compare, if somewhat tenuously, with the preoccupations of original

Romantic artists and philosophers, namely their turn 'toward a grasp of inner meaning and intentionality' (Barry and Melling, 1992, p. 21) in all personal quests for truth and knowledge. Certainly, Campbell's choice to construct a theory privileging the experiential and hedonistic aspects of consumption over and above the economic and utilitarian ones has resulted in his undertaking being credited as 'ambitious and challenging' (Bowlby, 1988, p. 139) and 'subtle and innovative' (Falk, 1994, p. 150). For Campbell, his identification of consumption as a phenomenon of imaginative, autonomous, self-illusory hedonism is still the 'best way to understand modern consumption in general' (1995, p. 119).

In order to explain the dynamics of modern consumerism, Campbell devotes the first half of his book to a theorization of two, clearly differentiated types of hedonism – traditional hedonism and its successor, modern hedonism. Campbell subsequently argues that a commitment to Romantic principles facilitated such a transition. The model of traditional hedonism, based upon the concepts of need and satisfaction, involves the hedonist extracting pleasurable sensations from social and cultural interactions. The centrality of the body and bodily stimulation is reinforced by Campbell's listing of traditional hedonistic activities – 'eating, drinking, sexual intercourse, socialising, singing, dancing and playing games' (1987, p. 69). Here, pleasure and fulfilment are achieved through immediate and direct, tactile and sensory experiences.

According to Campbell this traditional type of hedonism has been supplanted through modernity by an equally hedonistic enjoyment of imagined or anticipated emotions. Although, in Campbell's own words, it is an 'exceptionally difficult exercise' (1987, p. 76) to gain direct pleasure from the imagination, modern hedonists have gained the capacity to control and decontrol imagined emotions. Pleasure is intensified through this process of 'emotional management' rather than through tactile sensation. Mental images are constructed and then consumed 'for the intrinsic pleasure they provide' (Campbell, 1987, p. 77). Campbell therefore proposes a 'hybrid' model of, effect-ively, rationally managed or (de)controlled passion, in which the more usually polarized relations of reason and emotion are seen as harnessed together through the construction, control and enjoyment of imagined pleasure. As Campbell puts it:

... in modern, self-illusory hedonism, the individual is much more an artist of the imagination, someone who takes images from memory or the existing environment, and rearranges or otherwise improves them in his mind in such a way that they become distinctly pleasing. No longer are they 'taken as given' from past experience, but crafted into unique products, pleasure being the guiding principle. In this sense, the contemporary hedonist is a dream artist, the special psychic skill possessed by modern man making this possible. (1987, p. 78)

This, as Falk (1994, p. 53) comments, meshes well with, if not updates, Elias's (1978) 'civilizing process', involving a shift from the expressive to the experiential dimensions of corporeality and its modes of transgression.

Hedonistic daydreams are void of any imperfections that 'reality' may entail, thus deliberately cultivating idealistic, 'as-if' emotions (Campbell, 1987, p. 189). Indeed, Falk characterizes them as 'auto-effective and masturbatory forms of imaginary "self-consumption"' (1994, p. 112). Given its structuring around psychic pleasure, then, modern hedonism can be conceived as autonomous, imaginative, mentalistic, but not materialistic in the least. To Campbell it qualifies as a purposeful activity, one that involves a 'voluntaristic, self-directed and creative process' (1987, p. 203).

An important issue to expand upon at this point concerns Campbell's own particular approach to the dualistic legacies of Western culture and society, including the supposed age-old struggle between mind and body, reason and emotion. In many ways, as outlined above, Campbell's theory can be read as a bold and innovative attempt to overcome these former dualities, or to bring them at least into a closer alignment. Problems nonetheless remain here, resulting paradoxically in a somewhat disembodied approach to consumption and a similarly ethereal or partial account of emotions – one which masks as much as it reveals about the embodied nature of emotions in social life and their intimate relations with rationality (Williams, 2001). If mind and body do not exactly come together through a fully embodied approach to consumption, then the same may also be said of relations between reason and emotion. Emotions, it is clear, display a variety of relations with rationality – relations which Campbell's own hybrid emphasis on the rationally controlled decontrol of emotion only partially captures. These relations, for sake of clarity and simplicity, may be schematically outlined and summarized as follows, and have been elaborated upon elsewhere (Boden and Williams, 2002).

(i) A relation of domination

Within this traditional or orthodox Western viewpoint, emotions are banished or driven out, displaced or replaced, by the steady (male) hand of reason. Unqualified support for this strongly oppositional viewpoint is in fact, on closer inspection, quite difficult to find. Emotions, for example, have an important role in the work of rational philosophers such as Aristotle and Spinoza. Even Weber himself, the sociological heir to the Kantian tradition, may be read in a somewhat more favourable light than many of his critics give him credit for, concerning his treatment of emotion and his (incapacitating) fear of the irrational (Albrow, 1990). The domination theme does, nonetheless, serve to capture, in spirit if not content, an important point of reference in the history of Western thought, or perhaps more correctly, the advent of rational modernity and the quest for 'dispassionate rationality' to which it has given rise. Emotion, from this viewpoint, is indeed the scandal of reason, conceived in instrumentally rational terms (Bauman, 1992).

(ii) A relation of liberation

If the traditional, orthodox viewpoint is premised on the formal opposition between reason and emotion – the latter denounced in favour of the former – then the same may be said, albeit in reverse, of those alternative traditions of Western thought and practice, in which emotion is championed over the supposedly stifling hold of rationality. What we have here is a situation in which the opposition between reason and emotion is more or less radically reversed rather than overturned – a substitution of the positive and negative polarities in this age-old debate. Romanticism, of course, with its own (one-sided) appeal to emotion vis-à-vis the excessive rationalism of the Enlightenment, fits more or less readily within this latter viewpoint. Emotions, from this stance, stand in need of liberation from the calculative hold of rational modernity and the stifling emotional legacies to which it gives rise.

(iii) A relation of calculation

The limits of both (i) and (ii) above in turn pave the way for a somewhat more complex, subtle and sophisticated understanding of reason/emotion relations. This appears to be a calculation viewpoint, traceable across the course of Western history, but gathering increasing force or momentum within the current era. It is not so much a question here (as these very terms of reference suggest) of emotion *dom-*

inated by or *liberated* from reason, as the management of the former by the latter, for better or worse. What we have, in effect, is a channelling of affect through the cultivation and calculative deployment of emotion in the service or under the guidance of rationality. A variety of work may be drawn upon in support of these contentions – from Elias's (1978) 'civilising process' to Hochschild's (1983) 'managed heart' and from Giddens' (1991, 1992) 'reflexive self' and 'pure-relationship' to the 'postemotional' claims of Meštrovic (1997). Emotions become 'things' to be managed or monitored, manipulated or manufactured in this way or that – labourers put to work according to the latest rational imperatives or commodified through the market dictates of late/postmodernity. As for Campbell's own analysis, this perhaps, without violating too many of its assumptions, may be more or less happily accommodated under this calculation rubric; one premised on a hybrid, rationally ordered world of managed emotions, pleasurable or not.

(iv) A relation of unification

Here we arrive at a fourth and final viewpoint on the relationship between reason and emotion, one in which their 'marriage' is well and truly 'consummated'. It is not simply, as in (iii), a question of rationality dominating or managing emotions, but of their more or less happy or harmonious convergence for a supportive or synonymous unification. A growing body of literature may be drawn upon here, in support of these contentions – from Damasio's (1996) exposure of *Descartes' Error* and the affective basis of effective decision-making, to Barbalet's (1998) own insightful exploration of the passion for rationality, and from Johnson's (1987) and Lakoff's (1987) demonstration of the bodily basis of meaning, imagination and reason, to feminist reconstructions of being and knowing (Jaggar, 1989; Rose, 1994). The opposition between reason and emotion, seen in this light, is indeed far less 'durable' than belief in the opposition itself (Barbalet, 1998), masking as much as it reveals about the precise nature of this relationship, including particular types of emotion and particular types of rationality in particular types of contexts. Rather than repressing emotion in Western thought and practice, therefore, it is necessary to fundamentally 'rethink the relation between knowledge and emotion and construct conceptual models that demonstrate the *mutually constitutive* rather than oppositional relation between reason and emotion' (Jaggar, 1989, p. 157, my emphasis). The implications of this final viewpoint are clear – the relationship between reason and emotion in consumption, as elsewhere, is not simply oppositional or even that tensionful, but one which is both constituted and consummated in more or less happy, harmonious ways.

Returning more squarely to our discussion of the key arguments of Campbell's theory, having identified self-illusory hedonism as the spirit of modern consumption, Campbell turns his attention to exploring the cultural ethic underpinning or animating this spirit. Romanticism, it is claimed, is implicated as a primary facilitator of the condition of modern hedonism, and by extension, modern consumption. Theorizing the ways in which Romanticism, or a Romantic ethic, may connect to consumption necessarily begins with a reconsideration of the consumer revolution and its chronological coincidence with the original Romantic Movement. Drawing from Campbell's earlier work, McCracken states that Romantic ideology and the growing commercial nature of society became entwined:

> ... new patterns of consumption were both cause and consequence of Romantic definitions of the self. The Romantic insistence on the uniqueness and autonomy of the self, and its insistence on the realisation of the self through experience and creativity, both drew from, and drove, the consumer revolution. (1990, p. 20)

Nenadic makes a similar connection:

> Though critical of the debasing power of the market, popular manifestations of Romanticism were intimately tied to modern commercialism. Indeed, the movement flourished throughout the western world, and was particularly popular among the middle classes, because its cultural products were manufactured and marketed by some of the most commercially minded producers of the age and because it was tied to the spirit of modern consumption. (1999, p. 210)

Whilst appreciating that original Romantic artists and philosophers did not intend to endorse a consumerist ideology or ethic, their values, beliefs and lifestyles lead Campbell to insist that the Romantics 'brought about a state of affairs generally conducive to modern consumerism' (1987, p. 208). As a reactionary discourse to the modern 'disenchantment' of the external world, the historical significance of Romanticism centres on its 're-enchantment' of the individual psychic world. The philosophical framework of the Romantics espoused an

emotionalist world-view, positioning the 'cult of the self' at the fore-
front of human existence.

Modern consumers, it is argued, in their practices of self-illusory
hedonism and in defence of their rights to self-express and self-define,
seem to be engaging with and displaying many of the characteristics,
values and beliefs typically attributed to original Romantic artists –
their creative genius, continual self-dramatization, their visionary
powers, an idealist or perfectionist outlook, their sensitivity to pleasure
and propensity to spontaneous, intense emotion, a compulsion to
improve upon reality, and the distinct and fascinating nature of each
individual's 'self'(adapted from Campbell 1987, pp. 152–3). Moreover,
Campbell argues that not only did this Romantic ethic initially create
the capacity for modern hedonists to consume imaginatively, but the
'self'-centred legacies of Romanticism have continued to renew or
foster the spirit of consumerism ever since.[1]

Yet it is the specificities of modern consumerism, for Campbell,
which paradoxically account for the inevitable failure of material
goods to live up to the imaginative capacities of the individual.
Ironically, the more proficient one becomes at creatively imagining
emotions and sensations, the more likely it is that 'real' consumption
fails to deliver a comparable intensity of pleasure. This establishes a
cyclical pattern of consumer frustration in which actual consumption
is typically a disillusioning and dissatisfying experience. The implications of this cycle of desire and disappointment for the market
economy are tremendous. In their quest to experience in reality,
through the medium of material goods, the dramas of their imagination, modern hedonists are ceaseless in their demand for original,
novelty commodities. Consumer wants become insatiable and inex-
haustible as they search for that elusive, completely satisfying consuming experience amongst the seemingly endless supply of new products.

It is a commonplace now in consumption studies to believe that
today's consumers are mentally very busy. 'Consumption,' Bocock suggests, 'is more than ever before an experience which is to be located in
the head, a matter of the brain and the mind, rather than seen as the
process of simply satisfying biological bodily needs' (1993, p. 51).
Ramifications of Campbell's theory permeate consumer culture literature, standing as testament to the scope of further research which
seeks to address the imaginative and emotional drives of consumers.
Corrigan (1997), for example, argues that the defining feature of contemporary consumption is the autonomous control of the consumer's
emotional reactions, relating his claim, via Campbell, to the historical

precedent of Puritanism and its insistence on the suppression of 'natural' emotion in favour of the cultivation of 'artificial' ones more functional to the capitalist project. Lury, however, debates whether consumers actually have the capacity to control and decontrol their emotional responses to commodities in this way. 'Is this oscillation really typical for most people?' she asks, 'Is aesthetic knowledge accessible in the same way by all individuals?' (1996, p. 77). Featherstone (1991) nonetheless suggests that the self-conceptions of modern consumers contain elements of the canonical Romantic hero, with consumers situating themselves as the main protagonists in their own narratives of consumption. Not only is it now being recognized that consumption has moved into a more imaginative, hedonistic phase, but that consumers themselves are adopting more reflexive and self-conscious attitudes towards the experience of consuming.

Theorizing consumption as essentially hedonistic has important methodological implications, and symbolically realigns the goalposts of consumer research to include not just the visible practices of consumption but those that occur in the imagination. To a certain extent, research agendas in consumption have taken this into account and, as such, a number of studies can be cited which seem to engage with the central argument of the Romantic ethic thesis – from Urry's (1991, 1995) considerations of the Romantic tourist gaze to Bagnall's (1996) research on the imaginative consumption of heritage-based tourism (see also Craig, 1989; Dungey, 1989), and from Fournier and Guiry's (1993) exploration of pre-purchasing dreaming to Moeran and Skov's (1993) analysis of the continuing Romanticism surrounding the romantic date, despite its commodification.

To summarize, consumption for Campbell is much more than economic conduct. The 'spirit' of modern consumerism can in contrast be defined as the move towards self-illusory hedonism. This involves the autonomous imagination of emotion without dependence upon tactile stimulation from material consumption. Pleasure is extracted from the construction, control and consumption of such imagined emotions. Self-illusory hedonism has its sources in Romanticism and a Romantic 'ethic', it is claimed, continues to promote this activity. Campbell's theory therefore helps to explain the self-satisfactory nature of consumer longing by distinguishing between potential and actual pleasure. Consumers often adopt strategies of delayed gratification, postponing the moment of actual consumption to revel in the pleasures of anticipation. Moreover, consumers demand new and exciting consumables both to fuel their imaginations and as an attempt to realize their daydreams. To a certain extent, then, Campbell's treatment of consumption implicates consumers in their own manipulation (hence the term 'self-illusory'), a manipulation which itself produces pleasure.

Mediating the Romantic ethic: autonomy and manipulation

Whilst the Romantic ethic thesis has proved influential in the field of consumption studies, it is not however without its problems. Part of the problem is Campbell's emphasis on the Romantic dimensions of consumption as autonomous hedonism, and the subsequent role this plays in generating consumer desire. Clearly, the concept of autonomous hedonism separates the Romantic ethic thesis from other more manipulationist theories of consumption. Yet, given its central importance to Campbell's work, a number of issues relating to autonomous hedonism remain unclear. What exactly, we may ask, have modern hedonists achieved autonomy from and is the more important question to find evidence against such autonomy? In order to explore these issues, this section proposes that three forms of autonomy are in fact present in Campbell's theorization of modern hedonism. These appear to be autonomy from material consumption for imaginative and emotional satisfaction, autonomy from media power and the manipulations of consumer ideology, and autonomy from the social relations surrounding consumption.

Taking these autonomies in turn – which, it should be stressed, in no way implies their independent existence from one another, but their separability for analytic purposes – the first, autonomy from material realization for imaginative and emotional satisfaction, has distinct Romantic connotations. If, as Campbell's Romantic ethic would have us believe, the actual consummation of the hedonist's desire is always a disappointing letdown, material realization, it seems, is and always has been a poor substitute for the creative imagination. In this sense, Campbell implicitly echoes Praz's description of how Romantic ideology conceptualized the creative act, an act which was defined primarily through its retention of autonomy from crude materiality:

> The Romantic exalts the artist who does not give a material form to his dream – the poet ecstatic in front of a forever blank page, the musician who listens to the prodigious concerts of his soul without attempting to translate them into notes. It is Romantic to

consider concrete expression a decadence, a contamination. (Praz, 1962, p. 33)

Yet whilst its roots may lie in Romanticism, the concept of autonomous hedonism is quickly put to use by Campbell to explain the impetus behind much actual consumption. Once 'modern' hedonists have, unlike their 'traditional' ancestors, mastered the essentially mentalistic exercise of rationally controlling and decontrolling their emotions they become all too eager, it seems, to extend their calculative daydreams into the material realm. It is not clear, though, how and when this step from the Romantic's purposive distancing of the creative imagination from material expression to trying to excite or satisfy it through actual patterns of consumption takes place, either historically or theoretically. What remains problematic, therefore, is why modern hedonists are initially prompted to realize their fantasies in this or that commodity, a key development which, in effect, imbues them with the identity of a consumer. At the very least, it is questionable why they should continue to assume such an identity so long after it has (supposedly) become apparent to them that the imaginative anticipation of consuming a product is infinitely superior to the 'real thing'. Admittedly, however, once totally immersed in the self-perpetuating cycle of 'desire-acquisition-use-disillusionment-renewed desire' that Campbell suggests lies at the heart of modern consumption patterns, it is perhaps easier to understand (theoretically at least) why modern hedonists persist in their quest for a consumable, material embodiment of the illusory ideals they possess or are given.

Campbell, then, as this suggests, never fully explains why his rationally calculative dream artist would wish to exercise their mentalistic capabilities using materials that are, indeed, 'materialistic'. Following on from this, one might also query why modern hedonists do not appear to be (or are perhaps prevented from?) defending their right to remain forever contented in the more pleasurable, anticipatory pre-acquisition stage of consumption. In fact, as I have said, the central puzzle in all this – the question of why modern hedonists should ever need to turn to material consumption for satisfaction – becomes all the more puzzling when such post-purchase satisfaction appears to be highly elusive. Looking for answers to what may have facilitated the transition from modern hedonism, especially one that is characterized as 'autonomous', to consumer demand, one must surely implicate the influence of external factors – the social, cultural and commercial influences to which any act of consumption is inextricably tied.

Understandably, critics of the Romantic ethic thesis are not satisfied with how Campbell fails to analyse and, in doing so, seriously downplays, the role of commercial pressure in stimulating either hedonistic activity or material consumption, or indeed in forging their link. The second of the autonomies I have extracted from Campbell's profile of the modern hedonist – autonomy from media power and the manipulations of consumer ideology – has been critically addressed before (Brown *et al.*, 1998). The central contention here, it appears, is whether consumer desire, as insatiable emotional and imaginative longing, can be regarded as a cultural inheritance of Romanticism, or is rather a consequence of the very industry it turns to for satisfaction.

To muddy the waters still further, though not necessarily in an either/or way, one could argue that modern consumers who possess an obviously 'Romantic' sensibility – stereotypically one that is idealistic, fanciful and visionary and therefore somewhat susceptible to believing advertising promises – can be seen as an exemplary personality type given the manipulative, ideological control of consumer industries. Critics of mass culture such as Packard (1957), Marcuse (1964) and Brooker (1970) have long suggested that media and market institutions purposely mobilize a ceaseless drive for novelty to ensure that consumers become receptive to the blandishments of new opportunities for consumption. This strategy, rehearsed many times before, certainly seems to 'fit' with Campbell's own admission that the practices of autonomous hedonism largely occur in forms of non-utilitarian consumption which do not involve 'mundane objects' (Belk, 1998). Only new, exciting, experiential consumables qualify as facilitators of autonomous hedonism, leaving practical necessities beyond the realms of the Romantic ethic and the part it plays in modern consumption. It should also be recognized at this point that much consumption is repetitious – a matter of routine embedded in daily, habitual practices which demands little or no forethought nor consequent reflection. Again, these points suggest that Campbell's theory offers, at best, a partial account of the consumption experience – one that ignores these mundane, unthinking acts of consumption and the 'disenchanted' concerns to which they speak.

Given this, one might well wonder if the 'emotions' of a Romantically inclined consumer, however disembodied Campbell's theory (unintentionally) makes them, may simply cause such consumers to become more receptive to the appeal of new products or whether it leads them to actively demand them. Certainly, consumers may defend their autonomy to the bitter end, conceptualizing themselves as the main protagonists or 'heroes' of their own narratives of consumption (Vander Veen, 1994). Yet, in many ways, these very same self-conceptions, underpinned as they are by the belief that each consumer must take responsibility for constructing their own uniqueness and individuality through consumption, are evidence of the ideological stronghold of contemporary consumer culture and its rhetoric.

To the manipulations of commercial ideology we may add those of patriarchy, or perhaps more precisely, the imbrication of the two and their influence upon consumers, especially women. Feminists, for example, have focused upon the role consumption plays in constructing gender identity. A variety of work can be drawn upon here to argue that consumer desire can and has been mobilized for strategic purposes. Writing about domestic consumption in the Victorian period, for example, Loeb (1994) shows how early advertising positioned women as the primary consumers for the family unit, a role promoted as a moral duty to reinforce their existing 'angel in the house' status. Much feminist work on popular romantic fiction, moreover, has exposed this type of literary consumption as selling the 'bourgeois fairy tale' of monogamous heterosexual martial harmony (Cranny-Francis, 1994), thus perpetuating a collective false consciousness of women, or at least of those who read such texts. To these illustrations we may add the more pervasive multiple regulatory and disciplinary regimes women are encouraged to enter into in order to conform to the market dictates of an ideal 'feminine' appearance. The ensuing continual, reflexive self-evaluation – the 'work' of consuming femininity (Winship, 1987), that is to say – serves to commodify women as consumable objects of the male gaze. Such issues, as well as many more raised by feminist work on consumption, must be recognized in any discussion of consumer autonomy.

Following on from this, research on consumption must also recognize the reciprocal interplay between the conceptualization of 'reason' and 'emotion' and the experiencing, as well as the *gendering*, of these in consumer culture. McCracken (1990), for example, has rightly argued that 'rational' consumption remains thoroughly cultural in character, with the commercial sector not only shaping the possibilities for consumption but also those very emotions that are amenable to managed (de)control. Even if, in the most Romantic of senses, the autonomous creative capacities of the imagination remain wholly uncompromised by consumer ideology (or, for that matter, any other ideological discourse) this does not rule out the fact that acts of consumption, whether 'real' or 'imagined', are still structured by social characteristics.

This in turn leads me to consider a third implied autonomy – autonomy from the social relations surrounding consumption.

To be sure, Campbell's Romantic ethic is socially and culturally located. In the concluding pages of his theory, for instance, we are told that the Romantic ethic does not have a universal contemporary appeal (1987, pp. 224–7). What might be termed the 'Romantic habitus', in effect, is apparent only in a very specific elite age, gender and class grouping. This in itself raises concern over who can legitimately experience and speak with authority about the Romantic aspects of consumption. As O'Guinn comments:

> Also troubling is that Romanticism is solely the experience of the Romantic. Romanticism is at least partially a trait, predisposition, or a learned interpretive orientation. Adherents constitute a culture. It describes the everyday experience of the Romantic, but perhaps only that of the Romantic. For the rest of us, many aspects of life may be fundamentally different or God forbid, simply mundane. (1996, p. 85)

Campbell's reliance upon Romanticism to explain the modern consumerist spirit therefore problematizes the theory's applicability to social groups other than the Western, middle-class youthful male Campbell uses as his default consumer. Romanticism, for example, was specifically a European movement, but interpreted in different ways elsewhere. It remains unanswered if or how a Romantic ethic may manifest itself in the cultural plurality of consumers nowadays. Likewise, in gender terms, Belk (1998) highlights the irony that consumer desire from the Romantic period onwards is usually conceptualized as 'feminine', since Romanticism was, historically, a distinctly masculine phenomenon. This contradiction is made even more ironic by Campbell's assertion that, unlike men, women do not develop 'Romantic' personality traits through the active (albeit largely mentalistic and disembodied) denial of a 'Puritan' character ideal, a factor which effectively (within the bounds of his theory anyway) disqualifies women *en masse* from ever having any real motivation to consume Romantically. Where this leaves women standing conceptually in relation to the practice of autonomous hedonism is ambiguous to say the least.

Despite identifying the predominance of Romantic values in a particular cultural grouping, the portrayal of the consumer as mentalistic and self-directed consequently de-emphasizes the broader embodied and socially embedded nature of consumption. By this I mean, for instance, consumption put to use for the purposes of social emulation and imitation, as a means of social display and communication, or as a strategy in the power games of competitive social groups (Bourdieu, 1984). Featherstone (1982), Turner (1984), Falk (1994) and Babbes and Malter (1997), moreover, have all discussed the important role of the consuming body, embodied cognition and the body in consumer culture. Seen in this light, one might argue that Campbell's Romantic ethic comes close to the divorcing of consumption by (some) postmodern consumer culture theorists from the embodied, and hence embedded, social structure and relocation into the disembodied and disembedded realm of the 'hyperreal' (Baudrillard, 1998). Indeed, echoing a critique more typically aimed at theorists of postmodern consumer culture, Uusitalo (1996, p. 93) similarly calls for accounts of hedonistic or Romantic consumption to guard against declaring 'the end of the social' by celebrating such acts as subjective and autonomous. As for Campbell's archetypal modern hedonist, however Romantic he might be, he in many ways remains a largely undersocialized and disembodied individual.

To summarize, the Romantic ethic thesis fails to convincingly incorporate the interconnections between autonomous hedonism, consumer desire and external determinants within its logic. Its argument is thereby further problematized by the neglect of commercial pressure or social structural influences upon the cycle of 'desire-acquisition-use-disillusionment-renewed desire'. Whilst Campbell may be correct in highlighting an ongoing historical connection between Romanticism and consumption, one must also acknowledge that examples of the commodification and management of emotion in contemporary consumer culture challenge the very tenets of Romantic ideology. This is not, however, to side despondently with the manipulationists and accept that autonomous consumer agency is a near impossibility in an age of external temptations to consume. It is simply to suggest, optimistically perhaps, a more complex dialectic between some sort of self-directed hedonism and the machinations of commercial ideology.

The Romantic ethic and romance: an all-consuming relationship?

One way of envisaging the future destiny of the Romantic ethic in academic research may be to examine the pervasiveness of the practice of self-illusory hedonism. In doing so, perhaps the most obvious place to begin would be with the experience of emotion, the role of the imagination and the function of consumption in romantic relationships. For a long time though, it seems, feminist perspectives have enjoyed a stronghold over theorizing love and romance, leaving the development of alternative constructions under-explored. However, Campbell himself has suggested that the cycle of 'desire-acquisition-use-disillusionment-renewed desire' is not necessarily limited to the consumption of material goods, but equally applies to interpersonal relationships, especially romantic engagements.

As I have already shown, the Romantic ethic thesis can and has been critiqued for neglecting to consider the role of external factors on consumer desire, such as commercial pressure and social structure. Yet in its emphasis on the individualistic imperatives of consumers, it is equally neglectful of the importance consumption can have in particular interpersonal contexts – a neglect which appears somewhat ironic given that the specificities of romantic love and the kind of interpersonal relationship it signified were formulated and stabilized during the Romantic period (Stone, 1977). Certainly, as Miller's (1998) empirical research has demonstrated (with reference to the reinforcement of family bonds), consumption can constitute relationships with loved ones. In this respect, not only does consuming often become an act of devotion, it is also a method of 'making' love (last). Where then we may ask, as final issues in this chapter, does imaginative hedonism stand in relation to changing and evolving meanings of romance and romantic relationships? What happens, for instance, to Campbell's Romantic ethic when a significant human 'other' disturbs the (projected) relationship between self and commodity?

It is necessary to begin with a brief look at how the concept of romance has been constructed since the Romantic period – noting, in particular, how despite its commodification, romance is still equated with 'authentic', intense emotion. Certainly, contemporary descriptions of something as 'romantic' do seem to retain many of the phenomenological significations embedded in the word through history, especially those imbued with Romanticism. As Shideler comments:

> One characteristic unites all the events that are properly termed romantic: *the shock of an intense personal experience.* Something is suddenly and shatteringly discovered, involving the whole of one's being in an integrated response. Dante described it as a '"stupor" or astonishment of the mind'; modern philosophers speak of the 'existential shock'. It is essentially a moment – brief or prolonged – of

violent change, after which nothing will ever be the same again, and it has two salient features: givenness, and passion. (1962, p. 31, original emphasis)

The meanings and importance attached to love by the Romantic movement – in particular, romantic love as a deep, incorruptible humanitarian impulse – can to a certain extent be interpreted as an attempt to rehumanize the 'aggressive individualism' of 'primary economic relationships' fostered by the Industrial Revolution (Williams, 1958, p. 42). Giddens (1992) also suggests that ideals of romantic love functioned to strengthen many of the values of liberty and free will that were central to the revolutionary age in which the Romantics lived, and that these values, along with more long-standing historical associations with mysticism and religious fervour, have been retained through modernity.

The emotional experience of romantic love influenced, and was in turn influenced by, the poetic imaginations of the time. Jaggar (1989) argues that it was during the Romantic period that the 'emotions', previously referred to as the 'passions', became conceptualized as intense, irrational urges that were as sufferable as the uncontrollable forces of nature. Emotions would not and could not be manipulated at will, thus making 'love' potentially subversive in character. Furthermore, this celebration of 'fleeting moments of bliss' led the Romantics in general, and Shelley in particular, to endorse the hedonistic impermanence of intense, absolute, passionate love over and above the life-long 'for better or worse' assumption of the Christian marriage vows (Schenk, 1966, p. 156). The emotional aspects of romantic 'agapic' (that is, near-religious and spiritual) love were 'incommunicable', 'inexplicably bestowed upon someone', they could not 'be held accountable' and were 'irreducible by the scrutiny of analysis' (Illouz, 1997, p. 211). Romantic love, in effect, was the only 'truth' worth knowing, the only emotion worth feeling, and to some poets, the only theme worth writing about. 'The Romantic literary work is not only "about" love', Izenberg argues, 'it is love that makes the work possible, love is its shaping spirit, the force that potentiates imagination' (1992, p. 62).

Illouz's (1997) account of generational developments in the concept of romantic love illustrates its subsequent domestication and commodification. Victorian culture inherited the idea of romantic love as an 'authentic', spontaneous emotion and as a means to knowledge and expression of the self from the Romantics. The experiencing of anguish, doubt and disillusionment had long characterized the quest for romantic fulfilment and heightened the ecstasy of its achievement. Yet, the idealistic excesses of the Romantic conception of romantic love soon became interwoven with Victorian values of virtue, reason and a high sense of morality. Narratives of love began to lose their tragic and dramatic extremes, as personal happiness and familial stability became the most sought-after achievement within intimate relationships. The subsequent deification of and dedication to each other ushered in a more privatized and secluded norm of couplehood.

The late Victorian period, however, witnessed the impact of commercial culture upon contemporary understandings of romantic love. This had the effect of simultaneously reinforcing and challenging the historical associations romantic love had with literary Romanticism and its privileging of romantic love as a secular, embodied expression of religious or spiritual exultation. By the end of the nineteenth century, the new ideological transmitters of culture, such as magazines, advertising texts and the rapidly growing entertainment industries, did indeed begin to equate certain acts of consumption with the properties of romantic love. With their experiential promises of hedonistic thrills, 'authentic' emotions and exoticism, commercially defined quests for romance offered a commodified alternative to the early Victorian idealization of heart-rendering struggle and practical domesticity without losing any intensity of feeling. As a result of these commercial developments, therefore, romance became a type of marketing strategy employed primarily for its function of consumer enticement.

The longstanding intimate and complex relationships between romantic ideology and socio-cultural influences (of which perhaps market forces are the most significant[2]) suggests that 'romance' and the particular type of emotion it signifies (and in turn is signified by), may always have been a construct – one that has been celebrated by poets, exaggerated by marketeers and misused by male power. It has nevertheless remained an important and enduring feature of courtship, and indeed, as we shall see in the chapters which follow, of the contemporary, commercialized wedding narrative.

So in what ways might we embody a consumer identity when searching for romance? According to Campbell (1987), like Giddens (1992), the experience of 'falling in love', for want of a better phrase, is a largely disembodied, mentalistic, intensely self-reflexive process – one which, intentionally or otherwise, downplays the sensual, erotic dimensions of embodiment, including sexuality (Jackson and Scott, 1997). Desire for an 'other' is premised upon the act of 'projective

identification' in which the qualities of a potential partner are intu-
itively grasped through imaginative or psychic communication. Acts of
self-illusory hedonism, in other words, can provide an ongoing
impetus for romantic attraction:

> Here, the required novelty is guaranteed by the very number and
> diversity of persons which an individual will normally encounter in
> a life-time of social interaction, consequently ensuring that there are
> plenty of 'strangers' upon whom one can project one's dreams.
> (Campbell, 1987, pp. 93–4)

Such theorizations seem to imply that romantic relationships are primarily entered into for the purposes of realizing or expanding the self,
effectively making the experience of falling in love much more of a
'self-ish' act than a 'self-less' one.

All this again places considerable emphasis on individuals as
autonomous, calculating agents, responsible for the organization and
management of their own romantic destinies. It also takes much
emphasis away from the individualities of their prospective partners. In
a similar vein, Illouz (1997) argues that new forms of 'consumerist
love' have commodified and rationalized romantic relationships.
Romance, she proposes, is unable to stand above the realm of commodity exchange and has become thoroughly intertwined with the
discourses of consumer capitalism. The conditions of late modern
culture have imbued 'the affair' with the values of consumer rationality
and, at some levels, made it representative of lifestyle and identity-
based choices. Shopping around for a better deal in the marketplace of
potential partners certainly acts as a foil to the assumed permanence of
conventional romantic narratives. At the same time, however, through
commodification, romantic encounters have begun to lack authenticity, spontaneity and sincerity. Love and romance have become staged
and exteriorized emotional productions, leaving 'consumers' with an
ironic awareness that many times before others have acted out the very
same scripted romantic conventions they are currently rehearsing.

Perhaps not surprisingly, given the supposed infiltration of consumer ideology into romantic relationships, Illouz's own research highlights a definite shift away from idealizing love in ways akin to the
original Romantic vision of love as a near-religious, intense and
absolute fusion of two beings – mind, body and spirit – towards conceptualizing relationships using work or marketplace metaphors (e.g. as
'hard work', as a 'process of bargaining'). Moreover, the phenomeno-

logical indicators of falling in love – the overwhelming, spontaneous embodied emotions so celebrated by Romantic ideology – are rapidly being dismissed by some as irrational, untrustworthy and highly suspect for the development of future stable relationships. Hochschild (1994), for instance, has noted the 'cooling' of emotional advice in women's magazines regarding relationship management. On the other hand, this change in attitude may be indicative of a growing awareness that distorted or fabricated cultural representations of romance do not always resonate with 'real-life' involvements, leading to disappointment and despondency and perhaps an altogether more realistic assessment of such relationships. So too, as Illouz points out, 'love at first sight' – a mainstay of the Romantic's conception of love and an infallible indicator of true passion – has been deconstructed and demystified through the contemporary separation of sexuality from love. From her own research, 'lust at first sight' or simple 'infatuation' seem more accurate descriptions of seemingly instant attractions.

Yet, returning to Campbell, his work, for better or worse, can be interpreted as an attempt to trace the legacies of Romanticism through to the present day, particularly within the sphere of consumption. A similar approach to romantic relationships is needed as a means of challenging much recent sociological scepticism as to the possibility of experiencing 'authentic' emotion[3] in what, in so many other ways, is an inauthentic, commodified age (Ritzer, 1995; Meštrovic, 1997). As Duncombe and Marsden (1998) suggest, we may experience as 'authentic' that which others (i.e. sociologists and other cultural critics) dismiss as inauthentic or false consciousness. Who, however, is kidding whom?

Perhaps a useful starting point here in such an endeavour would be to problematize the overly simplistic assumption that the commodification of romance will necessarily prevent spontaneous romantic encounters and authentic emotional responses to a person or product. Leading on from this, one might begin to question whether a rigid opposition needs to be maintained between the original Romantic emphasis on the 'real thing' – that is, immediate, authentic, uncompromised engagements with nature, society, the self – and emotional experiences that are facilitated through the consumption of appropriate products. Whilst authentic emotion may remain resistant to total commodification, surely, one might argue, consumption has the capacity to potentiate or enhance the experiential indicators of Romanticism (whether conceptualized as ethereal or corporeal).

It is feasible, for example, that the construction of, and participation in, scenarios conducive to romance, whether heavily reliant on consumption or not, may correspond to a continued longing for a more genuinely experiential type of Romantic exultation – one that may be seen to be highly elusive in the supposedly rational, disenchanted era of late modernity. Equally, one could argue that certain acts of consumption have been explicitly 'Romanticized' in order to facilitate a more full-bodied emotional and imaginative interaction between self and commodity. As Brown's (1998) research has shown, modern manifestations of the Romantic quest are all too apparent within the consuming passions of a shopping trip, whereby consumers willingly suffer the heart-rendering highs and lows of anticipation and dissatisfaction before experiencing 'love at first sight' when finally united with the product of their dreams.[4] Although transplanted into the sphere of consumption, such behaviour implies that the desire to fulfil some innermost Romantic yearning, by whatever means, remains undeterred. 'Romance,' Evans agrees, 'has a real foundation in human experience, however distorted and absurd it may become through commercial exploitation' (1998, p. 274).

Given these points it seems that future research agendas should consider more carefully the link between 'Romantic' (that is, to repeat, having explicit or implicit connection to the original Romantic movement) and 'romantic' (referring to its general usage to describe a quality of interpersonal relationships) influences upon, and dimensions of, consumer desire and it associated emotions. In doing so, the development of modern conceptions of romance must be related to the specific historicity of the Romantic tradition and its changing configuration, as well as to the rise of consumerism. The longstanding thematic and conceptual connections between literary Romanticism, romance and emotion may facilitate the possibility of more hedonistic forms of consumption occurring if this consumption involves a romantic event, place or relationship. Moreover, as Ruth *et al.* (1999) highlight, evaluations of romantic relationships are strongly linked to gift-giving occasions and their subsequent re-interpretation over time – the implication being that trajectories of relationships and trajectories of consumption are intimately entwined. Consequently, for researchers wanting to engage with Campbell's theory and tease out the implications of a 'significant other' disturbing the (projected) relationship between self and commodity, there seems to be a variety of possible sites of interest – the romantic date, weddings, honeymoons and other romantic trips, Valentine's Day and anniversaries, not to mention the day-to-day instances of gift-giving and other expressions of sentiment that take place in romantic relationships.

Conclusion

A series of issues and arguments have been raised in this chapter concerning Campbell's treatment of consumption, emotion and Romanticism in his Romantic ethic thesis. In concluding this chapter I draw these points together, showing their relationship with one another and, in the process, thinking through their insights and limitations.

The chapter has argued that Campbell provides a limited or partial account of emotions in consumption. Emotions are treated as primarily mentalistic, unmediated, autonomous and controllable entities. As a consequence of this, a somewhat disembodied and socially disembedded profile of the emotional consumer is promoted – one in which his or her emotions (as autonomous mental functions) exist in a vacuum from extrinsic constraints. In fact, it appears the case that by reading emotions through Romanticism, Campbell ends up with an unbalanced account of emotions and their role in relation to rationality and reason – the latter needing, somehow, to (de)control the former. Not only is Campbell's view of emotions limited to mental functioning, when these 'emotions' are placed in the context of romantic interpersonal relationships their status as partial, ethereal entities, wholly subject to the manipulative will of each 'consumer', becomes even more apparent. One problem of Campbell's theory therefore stems from its siding with rationality and reason as a means of (de)controlling emotion, and leading on from this, its failure to recognize more complex and constitutive relationships between the two.

Campbell may indeed be commended for his attempt to place Romanticism onto the sociological agenda (at least with respect to consumption and emotion). His theory succeeds in problematizing any interpretations of Romanticism as a historically bound movement, the ideology surrounding which supposedly fizzling out by the mid-nineteenth century. However, in the final part of this chapter I began to reveal the largely 'unromantic' view of Romanticism he offers. Campbell's own approach to emotions in the consumption experience, conceived as it is via Romanticism, seems largely neglectful of some of the core preoccupations of Romantic ideology, of which the obsession with romantic love and its absolute, uncontainable and even subversive quality is but one theme I have chosen to focus upon.[5] In doing so, I sought to problematize Campbell's own reading of Romanticism itself and the continuities of Romantic ideology in contemporary social and cultural activity.

This discussion brought me to consider the continuities and discontinuities between Romanticism and the changing and evolving meanings of romance, including its partial commodification. On the one hand, I pointed to a possible affinity between original Romantic discourse on love and the conceptualization and experiencing of romance or romantic love nowadays. I further argued that the intimate, historical connections between Romanticism, romance and romantic love justify the claims of Campbell's theory being researched in the context of a romantic consumer event. An event like the wedding, therefore, because of its traditional romantic connotations, its increasing commodification, as well as its potential for aesthetic and phenomenological impact, offers a highly suitable case study for assessing whether such arguments can be empirically substantiated.

On the other hand, though, in this chapter I did not want merely to celebrate romance for its continued affinity with Romanticism and, in the process, disregard several decades of important feminist work implicating the ideology of romance in the subordination of women. Nor did I want to gloss over the probability of consumer culture and its rhetoric having intensified and exaggerated many of the values prized by the original Romantic movement, including its conception of love. On the contrary, I wished to highlight the scope and breadth of Campbell's Romantic ethic for future research agendas on consumption and beyond – my own study indeed pursuing the relation between 'Romantic' and 'romantic' aspects of consuming for a wedding, whilst remaining alive to the influences of both patriarchal and commercial ideologies and their ability to affect consumption.

3
'Superbrides': Wedding Industries and Consumer Cultures

This chapter examines the role of the media and commercial stake-holders in articulating and sustaining the tension between Romanticism, fantasy and rationality as key dimensions of wedding consumption. As a context setting exercise, I begin by highlighting the scale and scope of the wedding industry in an international context. Two types of media are then analysed as evidence of the development of a wedding consumer culture in Britain. First, I draw examples from the coverage of celebrity and unconventional weddings in the popular presses to reveal the criteria successful wedding occasions are judged upon. This section highlights the current media emphasis upon the wedding as a spectacular, within-reach consumer fantasy. I then provide a more sustained analysis of six British bridal magazines, part of the ideological output of the contemporary wedding industry, which do not exist in a vacuum from those other media sites transmitting wedding imagery. Such publications function to give meanings to the pre-wedding build-up as well as to the day itself. These meanings are inextricably tied to consumption and are evident in the construction of bridal identity and the commodification of wedding types.

I deconstruct the recently formed consumer identity of what I term the 'superbride' to reveal two underpinning aspects of her personality – the rational 'project manager' existing alongside the emotional 'childish fantasizer'. Indeed, theorizing the bridal identity as such a split personality leads me later in this chapter into a more general discussion about the operation of a reason/emotion dualism in the conceptualization of wedding consumption. It is in the context of the tense yet constitutive relationships between reason and emotion, rationality and fantasy that I revisit Campbell's (1987) Romantic ethic thesis and evaluate, through media evidence, the claims he makes about self-

46

illusory hedonism and the possibility of its autonomy from the manipulations of commercial institutions. In doing so, I also consider what
strategies the wedding industry uses to encourage acts of 'Romantic',
imaginative consumption in anticipation of the big day and how these
acts interconnect with changing meanings of romance.

Wedding industries and consumer cultures: contextualizing the bridal magazine

To preface the following case study of British bridal magazines it is
necessary first to locate such publications in relation to the development of wedding industries worldwide and, what might correspondingly be termed, wedding consumer cultures.

Our first ports of call in such an exercise are existing scholarly
studies of the wedding which highlight the emergence of consumerism
as a significant factor. Earlier studies of the wedding, however, must be
historically contextualized. Diana Leonard's *Sex and Generation* (1980),
for instance, explores how the institution of marriage is reaffirmed in
both obvious and subtle ways by the ceremonial cycle of the wedding.
Her approach is explicitly feminist, using the wedding as a 'window'
on the labour relationship that Leonard argues structures relations
between husbands and wives. As such, consumption is not prioritized
as a theme, although the beginnings of a wedding industry are noted.
All informants who were planning a church wedding, for example,
consulted the two specialist bridal magazines of the time (*Brides and
Setting Up Home, Brides and Home*). The research also highlighted gendered attitudes towards this growing commercialization of the
wedding. Grooms and fathers of the bride appeared to be resentful of
the extra financial commitment involved, while brides and their
female kin were embracing their new roles as wedding 'customers' in
the hope of making their wedding day 'different and distinct from all
others' (1980, p. 257).

In *The Beginning of the Rest of your Life?* (1988), Penny Mansfield and
Jean Collard wanted to generate information about 'normal' marriage,
especially given the contemporary societal and political preoccupation
with the problems of marriage, or as they phrase it 'this obsession
with marital mishap' (1988, p. x). The study is set in the context of contemporary fears that the '"me" decade' and the 'struggle for self-
actualization' (1988, p. x) were leading to rising divorce rates. Mansfield
and Collard therefore concentrate on exposing the contradictory images
of marriage and married life (such as, its assumed permanency despite

the reality of rising divorce statistics), and consequently downplay representations of the wedding day or its build-up and the relationship of these to common assumptions of what it means to live a married life.

The first research to consider consumerism and market forces as becoming increasingly integral to the wedding occasion was Simon Charsley's *Rites of Marrying* (1991). The subtitle of his book, *The Wedding Industry in Scotland*, reflects its focus and indicates that Charsley considers commercial factors to be as significant an influence upon 'rites of marrying' as the more usual influences of tradition, religion or family. Charsley therefore breaks new ground in considering the characteristics of the wedding industry and its current influence upon marriage practices in Glasgow. The research also asks whether the growing 'wedding industry' might become 'an engine of change' in the future (1991, p. 194), expanding the occasion into a more elaborate, costly and conspicuous affair. In fact, the research found that such an escalation of wedding consumption was already taking place. Charsley argues, for instance, the wedding industry at that time consisted of three main elements – the celebrant, the photographer and the reception manager – each agent hoping to persuade marrying couples that they possessed the professional skills required to make the wedding day a success. The wedding industry is therefore portrayed as a series of experts or skilled professionals, individuals or groups of people who offer their practical services to the wedding party. The industry, as Charsley conceives it, had the effect of making wedding preparation more of a collective enterprise that extended well beyond family and close friends, into the commercial sector. The wedding industry is however, on occasion, viewed from a distinctly manipulationist perspective – as he puts it, 'Once within its grips their room for manoeuvre is usually highly circumscribed' (1991, p. 89). At no point though does Charsley enlarge his frame of reference to fully consider whether the wedding industry actually generates and is generated by ideological discourse (like traditional romantic narratives). Despite such an oversight, this research can be credited for initiating further critical discussion on the wedding as a consumer event in which, in retrospect, a still nascent wedding industry, however it is to be conceptualized, plays a crucial role.

Weddings have also proved fruitful territory for socio-anthropological work in interpreting and understanding the culturally specific rituals associated with marriage – whether highly commercial or otherwise. For instance, Pnina Werbner's (1990) anthropological fieldwork on Pakistani weddings in Manchester charts the symbolic and literal transformations of both the bride and groom in a sequence of performative phases en route to the validation of the couple's sexual union through marriage. These performances structure the pre-wedding build-up and are heavily reliant on the use and often literal consumption of particular objects, such as sweets, oils and milk, which possess symbolic value associated with traditional rituals in the Pakistani homeland. Werbner argues that such objects and their ritual use help immigrant Pakistanis define and retain their own cultural integrity in their 'host' country. This is because the associated symbolism of such objects and rituals is deemed to be 'less subject to a contextual modification in their meaning' when used outside the homeland (1990, p. 261). In these particular wedding occasions then, acts of consumption are not 'commercial' as such. Ironically, though, since Werbner's research, one of the key wedding rituals she documents – the art of *mhendi*, decorative henna body designs – has proved to be unresistant to Western consumer culture. Since Madonna's 'Frozen' video, it seems, this key element in the process of beautifying the Pakistani bride has been appropriated as a popular fashion accessory.

Ofra Goldstein-Gidoni (1993) has studied the contemporary Japanese wedding industry, using Hobsbawm's (1983) idea of the 'invention of tradition' to understand how the industry manipulates both traditional and Western cultural referents and repackages them into an invention of what comes to be regarded as decidedly 'Japanese'. Expressing this 'Japaneseness' is a primary motivator in wedding production and consumption. Goldstein-Gidoni structures the research around her experiences as a part-time employee in a Japanese urban wedding parlour, since 80 per cent of weddings in Japan are currently held in such commercial institutions:

> What I witnessed was a well organised, terribly efficient 'lubricated' machinery for the production of weddings. Observing brides running hastily from one 'station' to another, always urged on by the 'producers' who had to keep to a strict timetable, brought home to me an image of an *assembly line*. It reminded me of an insider's account of factory floor work in one of Japan's biggest industries. (1993, p. 52, original emphasis)

In fact, economic metaphors permeate the researcher's observations. Marrying couples are viewed as 'customers', brides become 'products' or 'commodities', the wedding parlour and its workers are the service and facility providers – the implication being that the Japanese ceremonial occasions industry has completely commodified the wedding as well as its central actors.

Cele Otnes and Tina Lowrey (1993), themselves market researchers rather than sociologists of consumption, note that by the early 1990s wedding consumption had become a topic of increasing interest. They therefore formalize this focus, seeing the American wedding as 'a consumption-orientated rite of passage' (1993, p. 325) and go on to research the attribution of 'sacred' or 'profane' qualities to wedding artifacts by brides. Employing Belk *et al.*'s (1989, p. 13) definition of 'sacred' consumption as 'that which is regarded as more significant, powerful and extraordinary than the self', the research found that the bride's dress and ring, the wedding music and decorations, the photographs, the church and the minister were most likely to be described in such a 'sacred' fashion. This leads to a 'hierophanous' wedding experience for brides, whereby the artifacts in question are discovered and consumed in a magically intense, revelatory fashion. 'Sacred' artifacts possess a special aura, making them very different from ordinary, mundane consumables and implicating them in the attempt to live out fantasies, especially that of being the fairy-tale bride/princess. Whilst sacred wedding consumption evolves around the creation of a suitable wedding ambience or atmosphere, other artifacts acquire a corresponding 'profane' status. Defined by Belk *et al.* (1989, p. 325) as 'ordinary and lack(ing) the ability to induce ecstatic, self-transcending, extraordinary experiences', 'profane' items shared a commonality with everyday items, often making a fleeting appearance at the wedding (such as the ring bearer's pillow) or merely being disposable (such as flowers). Items with an overtly economic dimension, moreover, like the wedding present list, were often deliberately excluded for fear of 'desacralizing' the occasion.

A later publication by the same researchers, based upon the original fieldwork, highlights the importance of gender divisions in structuring both participation in, and enthusiasm for, wedding preparations. It was found that the majority of grooms who took part in the study did not rate *any* artifact relating to the wedding ceremony as holding any real significance for them. None was 'sacred', in effect, all were 'profane'. Notable excitements and enthusiasms were articulated only in reference to the reception and the photographs. In particular, grooms valued the reception as a group celebration, an occasion of fellowship and camaraderie, in which guest convenience and provision was paramount. Lowrey and Otnes argue this to be in stark contrast to the bride's concentration on the wedding ceremony itself in which the spotlight shines exclusively on her. The overriding attitude of grooms towards their forthcoming wedding and its associated preparations appeared to be one of deference, neatly summed up by one groom as 'whatever would make her happy' (1994, p. 173).

More recently, the nature and meaning of an 'alternative' wedding occasion has become a research focus. Kim (1996) has looked at wedding chapels in Las Vegas in an attempt to open a doorway into contemporary American culture, a culture in which he finds two pervasive themes – individualism and commercialism. At the time of this study, the number of weddings conducted annually in Las Vegas was just under 100,000 (the 1994 figure stood at 99,727), with the Las Vegas wedding business grossing above $100 million in the same year. Besides documenting the sheer scale of such an industry, the research builds up a profile of typical Las Vegas weddings. They are fairly cheap, starting from only $29, offer a speedy service, are often the result of spontaneous decisions to marry and usually take place with fewer than two guests present.

The sensory overload that tourists and wedding consumers alike confront on arrival in Las Vegas is described:

> As I enter the city, I roll past signs reading 'Immediate Wedding Service' – 'Open 24 hours' – 'All Checks OK' – 'Visa and Mastercard Welcome' – 'World famous drive-up wedding window' – 'Joan Collins married here' and the most curious of all 'Romantic and Authentic'. (Kim, 1996, p. 33)

Such a promotional culture, advertising fame and celebrity, convenience, affordability and speed, typifies the status of Las Vegas as a city of heady, hedonistic pleasure. The meanings surrounding Las Vegas weddings and the ways wedding chapels market themselves draw heavily from this virtual culture. Here, in Kim's analysis, we can discern the clear influence of contemporary debates taking place more generally within sociology concerning the conditions of postmodernity. Using Baudrillard's postmodern consumer culture theory, for instance, Kim suggests that the sign-value of the city of Las Vegas is of overwhelming significance to the couple's decision to marry there. Las Vegas weddings offer the whole package – thrills (you can marry mid-bungee jump), unconventionality ('Elvis' can be your witness), spectacle (you can say 'I do' while riding in a 35-foot long limousine) – not only do they offer this, but they offer it quickly, fairly cheaply, without the involvement of other parties and without the connotations of permanence the traditional church wedding carries. The Las Vegas wedding therefore appears to offer instant gratification for its 'consumers'.

Kim goes on to position the experiences of getting married in Las Vegas and the consumption decisions this entails within wider debates on desire and disillusionment in consumer culture. The wedding industry, it is argued, both at an individual and an ideological level, creates, stimulates and fully organizes the desire of the marrying couple. The Las Vegas wedding industry promotes itself as being able to realize every couple's wedding fantasy, however unconventional. 'Weddings are no longer traditional ceremonies,' Kim argues, 'but have become products of imagination, realizations of one's most romantic fantasies' (1996, p. 143). Whilst the dream of a big traditional white wedding still held true for many Americans, Kim found that more than half of his respondents (54 per cent) had themselves already experienced this 'ideal' and were disillusioned and disappointed enough by the failure of an earlier marriage not to invest time, money and effort striving to replicate it. Alternatively, brides and grooms conceptualized the Las Vegas wedding experience as their new 'ideal', centralizing themselves and their own desires over and above those of their family and friends. According to Kim, such an intense privatization of the wedding event emphasizes the 'individualistic spirit' governing consumption matters in a postmodern climate. It also, worryingly perhaps, symbolizes the couple's isolation from wider social networks.

The most explicit critique of the wedding and wedding consumption to date comes from Ingraham (1999). Her exploration of the US wedding industry argues that Westernized 'white weddings' are heavily implicated in 'romancing' – that is, creating an illusion of – the institution of heterosexuality, and in upholding dominant race, gender, class and labour relations. Indeed, locating her work within the genre of critical heterosexual studies, Ingraham develops Rich's (1980) notion of 'compulsory heterosexuality' to highlight how an uncritical acceptance of the 'white wedding' and the traditional romantic ideology that accompanies it prevents other types of 'romantic' relationships (such as gay relationships, inter-racial relationships, remarriages) from being imagined or represented in popular culture. In this respect, Ingraham's discussion of the use of gay men and lesbian characters in the wedding storylines of popular films and television shows ('Gareth' and 'Matthew' in *Four Weddings and a Funeral*, for example) is both original and illuminating. They appear, she argues, always 'in the service of heterosexual superiority' (1999, p. 162). The continuing dominance of the 'white wedding', moreover, in America as in other Westernized countries, is no accident, reflecting and in turn legitimating those socio-cultural groups that can have unrestricted access to this rite of passage.

From this brief summary of work to consider the commercial nature of the wedding in any significant sense, a number of observations can be made. First, considering its ubiquity, the wedding is relatively little studied. One could reasonably infer that as consumption 'took off' as a research priority in sociology as a whole (mid-1980s onwards), its importance became more central to the study of weddings, as indeed it did to the study of other rites of passage and calendar events. For example, Christmas (Miller, 1993), baby showers (Fischer and Gainer, 1993), Valentine's Day (Otnes *et al.*, 1994), and even death (Gabel *et al.*, 1996), have recently been reconsidered as sites of commercial consumption. This led, as we have seen, to a number of wedding studies in the 1990s focusing upon the wedding as a commodified and consumable occasion. Yet despite these developments, questions concerning the production and consumption of a wedding have tended to limit themselves only to acknowledging the input of individual professionals who have direct influence over the marrying couple. As a result of this, no critical, sociological investigations of the ideological output of the British wedding industry or of the depiction of weddings in the popular media have been conducted.[1] Neither has there been a British study to consider how wedding consumption may have changed in the light of the licensing of approved venues for civil marriages in 1994.

It therefore appears somewhat ironic, given this sociological oversight and, moreover, the reality of divorce rates, that wedding industries are not only apparent but booming – estimated in Britain to be worth £4.5 billion, with an average spend of £14,000–15,000 on the occasion.[2] I use the term 'wedding industry' to denote the opportunities on offer to consumers to achieve the weddings they desire as well as the methods used to generate these desires in the first place – for example, bridal magazines, the media, Internet wedding sites, wedding professionals and service providers, business promotions, wedding exhibitions and 'fayres', regional wedding directories and CD-Rom wedding planners. It is also worth mentioning here that more and more couples are creating their own wedding web-sites, showing that weddings are not only becoming tied into consumer culture but also new communication technologies. As we shall see, the wedding industry constructs people getting married as consumers as well as giving them ideas about how to express this role. The production of a wedding, or more precisely, the production of meanings surrounding the wedding, therefore takes place at an ideological level as well at the more 'hands on' stages.

The wedding as media spectacle

After surveying academic work which points to the growing commercial dimensions of the wedding, it becomes necessary to examine changing media representations. Media coverage of celebrity and unusual weddings plays a key role in developing a popular wedding consumer culture, in part through identifying and celebrating the crucial elements of the successful wedding. Currently, the popular media and its depictions of appropriate or inappropriate wedding consumption heavily influence the wedding industry and the demands of consumers. One cannot fail to notice the newfound eagerness of the popular media in Britain to devote the space, time and opinion traditionally reserved for royal weddings to the weddings of the famous, celebrities, and, increasingly, to the more bizarre wedding preferences of the general public.

Over the last few years (1998–2002) the weddings of Prince Edward and Sophie Rhys-Jones, Victoria Adams and David Beckham, Michael Douglas and Catherine Zeta Jones, Brad Pitt and Jennifer Aniston, Madonna and Guy Ritchie, Liza Minnelli and David Gest, and Joan Collins and Percy Gibson, to name but a few, have had to share the limelight in the British media with 'soccer mad' Steve Hilt, who married wearing his England strip (the *Sun*, 8 June 1998, p. 5), Kim Edward and David Goddard, who exchanged vows 25 ft underwater on a coral reef in Florida (*Sunday Mirror*, 18 April 1999, p. 21), Sarah Webb and Neil Horlock, who wed in a shark tank (*Sunday Mirror*, 10 October 1999, p. 29), Carla Germaine and Greg Cordell, the winners of a blind-date wedding competition (25 January 1999, national presses), and Jane Crinnion and Leo Hickman, who married on the Millennium bridge in London (the *Guardian*, 21 March, p. 3). This developing voyeurism, the interest in spectacular or unusual wedding imagery, has been paralleled by the marketing strategies of magazines like *Hello!* and *OK!* which negotiate exclusive deals to publish celebrity wedding photographs, both formal and more intimate in variety, ensuring their readers have a visual experience of the wedding in question that is unmatched by any other publication.

Several recent marriages, highly publicized in the popular press, help to illustrate the criteria used for judging successful wedding consumption.

These criteria, in turn, establish, clarify and reinforce some of the shared cultural assumptions currently surrounding the wedding, especially the correct balance between Romanticism, fantasy and rationality.

In January 1999 Carla Germaine and Greg Cordell beat over 200 other hopefuls to become Britain's first ever blind-date bride and groom. The event was organized by the Birmingham radio station, BRMB. In return for exchanging vows with someone who remained a stranger right up to and, indeed, during the wedding ceremony itself, Carla and Greg were rewarded with a substantial wedding package – an all expenses paid civil wedding at a premier Birmingham hotel and a Caribbean honeymoon, plus a £200,000 luxury flat and the use of a car for a year – that certainly would be a dream prize for any marrying couple. The media spotlight, from the days preceding the wedding ceremony until the predictable announcement just three months later that the marriage was over, was intensely focused upon the implications this competition had for the institution of marriage. Carla and Greg, and the radio station that masterminded the stunt, were condemned by the Church and the tabloids for mocking the seriousness of any decision to marry. This condemnation extended to what the bride and groom had prioritized instead – namely, the material benefits the competition had to offer. Here was a competition that prioritized form over content, style over substance, and ultimately, the wedding over the marriage.

As the *Daily Telegraph* (26 January 1999, p. 3) reported at the time, it was also a 'marriage' that had its foundation built upon the rational criteria of the radio station's selection panel rather than the 'romantic niceties of finding each other by chance'. This, too, added to the artificiality of the occasion. Despite the disturbing familiarity of the wedding scene, an impression no doubt heightened by the consumptive expenditure of BRMB, by its very nature as a media production, Carla and Greg's wedding lacked the romantic authenticity needed to justify the occasion. Wedding consumption in this case was deemed inappropriate as it failed to hold any deeply symbolic emotional or communicative meaning for the bride and groom other than identifying them in such roles. Carla and Greg's staged wedding was unable to reflect any of their personality apart from their longing for material gain and temporary stardom that presumably caused them to enter the competition in the first place. The roles of 'bride' and 'groom' seemed, in effect, falsified and dishonest.

Six months later, the 'Wedding of Decade'[3] took place between Manchester United footballer David Beckham and Victoria Adams from the British pop group the 'Spice Girls'. In a 47-page spread exclusive to *OK!* magazine, the whole wedding experience, from the initial ideas stage, through the fourteen months of planning, to the day itself, is described. The wedding was held at Luttrellstown Castle near Dublin and was structured around a Robin Hood theme twinned with the luxurious elegance their celebrated status afforded. *OK!* applauds the enormous, continual commitment Victoria and David gave to their wedding preparations, with professionals being employed only in their capacity to 'realize' the wishes of the bride and groom.

The pre-wedding media hype speculating on how the golden couple would choose to celebrate their marriage generated a culture of anticipation and longing to see the final product. The wedding achieved its 'ultimate' status because of the seemingly unrestricted consumption opportunities of a successful, attractive young couple who appeared to be getting married for the most authentic reason – love. Therefore, justification for choosing an elaborate wedding centred on two elements – having the financial resources to afford the cost[4] and having the emotional foundation of romantic love to give a strong sense of meaning and purpose to the whole event. Yet, although media opinion generally found Victoria and David's wedding to be one of successful, if extravagant, consumption, coverage of the event did include some criticism that aspects of it were 'tacky'. These slurs were premised upon the couple's supposed lack of legitimate cultural capital, implying that they failed to discriminate between good and bad taste when given more or less unrestricted access to everything the wedding industry had to offer. Additionally, despite the Archbishop of Dublin issuing the couple with a special licence allowing the marriage to take place at that location, the *Church of Ireland Gazette* later argued that the expense and consumption involved in the wedding stood in contention to the Church's longstanding condemnation of materialistic values.[5] Nevertheless, in Britain, to date, Victoria and David's wedding will be remembered in the popular imagination as the consumption-based wedding spectacle *par excellence*.

Celebrity weddings, however, especially those involving exclusive magazine deals and the inevitable mayhem that results from trying to ensure photographic privacy on the big day, are beginning to witness something of a backlash from the British media. Celebrity couples refusing to turn their weddings into a commercial jamboree or media circus often receive positive endorsement for this very fact. The concept of a 'celebrity wedding', to some, seems to have evolved primarily as a form of self-promotion. Take reportage of the recent marriages of Liza Minnelli and Joan Collins in the British press as examples. Whilst there is ample attention paid to the extravagant expenditure and lavish consumption, lest we not forget the all-important magazine deals, implicit connections are made between the scale of these two spectacular weddings and the wavering celebrity status of their leading ladies. On one occasion, Liza Minnelli's wedding is interpreted, perhaps typically, as a 'cabaret' performance designed to enhance the star's position as a member of 'showbusiness royalty' (*Daily Telegraph*, 26 February 2002, p. 17).

In fact, media representations of what are taken to be overly-commercial weddings leads us briefly to a related digression – that of the promotion of a distinctly British notion of 'good taste' which frowns upon and avoids the excesses of (some) occasions across the Atlantic. 'At British weddings, less is considered more,' writes Judith Woods for the *Daily Telegraph*. Liza Minnelli's bevy of bridesmaids, she continues, of which there were 15 in total, including Gina Lollobrigida, Mia Farrow, Chaka Khan and Petula Clark, appears 'a long way from the original Victorian conceit of the maid who would assist the bride by carrying her train, holding her flowers and performing small tasks for her' (*Daily Telegraph*, 26 February 2002, p. 17). This implicit endorsement of the traditional British wedding, where simple, stylish consumption can revive the romantic nostalgia of days gone by and in turn combat an over-the-top, consuming for consuming's sake occasion, has also been further marketed by both the British and American wedding industries.

A number of wedding venues in England, licensed as approved premises by the 1994 Marriage Act, were selected and are promoted through their connection with internationally famous figures in British history. One can tie the knot, for example, at Newstead Abbey in Nottinghamshire, ancestral home of the Romantic poet Lord Byron, or in the Windsor family home of Sir Christopher Wren, one of Britain's most famous architects. It is also rumoured that the cottage where Shakespeare's wife Anne Hathaway once lived will soon be licensed for civil ceremonies. Such venues will no doubt receive further promotion, whether directly or indirectly, through the British Tourist Authority's current £25 million campaign which is prioritizing more historic, traditional images of British cultural heritage over and above the trendier 'Cool Britannia' concept marketed in the late 1990s. On the other side of the coin, not only does Charles and Diana's wedding still remain embedded in the American popular imagination as a perfect example of the traditional romanticism emanating from a British fairy-tale occasion (Ingraham, 1999), the Las Vegas wedding industry offers many '*faux*-Brit' ceremonies. These are typically promoted as 'Victorian' themed packages and aim to capture, in spirit if not in content, the supposedly distinctive quaint and quirky elements of 'Britishness':

> I say old chaps, why not have a truly upper crust wedding 'midst roses and lace, tailcoats and tiaras, and the musical strains of Bach and Handel as you waltz down the aisle ... a very proper affair. Even Queen Victoria would be amused.[6]

All in all, celebrity and unconventional wedding ceremonies have been firmly established as media events and as such now require the careful and extensive budgeting, planning and consumption as well as genuine love between the couple to be heralded a success. As the various examples illustrate, wedding success in the eyes of the media (and to a lesser extent, the Church) is calculated around the twin key criteria of authenticity and appropriateness and the right balance between them – authenticity with regards to the couple's emotional bond and their decision to marry, and appropriateness in relation to the amount of money, time and input the couple invests in consumption in order to symbolize and communicate these feelings.

Whilst I am not suggesting that celebrity emulation is the overriding concern of all marrying couples, media coverage of such occasions has a meaning-making function that helps to develop a popular wedding consumer culture. Where weddings differ from other fantasy-laden celebrity events (award shows, film premiers, exclusive parties) that remain at the level of fantasy for most individuals is in their accessibility and their ability to be replicated and experienced during the average lifecourse, whether this be as a bride, groom or guest. Thus if one is arguing that the popular wedding culture is influenced by media coverage of celebrity and unusual wedding imagery, it is logical to assume that this influence manifests itself as elements not only in a wedding culture of consumption, but one of opportunity, voyeurism, emulation, fantasy, longing and achievement.

Bridal magazines: creating the 'superbride'

It is my intention in the remainder of this chapter to analyse and unpack some of the ideological content within a significant part of the British wedding industry – the bridal magazine – in order to identify and discuss how such texts give meaning to the bridal identity during the pre-wedding build-up and the day itself. Throughout, I prioritize the role bridal magazines play in managing the tension between Romanticism, fantasy and rationality as facets of wedding consumption. Six British bridal magazines are used as a sample: *Wedding and Home* (June/July 1999), *Bliss for Brides* (June/July 1999), *Bride and Groom* (spring 1999), *Brides and Setting up Home* (May/June 1999), *You and Your Wedding* (May/June 1999) and *Wedding Day* (millennium issue, November 1999). (Please refer to Appendix A for further information about the design of both the magazine and the interview research.)

Bridal magazines imbue the wedding with a package of meanings that both influence and are influenced by the currently expanding wedding consumer culture. For example, the celebrity wedding depends for part of its appeal on the couple being 'like us' in also marrying and becomes used as one of a number of inclusionary strategies by bridal magazines to generate the sense of a shared commonality among those currently planning their wedding. Publications oscillate between fantasy, celebrity and real-life wedding imagery as easily as they intermingle information about the various networks of wedding production and consumption.

Feminist analyses of the media, especially those of popular women's magazines, argue that such publications make continual reference to other sites of cultural meaning (McCracken, 1993; Williamson, 1993). Bridal magazines are no exception. They too are thoroughly intertextual, polysemous texts. As well as producing meaning through significations informed by the wedding industry, bridal magazines rely upon their location within the wider genre of women's magazines to ensure their readers possess the cultural literacy to 'read' their texts. Certainly, a magazine's genre shapes its parameters of meaning, along with the expectations and investments of its audience. Women's magazines, for example, condition women to the popular representations of femininity and shape commonsenses about the consumption needed to imitate this imagery. In bridal magazines, as in women's magazines more generally, consumption dominates 'formally' and 'ideologically' (Winship, 1993, p. 48).

Genre identity also helps to construct the reader's 'sense of self' as they engage with the text (McCracken, 1993, p. 22). This process is intensified if the publication in question actively seeks to instil a strong sense of commonality not only amongst its readership, but also between the magazine's readership and its editorial team. Following McCracken's (1993, p. 257) categorizations, bridal magazines can be termed 'special interest' publications that display a strong awareness of the investments of its readership. This enables the magazines' producers to 'class' their audience as a more homogeneous, confinable section of the market than a mass-targeted publication can do, in turn serving the interests of their advertisers. Bridal magazines usher their audience into considering and completing distinct acts of consumption by grouping them into a single homogenous consumer identity – what I term, the 'superbride'.

Repeatedly, bridal magazines emphasize two supposedly universal characteristics of brides-to-be in an attempt to appeal to, unite and bond its all-female preferred readership under the identity of 'wedding consumer'. These two 'typical' character types can be distinguished as that of 'project manager' and 'childish fantasizer'. Brides are expected to be in calm control of their wedding, making decisions for the big day in a business-like, rational manner. In fact, bridal magazines construct the illusion that each bride retains full autonomy over her wedding choices. Repeatedly, brides are asked to decide what sort of bride they want to be for a day. Many examples were found demonstrating the categorization of brides: 'Millennium-minimalist bride' (*Brides and Setting up Home*, p. 36), 'Trend-setting brides' (*You and Your Wedding*, p. 95), 'Modern brides' (*Wedding and Home*, p. 78), 'Summer brides' (*Wedding and Home*, p. 116), 'Girls on a budget' (*You and Your Wedding*, p. 95). This categorization is evidence of the commodification of the event, although it is marketed as a result of greater consumer agency and choice.

Brides must make themselves knowledgeable enough to discern their wedding style and to make informed purchases to achieve coherence in this style throughout the whole wedding occasion. This new breed of 'superbride' is discriminating in her tastes, having the ability to filter out the tacky and unsavoury mistakes of other brides, as pointed out in the magazines. For instance, one panel of 'style experts' who rated the best and worst dressed brides of 1999 repeatedly condemned one celebrity bride for her 'weird outfit' which was 'such a mess' and radiated 'no elegance' (*Wedding Day*, pp. 76–8). Brides, moreover, are expected to have acquired literacy in wedding terminology and understand the concepts of PNT (pre-nuptial tension) and PWT (post-wedding trauma), thus demonstrating their status as fully-fledged members of the wedding community.

Yet this concentration on the rational characteristics of the bride is softened by a secret pink, fluffy feminine side that underpins her desire to dress up for a day and pretend to be a princess. Guiding their preferred, imagined audience through their wedding preparations, magazines writers become substitute motherly figures, or stretching the point, textual fairy godmothers helping all bridal dreams come true. In fact the 'let's pretend' motif is used to justify as much pre-wedding beautifying as the bride pleases: 'Getting married is a great excuse to mess around with lots of different pots, pencils and tubs of make up' (*Bride and Groom*, p. 27). Such imaginative play is 'naturally' extended into wish-fulfilment, in particular the desire to emulate popular ideal representations of femininity: 'I think all brides want to look like the models in magazines and look as good as they do, which is fine' (make-up artist, *Bliss for Brides*, p. 27). So too, fairy-tale wedding venues are marketed on the grounds of realizing childhood fantasies: 'Not only princesses get married in a castle' (advertisement for Naworth Castle, *You and Your Wedding*, p. 240). On the odd occasion grooms are invited to participate in wedding preparations they are advised to indulge their partner's 'truly feminine' side which is flourishing thanks to the bridal identity: 'She might not openly confess it, but it's every woman's secret desire to own a pair of glamorous marabou mules' (Groom's news, *Wedding and Home*, p. 122).

What we are witnessing through the bridal magazine's construction of a shared 'feminine' consumer identity is one example of how women are socialized into the role of the bride. This leads us to ask what particular pleasures do bridal magazines imply that the wedding offers women? Of equal importance is, which desires are induced in this process and how are they promised to be fulfilled?

The pleasures of the bridal identity

I'd always dreamt of looking like a bird in a gilded cage on my wedding day. (chirped by a 'real-life' bride, *Brides and Setting up Home*, p. 173)

One of the specific pleasures bridal magazines offer their readers can be termed the pleasure of ultimate femininity. This pleasure can only be assured, however, if concerted time, effort and expenditure are devoted to the construction of the bridal identity. Consumption, in terms of the entire wedding spectacle and the bride herself, is the primary method of ensuring success. This induced logic confers a duty to spend on the part of the bride as much as for her sake as for her extended wedding party. It also implies that the bride's creativity and effort will be used to good effect.

Through consumption, brides are expected to strive for 'still-life' perfection. This reveals a lot about the particular types of pleasure and femininity offered by the wedding. Overwhelmingly, femininity is conceptualized as 'picture-perfect', triggering visual pleasure for the bride as well as her audience for conforming to the cultural requirements of a successful bridal appearance. The ways in which women are shown to be creating and living out the bridal identity lead us to consider the relationship between gender, spectatorship and performance. For instance, theorists like Judith Butler (1990) argue that gender is an enacted performance. The current 'postmodern' culture, characterized as it is by eclecticism, shifting identities and boundary-blurring may suggest we have freedom to reinvent, play with and act out our gender identity in what appears to be an almost unrestricted circuit of ritual and performativity.

The covers of *Wedding Day* and *Bride and Groom* illustrate the performance of gender roles so central to the wedding occasion, and can be 'read' using the insights of Goffman (1979). *Wedding Day* (see Figure 1) depicts a youthful, pretty bride in a simple, traditional, white satin dress twinned with a white veil which cascades down beyond the representational frame of the photograph. The bride appears to be sitting outside on a lawn, holding her bouquet. A little girl rests her head on the bride's lap and appears to be in pleasant slumber underneath the falling layers of netting.

The gaze of the implied male spectator, presumably her groom, positions the image of the bride. She displays her femininity not only through the conventional markers of bridal identity (dress, veil, bouquet, ring) but, more tellingly, through her pose. The bride's head is slightly bowed as she peers out from the semi-covering veil. Her face is smiling, yet her mouth is half-hidden by the fingers of her left hand, one of which shows the engagement ring. She holds her fingers in front of her mouth in a playful, childish manner strengthening the inference that she just has or is about to realize her childhood fantasy, the fairy-tale wedding scenario that the young girl in the photo is now dreaming of. Through seeking the spectatorial male gaze and pleasing it by achieving the expected representation of a perfected, beautiful bride, her femininity has been confirmed.

Bride and Groom (see Figure 2) was the only magazine sampled to feature both bride *and* groom in the cover shot. Again, the photo has an outdoor backdrop. Tall, palm-like trees and a parasol protect the bride and groom from the breaking glares of sunshine. The couple stand close together. She is dressed in a simple tailored white jacket and a long-line straight skirt, whilst he wears a classic black dinner suit. Her wedding ring is visible. Both the bride and groom appear to be re-

Figure 1   Front cover of *Wedding Day*, November 1999.

latively young (in their twenties or thirties), she has blond swept back hair accented with a flower and he has short dark hair and slightly Latino/Mediterranean looks, fuelling the implication that theirs is a wedding abroad.

The groom appears relaxed; he stands confidently with one hand in his pocket, the other grasping the hand of his bride, and is smiling off

Figure 2   Front cover of *Bride and Groom*, Spring 1999.

into the distance. The bride retains eye contact with the reader, establishing the female-to-female identification between audience and publication. She is leaning slightly into the male counterpart for assurance and protection, letting his facial profile cast a faint shadow over the left side of her face, obscuring her eye. Such a telling visual portrayal of the bride and groom relationship accentuates the socially constructed meanings of masculinity and femininity. As the bride allows her physical presence to be obscured by her groom, so too may she soon have her whole identity submerged into the label of 'his wife'.

Many of the features and advertisements within the magazines sampled were found to fragment the female body. They imply that particular parts of the body if left in their natural state may spoil the overall ambience of the bridal identity; for example, feet: 'Honeymooners beware ... your hair cut may look perfect, your body so silky-smooth and hair-free but when it comes to looking gorgeous, forget looking after those feet at your peril' (Bride and Groom, p. 33), and hands: 'Brides' hands come in for close scrutiny as friends take a close look at those rings' (Wedding Day, p. 57). Others target the deeper layers of bridal identity to ensure that the bridal body underneath the dress is firm: Christian Dior's High Definition Body Contouring System 'Can make you feel more confident about your body contours' (Brides and Setting up Home, p. 60), smooth: 'The results are dramatic: skin tone and texture is improved and the appearance of fine lines and wrinkles is minimalized' with Borghese's Active Mud Treatment (Brides and Setting up Home, p. 61), fragranced: 'What more could a bride want than a perfume that promises laughter, sensuality and radiant femininity' (You and Your Wedding, p. 89), tempting: 'If you have your heart set on your new husband discovering a sexy, lace number on your wedding night then there is no reason why you cannot quickly change into something else after the reception' (Bride and Groom, p. 80), and accessible: 'This deeply feminine lingerie is part of a larger collection whose easy-to-pull ribbons should ensure no fumbling' (Brides and Setting up Home, p. 14). Moreover, current bridal fashions which favour the bodice-style gown further exaggerate the ideal 'hourglass' female form. Such imagery, combined with the consumption-led pursuits for aesthetic 'feminine' perfection encouraged throughout the magazines, place the spotlight on the 'figure' of the bride, long before she is due to have her big day.

So, as well as selling the bridal identity to us as a 'pleasure', bridal magazines in fact promote the disciplined female body – disciplined not only through diet, beauty regimes, costume, gesture and posture (expressed as a totality through the lived spatiality of the cover brides in Figures 1 and 2), but also through conforming to the more traditional proprieties of wedding etiquette and formality. The construction of bridal identity is undoubtedly a disciplinary project and can be termed the 'work' of consuming femininity (Winship, 1987). Brides must enter into multiple regulatory regimes justified on the grounds that such short-term restrictive behaviour will ensure the later pleasures of fulfilled femininity on the wedding day. This ever-increasing monitoring process of the bridal identity is accompanied by an increase in the array of products and advice on offer. Indeed, restrictive bodily regimes required to ensure a successful bridal identity, based as they are around the notions of control, denial and anticipation stand in ideological contradiction to the commercial discourses of abundance, choice and sumptuous satisfaction that the wedding occasion is tied to. It is in this sense that Foucault's (1977) reading of how the body is inscribed by controlling power relations can be applied to consumer cultures in order to show how any desire to sculpt bodily appearance is created through panoptic commercial ideology and the appropriation of external disciplines into continual, reflexive self-evaluation. Certainly, the bridal identity is subjected to a series of internal and external surveillance mechanisms. Perhaps given this fact it is time to acknowledge, following Naomi Wolf, that the wedding and the bridal identity it demands now equal 'the diet' in being 'the most political sedative in women's history' (1991, p. 187).

Whilst bridal magazines clearly employ a number of inclusionary strategies to generate the sense of a shared commonality between wedding consumers, simultaneously, however, through visual and textual representations of the homogeneity of brides featured, we can identify a clear profile of their preferred readership: young, slim, white women, in their twenties and early thirties who are getting married for the first time and have reasonable amounts of time and money to devote to the creation of their wedding. As a consequence of this, bridal magazines thereby exclude the full integration of other brides who do not fit such criteria into their imagined community.

Invitations to consume within the sampled bridal magazines were found still to be dependent upon traditional social categories like age, class, ethnicity or 'race'. Relatively few Black or Asian models, for instance, were pictured in advertisements or editorial features. One black model was used for a seven-page fashion spread entitled 'Silver Shadow', being booked presumably instead of a white model because the silver gowns would appear more flattering against her darker skin tone (*Wedding and Home*, pp. 78–86). Whilst all make-up and hair articles overwhelmingly made the assumption of the 'English Rose' skin tone and hair texture of its readership, *Bride and Groom*, in particular, did address the needs of other brides, albeit briefly: 'Asian skins tend to look ashen so avoid yellow based products' (*Bride and Groom*, p. 27). *Bride and Groom* also included an Iman foundation (part of the make-up range promoted by the black supermodel Iman exclusively for darker skin tones) in their 'tried and tested' feature, and included a black mother and daughter among their reader makeovers.

The 'ideal' bride is youthful and marrying for the first and the last time: 'Eternity is about being young, independent and, above all, happy' (editorial promotion of Eternity bridal wear company, *Wedding and Home*, p. 12), 'If you're walking up the aisle for the second time you probably don't want to wear a full-skirted ball gown' (*You and Your Wedding*, p. 23). Such examples imply that the older woman cannot live out the full bridal fantasy. Brides with visible disabilities were omitted from all wedding imagery and discussion, although one letter printed on *You and Your Wedding*'s 'Ask Us' page did enquire as to the availability of specialist dresses for bridesmaids in wheelchairs. So too, brides lacking the tall, slim silhouettes thought necessary to show wedding dresses at their best were notably absent. Two advertisements, one 'strictly for sizes 18–30 only' (picturing a larger black model) and one for 'smaller brides' (picturing a petite, Oriental-looking bride) further imply that such clientele are an exception to the bridal norm and have to be catered for by specialist designers.

Bridal magazines make very few concessions to the class situation of the bride (and groom), and the structural constraints this may have upon the desire and ability to consume. Within the genre of women's magazines, bridal publications are located alongside the more upmarket 'glossies' such as *Elle* and *Vogue*. *Brides and Setting up Home*, especially, seems to assume a wealthier, style-conscious readership. This is evident from the magazine's heavy promotion of Harrods, the world-famous exclusive Knightsbridge department store: 'To celebrate its one-hundred-and-fiftieth anniversary, Harrods is selling a patriotic version of that most covetable of kitchen items, the Dualit toaster. Specially designed for the store, the red, white and blue toaster, £169, is apparently being snatched up by style conscious brides' (*Brides and Setting up Home*, p. 26), and the couture bridal designers who are most often based in London: '21 reasons why your wedding plans should begin in Bond Street' (advertisement for Ivory shoes, *Brides and Setting up Home*, p. 44).

Moreover, *Wedding Day* dedicates thirty pages to the coverage of 'real' weddings, yet restricts its range of weddings portrayed to eight lavish occasions that are extraordinary in one way or another. For instance, Sarah Ferguson appears as a guest at one of the weddings, one is a Persian ceremony in an English mansion, one includes a live satellite transmission back to the groom's father in Australia, one is the first wedding to be held on the QE2. Like the models posing as brides and grooms on the other pages, these 'real' weddings are airbrushed to remove any signs of ordinariness or imperfection, fuelling the suspicion that the only place 'real' weddings can be observed in the popular media is on video outtake programmes such as *You've Been Framed*.

Bridal insecurities and the management of guests and grooms

We have seen, then, that bridal magazines socially situate their preferred reader. The bride's acts of consumption are also located within her wider social context and are usually portrayed as taking place amid a minefield of unwanted advice and input from the extended wedding party. This leads us to counter the earlier examination of the supposed pleasures on offer by the wedding with a consideration of which particular fears or frustrations become associated with it. It could be argued that bridal insecurities are purposely mobilized as a method of need stimulation. Certainly, anxieties can stimulate consumer desire and ensure potential consumers are receptive to the deeper psychological underpinnings of advertisements. For example, in several instances the magazines sampled justified particular aspects of wedding consumption as a strategy of risk elimination. Two major threats to the day itself and its preparation are continually identified – guests and grooms.

Bliss for Brides devotes the whole of its question and answer section (pp. 83–4) to solving the dilemma of how to 'keep *your* wedding yours'. The feature begins 'Everybody has an opinion on how to organize your wedding. You'll be grateful up to a point, but what do you do when useful advice turns into unwanted interference?' and proceeds to answer a series of bridal worries on how to be a forceful and determined wedding organizer without upsetting the relatives. Brides are reminded that to get what they want requires tactful, manipulative behaviour. For example, replying to one bride's concern that her mother's 'personal style is closer to Dame Barbara Cartland' than her own and that she wants to impose this 'style' upon her daughter's day, *Bliss* advise: 'Rather than embarrass your mother by exposing her interior design fallibilities, why not steer her towards other equally important, and ever so worthy aspects of the wedding organization, where well-intentioned but fundamentally flawed creative ideas can't do any serious damage? Ask her to make fudge, write the table place names or usher people into their seats at the ceremony. Whatever she does make sure your almost nauseating "thank-yous" pump plenty of air into her deflated ego.' The management and organization of people as well as consumables, it seems, is equally as vital to the construction of a successful wedding occasion.

To curtail the over-zealous enthusiasm and involvement of close family members (usually the bride's mother or future mother-in-law) *Bliss* go on to instruct brides to follow the shining example set by Sophie Rhys-Jones who had the British royal family to contend with when she was planning her own wedding: 'And despite offers from Buckingham Palace to take the entire arrangements out of her hands, Sophie has insisted that she wants to retain control of every aspect of the wedding from what dress she wears right through to the flowers in the church and the decorations on the table at the reception. Use her example and tell your mother-in-law that whatever size you and your fiancé want the wedding to be is the right size.' Neither should any bride allow her family or future family to try to make a claim on her wedding based upon economic justifications: 'Regardless of who is paying for the wedding the fundamental point to remember is that it is *your* day.' Weddings involving step-families, warring or divorced parents are also problematized, as they make the seating arrangements for guests at the reception a logistical nightmare. *Bliss* advises the better-safe-than-sorry tactic of seating only the bride and groom together at the top table, thus effectively limiting familial interaction.

Brides are also repeatedly warned that they must take action against the 'lad' culture their fiancé may be part of, since its 'bacchanalian excesses' could disrupt the already stressful pre-wedding build-up: 'You'll have enough on your plate organizing a wedding without wondering what your fiancé will get up to in his last, wild days of bachelorhood' (*Brides and Setting up Home*, pp. 174–5). This particular article, entitled 'Grooms Behaving Badly', pictures Martin Clunes from the popular British television series *Men Behaving Badly* looking worse for wear after a particularly riotous stag night (he appears to be naked, apart from bandages to his head and his arm, and carries a pair of handcuffs and the head of a fancy dress dog costume). The article educates brides about several coping strategies for taming their groom's 'laddishness' in the hope of eliminating such bad behaviour in time for the wedding day and the anticipated years of stable, monogamous couplehood ahead. One of these strategies involves the censorship of the groom's reading materials: 'Most women fear finding their lover's stack of pornography under the bed. However, a collection of top-shelf titles is better than discovering that your fiancé has a subscription to *FHM* or *Maxim*, since these are the instruction manuals for men who want to behave badly. It is essential that as the big day approaches you censor his reading matter, and ban the purchase of the above titles at least six months before the wedding.' Although presumably intended to be read as a humorous look at the ways 'typical' masculine and feminine characteristics become exaggerated on the road to marriage, this article firmly identifies the groom as bringing a serious element of risk into the wedding preparations.

Therefore, on many occasions, bridal magazines conceptualize wedding preparations as a series of potential authority struggles between the bride, groom, friends and family. For example, they imply that in order for the bride to have her fantasy day the groom has to subordinate himself to it, effectively making him only a 'silent partner' in the business of wedding consumption. These potential struggles for authority are never conceptualized as being between the bride and the wedding industry. In fact, it can be argued that bridal magazines treat the wedding as a welcomed collective enterprise, but only collective in the sense of the bride's reliance upon wedding industry professionals. Bridal magazines market themselves on sharing strategies with the bride for gaining and keeping control over her own wedding. Typically, this involves encouraging the bride to take control of all consumption decisions, evoking themes of agency, choice and self-responsibility to disguise the economic incentives driving the commodification of the event. Thus, the wedding becomes a carefully negotiated performance organized by the bride, aided by the industry, given meaning by the culture and kept at a secure distance from the unwanted influences of other involved parties.

The romance of it all: revisiting Campbell's Romantic ethic

To conclude this analysis of the meanings bridal magazines imbue the wedding with, it is necessary to return to the central thematic concerns of this book – the relationship between Romanticism, romance and consumerism – and, in doing so, revisit Campbell's Romantic ethic in light of the media evidence.

There is much evidence of the wedding consumer being encouraged to conceptualize their wedding in terms of a Romantic consumer ethic. For example, brides are asked repeatedly to exercise their imaginative capacities by conjuring up numerous mental pictures of the forthcoming event: 'Do try to imagine how you will look on the day in a dress with make-up, jewellery and flowers, not bare faced and dressed in jeans' (*Bride and Groom*, p. 29); 'Think of your wedding as a stage show where you look like the best version of you, not what you think a bride looks like' (*Bride and Groom*, p. 29). Often these invitations to imagine are located in wedding countdown features and so use the anticipation of sensation to fuel the longing and desire for the real-life experience. This serves to frame the wedding in a highly imaginative and emotional context, months and even years before the bride's own big day arrives. This effectively raises the bride's expectations for her wedding and sets a high standard for the day to live up to.

A few advertisements and features with obvious Romantic connotations were also found. These usually make some reference to the popular understanding of the original Romantic period and its historical associations with literature and natural landscapes: 'Love in the Lakes – the Lake District has always been associated with the Romantic poets and is perfect for an idyllic honeymoon ... Romantic extras such as roses, heart-shaped chocolates and even a champagne helicopter ride can all be arranged' (*You and Your Wedding*, p. 170). Moreover, for brides wishing to give their wedding even more Romantic authenticity, one can send out invitations inscribed with a 'Romantic quote' from Charlotte Brontë's classic *Jane Eyre* (*You and Your Wedding*, p. 26).

Although there is much evidence of bridal magazines encouraging brides to indulge in acts of Romantic, hedonistic consumption, weddings are more typically marketed as romantic events. To say that 'romance' and 'romantic' are clichéd, overused words when it comes to describing anything wedding-related would be an understatement. The classified section of *Bliss for Brides*, for instance, is turned into a battleground between advertisers for romantic supremacy in the marketplace of wedding music: 'Romantic jazz', '*The* romantic guitarists', 'The most beautiful and romantic music played for your wedding'. Romantic word (and picture) prompts are 'triggers of action' in consumption temptations to stimulate consumer desire through the appeal to a genuine human longing (Packard, 1957, p. 27). In bridal magazines consumers are encouraged to identify with the need to feel and express romantic love.

Typically, wedding consumption is legitimated using the model of a romantic relationship, with advertisers often employing the language of love to market their product: 'The heart already knows ... what the mind can only dream of ... trust your heart' (advertisement for Margaret Lee bridal designs, *Wedding and Home*, p. 62), 'You have chosen each other – now let H. Samuel help you make some other romantic decisions' (*Brides and Setting up Home*, p. 53), 'Fall in love with Estée Lauder' (*Bliss for Brides*, p. 18), 'How do you make sure that the accessories to your marriage match the overflowing feelings in your heart?' (article on creating dramatic weddings, *Bliss for Brides*, p. 110). Consumables stand in for feelings, providing a commodified alternative or prompt to direct, verbal emotional expression: 'As he put it on my finger he just said "Forever". It takes a diamond solitaire to make a man that romantic' (advert for De Beers jewellers, *Wedding and Home*, back cover). Emphasizing the romantic dimensions of a consumable implies that there is a purchasable alternative to undesirable (i.e. unromantic) states of being. Objects become duly desired for their romantic transformatory powers: 'Indulge yourself with glamorous lingerie and accessories that are made for romance' (*Wedding and Home*, p. 108).

Certainly, then, it seems that in the bridal magazine references to a popular understanding of Romanticism and its experiential indicators are increasingly blurred with more modern consumption-led definitions of romance to produce and intensify the expectation that the wedding must be emotional, imaginative and, above all, 'romantic'.

In relation to theories of Romantic consumption, the discussions of this chapter begin to problematize the logic that modern hedonists purposely delay the gratification of their mental constructions in the material realm for as long as possible in order to revel in the pleasures of anticipated sensation. Although there is a clear element of pleasure in the planning of the wedding, anxiety is just as marked. If wedding expectations have been raised (arguably for all concerned, but especially those of the bride) by the developing wedding industry and con sumer culture, then the months and years of pre-wedding preparations that typically involve much emotional and imaginative apprehension may instead constitute a strategy of risk elimination to secure a 'romantic' experience. Indeed, wedding consumption is a perfect example to illustrate this process since unlike holidays or the purchase of new clothes, for instance, brides do not usually see themselves as likely to have the opportunity to repeat it. This is perhaps why risk avoidance is so important and may explain why brides need so long to negotiate and perfect the wedding fantasy.

Therefore one could argue that the preoccupation of bridal magazines with the imaginative and emotional anticipation of the wedding day has two consequences – to generate consumer wants to act as a safeguard against unromantic outcomes, and to intensify the emotional, experiential pleasure of the wedding day itself after the induced anxiety of it not living up to constructed expectations.

If bridal magazines produce the expectation of a highly romantic wedding day then surely through their months of careful preparation, organization and consumption, consumers are consciously setting the stage to secure such an emotional experience. Bridal magazines repeatedly claim that consumer rationality is needed to enable a later romantic fantasy, namely that of living out the fairy-tale wedding scenario. They reassure us that the bride's exercise of reason and direction will not spoil her wedding fantasy but ensure its realization. This is evident in the depiction of the supposedly universal split personality of the bride – the 'rational' project manager existing alongside the 'emotional' childish fantasizer. Does this suppose that, in the context of wedding consumption at least, consumers are recognizing the constitutive relationship, or, perhaps given this present context, the 'marriage', between rationality and romance, reason and emotion – that is to say, the heart has its own 'reasons' for wanting to guarantee an intense, romantic wedding experience?

These points about the nature of a reason/emotion dualism in consumption activities entered into in order to facilitate romance propel us sharply back into the complexities of Campbell's 'hybrid' model of rational passion (i.e. through the construction and control of imagined sensation). Certainly, any discussion of the operation of the reason/emotion dualism in the context of wedding consumption and the possible existence of a Romantic ethic must take into account gender identity and consider the implications of consuming romance along gender lines–an issue taken up more fully in Chapter 5. If as Bulcroft *et al.* (1997) imply, romantic and consumer ideologies have distorted the lived reality of the honeymoon, and indeed, as I propose, shaped the wedding experience, the consequent 'creation of a *shared* reality' (1997, p. 464, my emphasis) between the bride and groom, actually contains a strong gender imbalance. Typically, it is the bride who invests greatest effort to facilitate a romantic wedding day and, as with the honeymoon, is responsible 'for orchestrating the emotional climate' (Bulcroft *et al.*, 1997, p. 479) of the whole event. Bridal magazines stand as testament to this fact, steeped as they are in images and ideologies of the 'superbride' who willingly takes on and enjoys creating her special day. The corresponding lack of publications aimed at grooms only serves to reinforce the welcomed absence of men from the all-female community of wedding consumers.

One must, therefore, remain suspicious of whether the wedding industry creates a 'shared reality' for each marrying couple, given the fact that its cultural output, encapsulated as we have seen in the bridal magazine, encourages only the immersion of the bride in romantic and consumer ideologies and the meanings these give to the wedding occasion. As Otnes and Scott (1996, p. 44) describe, traditionally the wedding is a ritual of transformation for both partners, involving 'not only a change in marital status but also a heightened state of consciousness ('love' , 'romance' , 'the most special day of our lives')'.

But for the bride exposed to the ideological discourses of bridal magazines and drawn into the wider wedding culture, interpreting the wedding through a romantic lens dominates. Yet, alas, with bridal magazines mirroring much romantic fiction in its abrupt discontinuation of the romantic narrative after the wedding day, we are left only to wonder whether married life will be able to match the emotional and imaginative rollercoaster of romance and consumption already experienced by the bride in her wedding preparations.

Conclusion

So, to conclude, in the light of the recent heavy promotion of wedding consumption in the media, three key dimensions of wedding-related consumer behaviour can be identified – Romanticism, fantasy and rationality. Two types of media have been analysed, although they do not exist independently of each other or the wedding industry. Depictions of celebrity or unconventional weddings in the popular presses celebrate the crucial elements of a successful wedding. They stimulate the desires of ordinary consumers to emulate these ideals, thus turning the wedding into a fantasy-laden cultural event that is dependent upon consumption. Bridal magazines also play a central role in developing a popular wedding consumer culture, tending to focus more upon promoting the bride as the heroic creator of her big day. The successful 'superbride' is a figure who manages to channel the rational and emotional aspects of her personality into the business of wedding consumption. This endeavour promises a continued cycle of pleasure and frustration right up until the wedding itself.

The media evidence presented in this chapter has supported the argument that consumption can be promoted and marketed as occurring equally in the imaginary realm as in the material one. Often labelled Romantic or hedonistic consumption, such primarily mentalistic acts are characterized as pleasurable, fantastical, emotional, imaginative, creative and expressive, and can involve the experiential consumption of a product, person or place. I have in this chapter, for example, emphasized the strategies the wedding industry uses to sustain the tension between

Romanticism, fantasy and rationality. These function to construct and reinforce ideas about how the wedding day and its build-up should *feel* and subsequently problematizes Campbell's (1987) claims that self-illusory hedonism is mainly autonomous from the media and other cultural output. How far *can* consumers retain control and autonomy over their own perceptions and desires whilst immersed in a wedding industry that seeks to construct and control them?

I have shown how what I term the identity of the 'superbride' is constructed in order to incorporate the relevance of the manipulative view of consumption into the Romantic theme. As we have seen, brides have to negotiate a complex, distorted identity, being producer and consumer, actor and audience, subject and object of their wedding. The bridal role, infused as it is with a consumer identity, is certainly a restrictive, regulatory existence. Yet although the wedding has become a commodified occasion, in the run-up to their big day brides are not only given the space to daydream, the industry demands it of them. What I have documented in bridal magazines in relation to wedding consumption is both the anticipation of emotion and the expectation of tension, and, most importantly, the constitutive relationship between the two. This can be taken as evidence that despite and, indeed, perhaps because of the bride's imagination being colonized by market forces, women can still extract some sort of pleasure out of the whole wedding experience.

As a final point, this chapter's focus upon the ideological content of bridal magazines, and by implication, that of the wedding industry, has highlighted several key areas for the interview data to address. For instance, in the following chapters, I ask how far popular wedding imagery informs my interviewees' understandings of the cultural requirements of a successful wedding experience. How do the couples who took part in this study regard the images of perfected, spectacular weddings that confront them when they are organizing their own big day? In other words, to what extent is wedding consumption perceived to be structured or predetermined by a wedding industry? I also go on to explore and develop the more specific themes of this chapter – namely, the role of the bride as 'consumer' and 'worker', the pleasures and frustrations of the bridal identity, the conceptualization of guests and grooms, as well as the relations between reason and emotion in wedding consumption.

4
Wedding Preparations: The Significance of Consumption

As we saw in Chapter 3, many weddings now have a different status from perhaps thirty years ago. What is now being celebrated is less the beginning of a romantic and sexual relationship than the confirmation of one that already exists. Moreover, at the same time divorce is prevalent in British society, a wedding industry continues to boom, with the average consumptive expenditure on the big day at an unprecedented high level. It is with this apparent paradox in mind that the following discussions proceed.

This chapter is the first of three to consider the interview evidence. I have structured these chapters temporally, each concentrating upon a particular stage of the wedding experience and its associated consumption matters. This present chapter covers the first of these stages, exploring what criteria couples take into account when planning their wedding and what constraints they perceive. Following on from this, Chapter 5 takes as its focus the immediate pre-wedding build-up along with the big day itself. Then, in Chapter 6, I concentrate upon the aftermath of the occasion.

This present chapter falls into three main sections. First, I set out the general criteria which couples take into account in their initial stages of wedding planning. In doing so, I demonstrate how consequent consumption choices are related to a number of factors which interact with each other and must be negotiated by the couple. The criteria most frequently referred to are: 1) style, 2) cost, and 3) 'traditions' and past personal associations, and are articulated in relation to the wedding's 'new' status as a highly commodified and commercial event in which notions of consumer choice are paramount. I then analyse forms of limited consumer behaviour in preparation for the wedding, pointing to evidence of what may be termed 'consumer ambivalence', which coexists alongside 'consumer anxiety'. Finally, I analyse the interview data in relation to some of Campbell's (1987) core concerns. In particular here, I focus upon the gendered dimensions of Romantic consumption, taking into account the influences of the wedding industry upon the conceptualization and experiencing of a reason/emotion dualism when consuming, and the embodied activities in which a Romantic ethic might be enacted and negotiated. Throughout this chapter, I argue that decisions about wedding consumption are not, as promoted by the wedding industry, exclusively a matter of stylistic choices, but that such decisions are underpinned by interpersonal relations alongside material and structural factors.

Wedding consumption: constructing criteria and making choices

After taking the decision to marry, brides and grooms 'in waiting' are faced with a series of key choices. Typically, such choices centre on the timing and location of the wedding ceremony and the reception, the costumes, music and flowers, the entertainment, the guest list, the catering and the photography. Equally, if not more important, are overarching choices about the style, theme, scale and ambience of the event as a whole. The expansion and significance of these key decisions can be related in part to the newness of the wedding as a commercial occasion. Certainly, as I have mentioned previously, weddings have always been structured around forms of 'consumption' of a sort, based around the symbolic and communicative qualities of material objects (most obviously, the rings and the virginal whiteness). Yet, today's new world of weddings (the explosion of which we can date around the passing of the 1994 Marriage Act – when weddings became 'more liberal' according to one bride I interviewed) seems to offer brides and grooms the opportunity of having an event felt to be appropriate and relevant to them, whatever their personal or social situation, and an event which they can actively shape and construct. This is perhaps why couples place tremendous emphasis on and pay special attention to the choices they make and the criteria behind these choices. These criteria may be thematically outlined as follows.[1]

(i) Style

Each couple's emphasis on their wedding as being of a particular style or type clearly demonstrates how ideas about consumption play a central role in the construction of the wedding as an 'occasion' or 'experience', one imbued with a strong element of fantasy. In the wedding, the bride is undoubtedly the main character, and the creation of her 'perfect' day is something she longs for and strives towards. As Robert and Sarah discussed:

> *Robert*: Even the most ardent feminists I've met have had registry office weddings but would have still liked the big church wedding. And I think every bride, every woman, dreams of being the Queen for the day.
>
> *Sarah*: I've always wanted to be since I was ten years old, ever since as far back as I can remember.

Coherence in stylistic choices was thought to be the primary means of realizing the wedding fantasy, whether a fully-fledged Cinderella-type romantic occasion (analysed in more detail in the following chapter) or a milder, toned-down version due to economic restraints or family context. Brides certainly engage with the wedding industry at several levels in these early preparatory stages and, because of their exposure to its ideology, can be argued to be imitating 'superbrides' in their attitudes and behaviour with respect to wedding consumption, as we shall see later. All but one bride in this study had in fact purchased several bridal magazines, nine had attended wedding exhibitions or fayres, and seven had visited wedding web-sites.

Along with the influence of the wedding industry, the present personal circumstances of the couple equally affected the type and style of wedding they wanted (or could afford). Some couples who had been in a long-term relationship saw a 'big do' as inappropriate or unsuitable to their lifestyle. As the following quotations illustrate, the 'uniqueness' of the wedding occasion and the traditions that characterize its build-up might be seen as largely redundant in this context:

> We didn't want the full, white ... well we've been together for eight years nearly so I mean we sort of didn't want a great big do. (Kate)

> Well we've lived together for five years, so it *is* symbolic, but not like as if we just started out. It is not really a beginning for us. It's not a starting point for us, but it's still nice. It's still symbolic that we've decided to make it legal I suppose. (Beverley, original emphasis)

> It stems back to the fact that, because we live together, it feels like just another day. It just feels like something that is going to take up

a day of our time. At this stage, I wish we'd never lived together. I would feel that the wedding would have *a lot* more importance because it would be to start our future together, in an old-fashioned sense. Maybe thirty years ago you got married to start your life together, but I feel we've already started ours ... which stems right back to the wedding list ... *we can't make a list.* (Patricia, original emphasis)

Taking these responses into account, it seems that brides are prompted to 'realize' the meaning of their wedding by thinking about stylistic consumption decisions.

Wedding consumption was significant in 'showing' guests (or their 'public') the success of their relationship and to stress that this present success will be lasting. A number of examples can be recalled here to illustrate this assumed equation of wedding consumption with the display or communication of feeling: 'It's important that everyone sees ... family and friends see the commitment we are making. You know, it's to show everyone that we love each other, want to spend the rest of our lives together and we want people to see that, to show our commitment' (Josh); 'It finalizes it and it shows you're committed' (Leon); 'It lets everybody else know, doesn't it? It's a sense of achievement' (Fiona); 'Public commitment. It's like our day in public' (Hayley); 'I think people just sort of expect that as people have been together for as long as Robert and I have, or any other couple, they do expect some sort of statement of commitment, I suppose' (Sarah). It becomes clear, then, that couples seemed concerned to send certain messages to their wedding guests – messages which relied upon material goods for communicating present emotion (and implying its continuance), thereby endorsing the consumption as communication thesis. Consumption, that is to say, was assumed to be the best method of emphasizing the 'point' of the occasion to those in attendance. In other words, it helped to create the sense of a significant 'occasion' for all, especially if it was not apparent why the marriage was taking place at this particular stage in the couple's relationship. As William put it, 'You want to keep guests entertained, don't you, for the weekend if you can; there's no point going otherwise.'

Accompanying these beliefs about the significance of wedding consumption was the expectation of subsequent reminiscing later in married life on the wedding day – an expectation which in itself seemed reason enough for lavish expenditure. Both Jessica and Robert seemed to articulate this type of justification:

I think it's always lovely to look back on that day and I'm sure we could have put our money to a lot better use, you know, financially, and a lot of it does seem completely frivolous to throw a year's savings up the wall in one day. But we both wanted a big wedding and I think if we didn't do it now you don't get that second opportunity. I think it's incredibly important to have something you don't regret. You didn't do it cheaply, you did it exactly the way you wanted it and you can always look back on that and think of it with fond memories really. (Jessica)

One of the things you are doing in a wedding is you're going to look back on your wedding day for the rest of your life. It's got to be memorable and therefore in order to make it memorable everything has to be of the very best quality, you'll remember that. (Robert)

(ii) Cost

The issue of cost seemed paramount to most couples in the study and underpinned their stylistic choices. 'Everything has been governed by it,' John told me. Couples themselves see this as a direct effect of the wedding's new status as an extremely commercial and commodified event (that is, something which is marketed as purchasable). For example, economic comparisons were made to weddings in the past in which expenditure was thought to be lower and not the sole responsibility of the bride and groom. As Nick says:

In my parents' day all the family used to chip in. It was a bit more of a family thing. People got married and went off to someone's house for the reception. Things obviously weren't as expensive as they are now.

Another couple agreed:

John: It's tradition now apparently that we pay for a best man's suit and it's all new. If you were a best man, the best man bought his own suit.
Louise: The same with bridesmaids.
John: And like gifts ... you always used to give your parents flowers or whatever. You never actually brought bridesmaids or the best man a gift, and there were never such things as these bonbonaires, favour things, there were never any of these on the tables. And this is not too long ago.

These points reflect the current emphasis on the production of a wedding fantasy through consumption – one which, because of the contemporary wedding industry, is thought achievable by 'ordinary' marrying couples, and not considered exclusive to the upper classes or to the famous. The cost of constructing the occasion they wanted drove one couple to revive the tradition of sharing out their wedding expenditure between family and friends:

> *James:* We're asking those who are coming to pay for the wine at the reception.
>
> *Tina:* We've asked people to contribute towards the cost of the wedding.
>
> *James:* Like, I'm asking four or five of my friends to club together and pay for the room for the wedding night, that type of thing ... well, it might sound a little thing ... but like the taxi from the reception to the hotel where we're having the wedding night, that could be forty pounds. So its like a small present really, something people would have on their list.

The financial comparisons and contrasts made between weddings in the past and this apparent new commercial world of weddings was intensified because the majority of my sample were marrying in the year 2000. The millennium year was heavily promoted in both bridal magazines and the popular media as likely to be a record-breaking year for the number of weddings staged. As a result of this, some couples in the study seemed acutely aware of their wedding being a costly affair in which they were competing with other marrying couples in the wedding marketplace:

> It was getting to the time of the year 2000 and, you know, everybody was putting the frighteners on that it would be booked up. It's panicked us more than anything, because if we make it the year 2000, is it going to bump the prices up? (John)

> August was effectively the date we had to pick because of the constraints of venues. Being 2000, obviously many people are getting married this year so it's ... we booked it quite a while ago, but even then places were busy. (Josh)

> When we booked it we'd got eighteen months to go and we felt absolutely ridiculous going in and booking it then. And we didn't

just book that, we booked absolutely every aspect about eighteen months ago. (Jessica)

The thing is, if you want first choice of everything you need to book at least a year, two years ahead, because if you leave it less than a year you are unlikely to get your second choices let alone your first. So I don't think you have any choice in the matter. (Robert)

Wedding professionals, according to one groom, appeared to be taking advantage of the expected high demand for their services:

I mean some venues that we went to actually have a look at, they've actually turned us away because at the time we were only having like thirty or forty people. But as time goes by and you save more money up you can invite more. And they actually turned us away saying 'It's the year 2000, we know we can get more people into a wedding, so I'm sorry but if you're having less than sixty you're going to have to make up the difference'. (John)

Most couples, therefore, realizing the total financial outlay that their wedding would require – a realization no doubt heightened by the perceived escalation of costs brought on by the millennium year – had to formulate a strict budget to govern and manage their consumption activities. This budget was often calculated meticulously ('Can you estimate how much your wedding is going to cost in total?' – Sharon, 'Can we *estimate*! You're joking ... if you want it to pence! – John, original emphasis) and became viewed as a 'big constraint' (Robert) on couples wanting to create their perfect, fantasy day. In fact, as most couples had to be 'quite strict' (Beverley) when constructing their guest list (because of the corresponding scale of expenditure, that is), wedding costs in turn became a limiting factor on social interaction.

Leading on from this, it must be recognized that in their preoccupation with wedding finances, couples faced limited consumption in other areas of their lives. As Louise and John explained:

John: We've had to really ...
Louise: Budget.
John: You know, if you've been used to going out a couple of nights and we've not been going out a lot, have we, and it's sort of like you've really had to buckle down and say 'Right, we're down to like X amount of spending money a week'.

You know, we've been taking so much out and that's had to cover like food, bills, well not bills they're all ... like food, petrol, spending money ...

Louise: A bit to spend.

John: So ... and we've had to stick to that for a long time now, haven't we?

Louise: We just can't wait till after the wedding just to go out and have fun.

John: Yeah, to actually get your wages and think everything's paid and be 'Wow, we've got all this much left' and it'll only be like thirty quid left at the end of the week but we've never had so much for so long!

Overall, then, at one level or another, cost-related issues were evident in the preparations of every couple in the sample.

(iii) 'Traditions' and past personal associations

When making key wedding decisions, some couples were concerned to carry on family traditions, perhaps buffering any sense of a commercialized wedding being too artificial or prioritizing style over substance. Specific churches, for instance, where other family rites of passage had taken place, were therefore chosen – although, it must be said, largely for their personal rather than religious significance:[2]

Patricia: His mother and father were married in that church. All his brothers and sisters had been married in that church. His twin brother is buried in the graveyard. His father, consequently, is buried in the graveyard of that church ...

Peter: It's our family church.

Patricia: And we felt, we just wanted to ... 'cause he's the last one to be married, we wanted to finish it off.

Beverley: It's a family church. My gran used to live just around the corner from there. My mom and dad got married there, all my sisters got married there, my brother got married there, we have funerals there. It's just like the family goes ... if there's anything to do like weddings or funerals, we seem to go to that church really.

Additionally, one bride wished to replicate certain aspects of her parents' wedding day, and, by extension, what was considered to be their largely successful marriage. Louise, in fact, made reference to imitating the style of her parents' wedding at several points in our first interview: 'I've always fancied a September wedding because that's when my mom and dad got married'; 'The flowers I've tried to have very much like my mom had, like lilies and roses'.

Continuity with the past was also a major criterion for a couple marrying in a newly approved location. Tina and James, in this respect, chose their wedding venue (a newly licensed stately home) because it was where they had their first picnic, and held their evening disco at the same pub where they had their first date. The couple's personal history together, in particular the formative stages of their relationship, imbued their chosen wedding venues with deep, symbolic value.

If either partner had been married before, the past also affected decisions but in the opposite way around – that is, couples looked for reversals of past histories rather than continuities. For one bride especially, the fact that her partner had already been a groom was the main reason for deliberately creating what she regarded as an alternative or unconventional style of wedding:

Dawn: Because William has been married before I just wanted …
William: You've said that about eight times now.
Sharon: If it's a factor that affects things …
Dawn: He had a very traditional wedding the first time around … I just wanted to do it very, very differently. So everything about ours is just absolutely not traditional, deliberately. So we are having a murder mystery on the evening. My wedding cake is a chocolate wedding cake. Everything about it is just out of the ordinary, deliberately.
Sharon: Why is everything purposely non-traditional? Because William was married before?
Dawn: Yeah, I didn't want there to be any comparisons made by William's family or even William. I didn't want him to think 'Oh Wendy's dress was *so much* nicer than Dawn's' or want his mom to think 'Oh …' [original emphasis]
William: But I *have* been married before you know. [original emphasis]
Dawn: Well because it is supposed to be such a special day I didn't want anybody to be able to draw comparisons. You know, I didn't want them to think it was better before and I thought if it was very, *very* different people wouldn't even be *able* to compare. [original emphasis]

Sharon: Is that an overriding theme in your preparations?

Dawn: Yeah, I think it is much of a motivation for me, wanting it to be different from William's first wedding.

Therefore, rather than the meaning of consumption diminishing in importance if the wedding involved a remarriage for either partner, its justification centred on establishing stylistic distinction and difference from the previous wedding. This in turn enabled the 'denial' of the previous marriage and the subsequent reinforcement of the uniqueness of this present occasion and the new relationship it celebrated.

Whilst the three previous criteria – style, cost, 'traditions' and past personal associations – were spoken about most frequently in relation to wedding planning, a number of highly individual or idiosyncratic factors were found to shape key decisions, especially the choice of venue for the wedding and reception. For example, Anne and Geoff chose a registry office that was 'quite convenient for the motorways' because they had family and friends travelling from different parts of the country. Taking the other extreme, Heather and Darren explained that they chose to marry in Sri Lanka because 'there's an elephant orphanage in Sri Lanka and you can arrive on an elephant instead of in a car'. Dawn and William, who had a wedding weekend in a country hotel, strategically selected their venue for its ability to accommodate only the specific number of guests they wished to invite. As Dawn put it:

We wanted somewhere that had got just enough rooms for the number of people we wanted but no more so that, a) there wouldn't be any strangers in the hotel, but b) we wouldn't have the issues of William's mom or my mom saying 'Oh if I pay for your great aunt Betty can she come? ' We can just say, 'I'm sorry there's no room'.

To these examples, we can also add Hayley and Nick's dialogue about why they chose not to have their reception at the same venue as their wedding:

Nick: Apparently it's not very good there.

Hayley: I've got friends who've got friends who married there and said the reception place wasn't nice.

Nick: It's nice to get married there, but afterwards it's just ...

Sharon: Why didn't your friend like it?

Hayley: She said the floor was really slippy. That's the main thing I remember.

Several points can therefore be made at this stage about the overall significance of wedding consumption for the couples in the study. First, drawing upon the evidence already selected, whilst brides often spoke of having a wedding appropriate to their present personal and socio-economic situation, and seemed content with this, consumption still appeared to function in a somewhat compensatory fashion through its assumed ability to 'enchant' or 're-enchant' the occasion. For example, a reinforcement or reminder of the symbolism of a legal marriage through appropriate consumption was still thought necessary if couples had already lived together, parented children and assumed a more or less 'married' existence. In fact, it could be further argued that since the roles of 'bride' and 'groom' have such a short-lived existence anyway, couples invest so carefully, financially and emotionally, in order to prolong the successful embodiment and associated experiences of these supposedly once-in-a-lifetime, fleeting identities.

Second, couples made a clear connection between the amount of money, time and effort they chose to invest in the big day and the importance they attached to it. Two grooms clearly articulated this type of reasoning: 'I think obviously from the amount of time and effort we've put in you can see how important it is to us' (Josh); 'If you don't think the wedding was important you wouldn't spend any money on it. There's a correlation' (Robert). Moreover, as a third point, careful wedding consumption (or, as we shall see later, deliberate non-consumption) was felt able to reflect or express their respective 'personalities' or 'philosophies', either individually or as a couple. Anne and Geoff, for instance, said they wanted a wedding 'in keeping with our mode of life and our philosophy', defining themselves as not 'particularly exhibitionist'. Similar connections were made by other brides and grooms: 'It just doesn't suit our circumstances, our needs, or us as a couple to have a traditional church wedding with a big white meringuey frock. It's just not us' (Dawn); 'I think we're quite confident, out-going people. We're not shy retiring wallflowers. I think it would be really nice to feel like that for a day, that you're the most special person there' (Josh); 'We're very casual. The idea of having a church wedding was out ... because everybody's got to dress up' (Stuart); 'I'm quite a gregarious person naturally. Quite outrageous. My dress will reflect what an outrageous person I am' (Sarah). Corresponding wedding 'styles' or 'typologies' were selected as a consequence of such identities: 'Low-key' (Anne and Geoff, Kate and Matthew); 'Very traditional, very romantic' (Sarah and Robert); 'A traditional fairy-tale lovely romantic day' (Jessica and Josh); 'A small family wedding' (Hayley and Nick); 'A standard wedding, because of the cost' (Natalie and Daniel).

Couples recognized that class, gender and age factors helped shape these viewpoints, suggesting that stylistic choices have a definite grounding in the social structural location of the couple. Two brides referred directly to their age as an influential feature in their wedding plans: 'We're not exactly spring chickens. It's not something when you get older that you really think of in the same way. It's almost sort of a technicality, isn't it?' (Anne); 'I didn't want white or cream because I'm too old, but I *did* want a wedding *dress*. So I think age, yes, you know your own mind better' (Beverley, original emphasis). Kate and Matthew, on the other hand, saw their class status as bearing some impact upon their decision to marry and presumably upon their style of wedding: 'I suppose you could say something about our class, we are both middle class. Perhaps that has a bearing on it, the tradition that we should be married.' Moreover, on many occasions, class and age relations were felt to be apparent in encounters between younger brides and bridal shop owners: 'I think they just see a young lass going in ... it's just her daydreaming. They feel as though they're above you' (Louise). Gender, as we shall explore more fully later in the chapter, was equally regarded as a significant feature affecting wedding consumption, the primary purpose of the day, for instance, being strongly linked by grooms to the desires and needs of the bride. As two grooms assumed: 'The bride doesn't like to be spoilt of her audience for the day. Queen for the day' (Robert); 'The celebration is for the both of you, but the day is more for the bride' (Stuart).

Failing to consume: anxiety and ambivalence

The predominance of cost-related issues in the preparations of my sampled couples leads me to consider to what extent certain acts of wedding consumption were limited or deliberately avoided. As Gould *et al.* (1997, p. 211) point out, consumers may wish to make statements about anti-materialism or non-materialism either by 'just not trying' to consume (ignoring various consumption solutions) or 'trying not to try' to consume (making an effort not to consume or, at least, to limit or modify consumption).[3] Certainly, the ideological base of the new commercial world of weddings does assume the occasion to have little resistance to the materialism which characterizes late-modern consumer culture. Are there examples then, we may ask, of the brides and grooms in this study 'failing' to consume? And if so, what reasons do they give for such non-consumption?

Anne and Geoff, for instance, as I have already highlighted in this chapter, opted for a 'low-key' wedding to fit in with their 'philosophy', spending just £500 on their wedding (which made them the lowest spenders in the sample by a significant margin – the next lowest spenders being Kate and Matthew at £3,000). They continually down-played the role consumption had in their wedding, 'We just don't want a fuss do we?' (Geoff), which led me to inquire whether their atti-tudes could be interpreted as an act of resistance against the increas-ingly materialistic or commercial nature of the occasion, to which they replied:

> *Anne*: I don't think it's as active as that. It's literally that we don't see any point in spending a lot of money on something that is just a day and that's not what it's all about.
>
> *Geoff*: Yes, yes, I quite agree. Resistance implies that you've got to have an opposition to the thing that you're going to resist and we just don't consider it, do we?
>
> *Anne*: No. It's up to other people if they're silly enough to spend that sort of money.
>
> *Geoff*: Yeah, if you're normally like that and decided not to do it, that's an act of resistance. But we don't even get anywhere near to that thought process.

This particular couple therefore did not agree that their 'low-key', low-cost and low-consumption occasion involved exercising a will *not* to embrace the new commercial world of weddings. According to Gould *et al.*'s categorizations, they appear then to be 'just not trying' to consume.

Although Anne and Geoff can be said to be the only exception to the rule among the sampled couples in 'just not trying' to consume for their wedding, several examples suggest that others were instead 'trying not to try' to consume. These instances typically involved resentment (often combined with sheer disbelief) of the high cost of certain wedding products and services, and of the recent, market-led elaboration of wedding 'needs'. This was followed by a realization that if the 'raw materials' for the wedding (such as flowers and headbands) or particular services (like the wedding photography) could be sourced, brides and grooms themselves could, with relative ease, make or under-take certain aspects of their own wedding. Matthew, Louise and

Beverley, for instance, can all be classed as 'Do-It-Yourself' consumers, as phrased by Cronin (2000):

> I made the bridesmaids' head-dresses in the end because when I looked at fresh flowers for the hair they started at £75 and that was one thing I thought 'Well, I'm not spending £75 for three brides-maids'. So I made them for about a fiver each and they were just as pretty. (Beverley)

> I mean, because I do a bit of photography anyway, I know the principles of it and so I don't want to spend £300 on a photographer. I mean my idea when I get around to it is to get somebody, like, well either hire a medium format camera and do it or either ... the University do a course so there will be students who can get the equipment out and literally hand me the film. (Matthew)

> I'd already decided we were having favours. But the prices, oh I think for what they are, are quite expensive. So basically what I've done, for the top table we're having those little fancy ones, bon-bonaires, we're having those for the ladies on the top table and then for the rest of the guests there are just like these little diamond cones and they have almonds in and a bow on the top. I've basically just bought the packaging. Instead of like one pound twenty each, I'm doing them for about fifty pence each and it gives me a bit of fun to do them. I've spent ages doing all the favours and things like that. I bought some arched candle holders, one for each table, but they were in wrought iron and everything else was in gold and cream. So I got some spray and sprayed all them gold, sprayed half of the kitchen as well! (Louise)

Limited or non-consumption can cause particular emotions in consumers. The interview data reveal several ways in which limited or non-consumption is framed in emotional terms. The most significant of these is perhaps 'anxiety' that low expenditure could be equated with a lack of emotional investment in the occasion, and can be most readily identified in how anxious couples were to justify or downplay their preoccupations with the financial side of the wedding. Mark, for example, said he must appear 'selfish and cold' to be so concerned about the costs of wedding consumption; John also made a number of similar remarks: 'It sounds horrible that it always comes back to cost', 'I know it sounds like we're real skinflints', whilst his fiancée was keen to point out that their concern to limit costs was never prioritized over good taste, 'We've done it basically as cheap as we can. Well ... not *cheap*, cheap nasty, but as *reasonable* as we can' (Louise, original emphasis). Three other couples also assured me that their limited consumption or their own 'DIY' wedding projects did not mean they were 'skimping' on the overall investment put into the day.

Leading on from these anxieties about the restriction or absence of certain kinds of consumption, we also find several occurrences of what Otnes *et al.* define as 'consumer ambivalence', that is:

> the simultaneous or sequential experience of multiple emotional states as a result of the interaction between internal factors and external objects, people, institutions, and/or cultural phenomenon in market-orientated contexts ... (1997, pp. 82–3)

The couples' discussions of their limited wedding consumption seemed to spark often contradictory emotional responses to earlier justifications and reasoning about the significance and meaning of their own consumer behaviour, one which now downplayed the link between their emotional and financial (consumption-based) investment in the day: 'It's like ... we're relaxed about what shoes we're going to wear and stuff. That's irrelevant really. We are there to get married, not show off our shoes' (Nick); 'I don't want to spend too much on it because I just think it's only for one day, isn't it?' (Harriet); 'At the end of the day you're just getting married. You take your vows and make your commitment to one another. It doesn't matter where you do it, really' (Louise); 'It's great to go all girly and say we're going to have loads of flowers and it's all lovely but it's not the be all and end all' (Jessica).

We might therefore propose that such examples of consumer ambivalence resulted from mixed feelings or uncertainties regarding the increasing commercialization of the occasion and the couple's own level of participation in the new wedding consumer culture, one which remained structured by their economic resources. As Craib (1995, p. 155) reminds us, 'emotional work' (in this case, in the context of consuming for a wedding) is highly reflexive and involves 'reconciling what goes on inside with what one is supposed or allowed to feel' – that is, for brides and grooms, trying to reconcile their own emotions with those suggested to them by the wedding industry. Such examples of 'emotional work', however, simultaneously imply a certain level of consumer autonomy. This is most evident in the ways consumers deal with possible feelings of envy or resentment that they cannot afford certain products or services by rationalizing that, after all, their wedding is 'only' one day.

Gender, shopping and the Romantic ethic

Having introduced the main criteria couples take into account when negotiating wedding consumption, I now turn to a discussion of perhaps the most important influence upon consuming for the big day – the influence, that is, of gender. In doing so, I begin to explore how and in what ways wedding consumption was undertaken. Central concerns here include: the impact of the wedding industry upon 'need' stimulation in brides and grooms, the issue of responsibility for creating the big day, the corresponding consuming 'roles' assigned to each gender, and the attitudes to associated activities (e.g. shopping) which help to construct and reinforce these 'roles'. A focus on these issues, I shall argue, highlights how the norms and values of a consumer society are highly gender-specific. This discussion will in turn enable the advancement and refinement of conceptual knowledge and analytical frameworks of Romantic consumption (in particular, Campbell's Romantic ethic), beginning not only to address its gendered nature, but also its relationship to the new commercial world of weddings and the socially and culturally constituted meanings of consumption upon which it is built.

Campbell (1997) has argued that gender is a crucial factor in an individual's predisposition to evaluate consumption either positively or negatively – the intimate connection between shopping and femininity in particular having certain implications for men and their conduct within consumer culture. Consuming for a wedding, moreover, has traditionally been women's business which, in turn, is likely to increase male aversion to it. Certainly, grooms' attitudes to wedding consumption in the initial preparatory stages did seem dismissive: 'It's not a bloke thing. Blokes ... they're not bothered' (John); 'It's a male–female thing isn't it?' (Leon); 'All my friends that got married, they've said that their wives organized practically everything' (Nick). Such attitudes, along with the allocation of consumption responsibilities they established, were felt to be the norm for the majority of marrying couples, causing any active, let alone enjoyed, involvement of a male in wedding consumption to be brought into question: 'A few of your friends have commented haven't they? Saying he's organized this or that. They have sort of said "Oh, what are *you* doing that for? Tina should be doing that"' (Tina, original emphasis). We might assume here that the majority of James's (Tina's fiancé) friends were male and that, to them, his willing involvement in an explicitly feminine activity problematized his masculine identity and legitimacy within his peer group (Campbell, 1997).

During the first interviews, couples were asked who had responsibility for planning and organizing the wedding. The following three responses were typical and displayed a clear justification for the 'role' of the consumer belonging to the bride, since the groom already personified the role of worker:

> *Sharon*: Who has main responsibility for planning and organizing the wedding?
>
> *Stuart*: She has.
> *Louise*: Well, he works long hours.
>
> *Alex*: [*to bride*] You really. I have to ... .
> *Harriet*: You're just at work. I mean, I work shifts so I can do a lot of things on my days off.
> *Alex*: By the time I get back from work it's 'zzzzzzzzzzzz' [*fakes sleep*].
> *Harriet*: You work twelve hours a day, six days a week, don't you?
> *Alex*: Almost, yes.
> *Harriet*: So when you come back you can't really focus on anything or do any organizing really.
>
> *Patricia*: Me. It's only because I'm female and we do take over! [*laughs*]. Plus I've got more time. I've actually been off sick, on and off, so I've had a lot more time at home, so any phone calls that needed to be made, I've done them. He's at work most of the time, till late in the evenings.

These roles, then, were regarded as fixed and complementary rather than flexible and interchangeable. They were also roles which, as we shall now see, developed in order to maximize the 'natural' organizational qualities and superior 'taste' and 'style' of women and to minimize the impact of the corresponding incompetences of men in this respect.

A largely caricatured version of the groom's assumed incompetences in wedding consumption was related to me by brides, their comments being only jokingly or ineffectually counteracted by grooms:

Jessica: Josh has had two responsibilities so far. Do you want to tell her what they are and how far you've got?

Josh: I've got to organize the men who do the suits, to meet up and get fitted ... and I don't even know the other one!

Jessica: Pick up the marriage licence.

Sharon: [to bride] And why have you organized most of it?

Jessica: Because I wear the trousers! [*laughs*].

Josh: No, it's just because you're more organized than I am. She organizes everything.

Jessica: Josh is hopeless, absolutely hopeless. The reason I'm strongly organizing it ... [*to groom*] because you'd think it would only need to be the second flower shop or the second bridesmaids shop and he'd be champing at the bits to get everything bought, 'Let me out of here!'

John: Women ... women, brides whatever, they all have more of an idea. I mean I'm colour co-ordinated but ... .

Louise: If I was to say go and get a suit, I'd hate to think what he'd come back with.

John: What?

Louise: Something like Austin Powers would wear.

John: Exactly.

All grooms emphasized the lack of consumption they required as compared to that assumed necessary for a bride. Here we can detect the failure or non-concern of the wedding industry to stimulate the 'needs' of the male wedding consumer (or indeed impose 'false' ones upon him; see Marcuse, 1964). As Campbell (1997, p. 109) suggests, if males are to participate in any form of consumption without having their 'masculinity' compromised, their shopping has to be justified as a 'purely purchase-driven activity related to the satisfaction of need' – one which, in keeping with conventional male ideology, has to qualify as an essential labour and not a recreational, leisured and pleasured activity having intrinsic value. Such attitudes are evident in the following interaction:

Leon: I would probably say it was more your day than mine ... slightly. It's like ... the groom ... you've got your suit and that's me sorted. And that's it ... done.

Fiona: But that's been your choice. You've not wanted to be involved in ... .

Leon:	No, but I mean … .
Fiona:	Flowers, invitations, flowers for the church … .
Leon:	No I don't mean that … .
Fiona:	Invitations … and … .
Leon:	No I don't mean that. I mean like you'll go into twenty shops just for a pair of shoes.
Fiona:	No I didn't.
Leon:	Twenty shops for a dress.
Fiona:	I went to three shops for a dress and I went to one shop for a pair of shoes.
Leon:	But it's like … you go out … you've been out quite a lot, haven't you, trying stuff on … and I went out more or less for one day.
Fiona:	Yeah, but you've got a suit to buy, I've got my dress, my tiara, I've got to buy underwear, my stockings, my shoes … and …
Leon:	Yeah, that's what I mean.
Fiona:	Yeah, but it's all to do with my outfit, it's no more … I mean we could go out and buy you some new pants especially for the wedding day if you want to.
Sharon:	Perhaps women get more pleasure out of shopping generally.
Fiona:	Yes, men find it aggravating, women find it relaxing.

Seen in this light, it is therefore no wonder that male participation in wedding consumption (or indeed 'joint' shopping) occurs at a bare minimum and is more or less regarded as incompatible with the 'feminine' shopping activities of the female wedding consumer.

Female wedding consumption can appear to be a distinctly 'feminine'[4] activity in several ways. As grooms correctly noted, it was frequently an activity which did not end with a purchase (or the satisfaction of a 'need', so to speak). For instance, Louise was accused by her fiancé of going out on 'loads and loads of shopping sprees' to no avail, whilst Jessica admitted that she continued attending wedding fayres after completing most of her consuming: 'By the time I went to most of my wedding fayres … I didn't know really why I was going because I didn't really have anything else to organize'. Wedding consumption was viewed by females as more of a social activity than a purely functional one, the enjoyment of which intensified if shared with another bride-to-be or a key female member of her own wedding party. Talking about the wedding too was itself experienced by brides as a pleasurable activity on par with active consumption:

Me and Fiona just do everybody's head in at work. All they've heard for the last eighteen months is weddings. It's good fun. Fiona has helped out, like I thought 'Oh that's a good idea'. Yeah, it's been nice to have somebody to talk to and you know she's not going to get fed up about hearing about it because she's just as excited. (Louise)

Some instances of consumption being a group activity for women were aided by particular fractions of the wedding industry. Sarah, for example, attended and shopped at the National Wedding Exhibition 'for about five or six hours, trundling around with all my bridesmaids' whilst Fiona and her friend enjoyed 'curling up on the settee with wedding magazines planning everything', adding to her groom, 'that's not something you'd do, is it?'

We have seen, then, how gender is already the major structuring factor in wedding consumption in these first stages of preparation and organization. On the one hand, the interview data highlight the 'failure' of most grooms (the exceptions being Robert, James and Matthew) through 'just not trying' to consume for their wedding – a 'failure' which is perhaps understandable if Campbell's contrasting male and female ideologies of shopping and the corresponding 'failure' of the wedding industry to stimulate the 'needs' of grooms are taken into account. On the other hand though, the widely accepted and assumed legitimate dominance or authority of females over most wedding consumption matters may bespeak a more general change in the status of women as consumers, and, in particular, as consumers guided by a 'Romantic ethic':

> The identification of male-related shopping attitudes focused on a rhetoric of 'need', in contrast to a female one centred upon a rhetoric of want and desire, has some interesting implications in the light of prevailing theories of the 'postmodern' consumer society. For since these characteristically present a concentration on the satisfaction of needs within a 'traditional' or premodern consumer milieu, while presenting the modern (or postmodern) mode as one that is centred on the gratification of wants and desires (Campbell, 1987; Featherstone, 1991), then it follows that men are 'old-fashioned' consumers while women are modern and sophisticated consumers. (Campbell, 1997, p. 175)

Certainly, in the light of what was said in Chapter 2, Campbell seems to have reversed his direction of thought somewhat since his earlier work, no longer assuming the default modern Romantic consumer to be a middle-class, youthful male. In fact, in support of Campbell's later claim, we can further elaborate his recognition of the importance of gender to acts of self-illusory hedonism. The possession of what might be termed 'a Romantic habitus', which effectively transforms 'ordinary' consumers into their own Romantic heroes,[5] did indeed appear to be clearly evident in the majority of brides taking part in this study. For instance, brides repeatedly related back their heroic consumption missions or quests to realize their fantasies, occasions which came to seem all the more challenging in the face of financial restraints, unhelpful wedding professionals and the disinterested posturings of grooms:

> *Louise*: I did reserve my dress somewhere, it was only a twenty pound deposit. So if ever they wanted to sell this dress they were supposed to phone me and tell me. So I went in earlier this year to try it on again just before I went for the bridesmaids' dresses, just because it was six months since I'd seen it and they'd sold it. So I went mad. I said, 'Have you got a picture of it yet?' 'No, no we haven't. We haven't got one we'll have to send you one'. She showed me a dress that was similar and I said 'It's nothing like that and if it is I don't want it, that's repulsive'. So ... erm ... I'd also seen this tiara and veil which I'd tried on with the dress. I'd already ordered them and paid for them. The following week I went to collect the veil and they just shoved it in a bag and I took it out when I got it home. It was really shoddy wasn't it?
>
> *John*: Mmm.
>
> *Louise*: So I rang them up straight away and took my veil back and said 'Well while I'm here I'd like to cancel my tiara' and they told me 'Well if it's already been ordered it's tough' and I said 'I know it's tough, you've sold me crap and I want my money back'. And she gave me all the money back but she gave twenty quid less deposit. And I said 'This isn't right', she said 'Yes it is, you cancelled the dress'. And then she started arguing with me and I said 'No way, the reason I cancelled the dress was that you couldn't provide me with a picture or didn't inform me that it had been sold. And she argued for ages, didn't she, but eventually she gave it me. So I wouldn't go there again. I cancelled everything from there and I've gone to somewhere else now ... Co-op. I

went in to order my dress. I tried about three or four on. This young lass was there and she was so helpful. I really enjoyed it. I came out beaming basically, 'Oh God, the dress I want. The dress of my dream'. She was really helpful and nice. I had plenty of time.

Wedding consumption was indeed experienced by brides more so than grooms as a strongly mentalistic activity, one that ebbed and flowed between pleasure and apprehension: 'Things that you never thought were important dawn on you while you're walking,' Hayley explained, although soon admitted to having 'a nightmare or two' about the impending event, whilst Fiona told me how she had been 'dreaming about it for months'. Moreover, brides considered their own minds and desires (and the 'heroic' consumer agency they seemed to relate to this) to be relatively independent from the perceived homogenizing and colonizing encroachment of the wedding industry's ideology. Two brides, who were interviewed together, stressed their independence from such external factors:

Dawn: I think Heather's very, very like ... creative, so a lot of my ideas have just come from having a vague idea that we wanted like a wedding invitation that was very different and sitting down and bouncing ideas off you and other people and then eventually coming up with something that you think 'Yeah that's what I want and that's different'. It's just a lot of thought, I suppose. A lot of thought, and a lot of discussion rather than looking at ... .

Heather: Pages and pages of different things.

Dawn: I mean Heather's come up with a wonderful idea for the place names and things like that. Just bouncing ideas off people.

Heather: I mean I've looked at Dawn's magazines but I've had no inspiration from them really.

It must be noted, however, that grooms occasionally made similar types of argument. The most explicit examples of this were Stuart's response to where inspiration or ideas for his wedding came from and James' remark that the consumers' 'mind' is not always their own: 'It may be our own creative spirits. It's in your head and that's it. In your mind. It's basically your own imagination. You've already got a picture in your head of what you want anyway' (Stuart); 'It's very easy not to have your mind. We don't want to be influenced by other people because we hate the thought of looking stereotyped'. On the whole, though, it was brides who claimed to be autonomously formulating a 'mental picture' (as termed by three brides) of their own big day, and then actively seeking to re-create it in a material form. Patricia, for instance, told me about her wedding dress:

> I mean, I actually designed ... erm ... went in and I'd got a mental picture, a rough idea of what I wanted, and I said to her 'Look this is roughly what I want' and she just got a piece of paper and went ... [*mimics the designer sketching*] ... down this piece of paper with this pencil, and just drew this really rough sketch and said 'Something like that?', and I went 'That's it!' You know, you think 'I'm never gonna get ...', you automatically think you're never gonna get something identical to what's in your mind ... so to me, I think that was the best thing ... yes, because I had got a ... you know ... a mental picture, and I went in and she could give me exactly what I wanted.

If the wedding consumer's mind constitutes one key site in which Romantic traits are readily apparent, then their 'bodies', by implication, constitute another. Issues of creativity, individuality and expressivity seem equally at stake here, for the bride at least – issues 'played out', so to speak, within her own bridal identity and upon her own bridal figure. Sarah, for example, explains how the decisions about her dress had a definite bodily basis as well as a concern to maintain stylistic coherence with the wedding venue:

> The reason why I chose it? I wanted something unique, I wanted something that was going to fit in with Marchand Hall, the colour scheme, the overall theme, things like that. Also I'd like to say that the other reason that I chose Timothy Duffy or any other designer dress is that it took a stone off me. The dress was very slimming, it covered up the worst aspects of my figure and also highlighted the best parts of my figure. So that's another reason why I chose designer because it actually does make the crooked man straight doesn't it?

On the other hand, Patricia emphasized how she had tried to grow her hair in order to increase the stylistic choices available to her on the big day:

Well, I've actually grown mine purposely ... I mean ... to purposely have an option, you know. At the moment I'm going on the theme of putting it up in some way. But, again, I haven't actually ruled out leaving it down ... but I'd like to know I've got the option there.

We can also add at this point that whilst brides frequently spoke of imagining and anticipating their wedding day, along with its associated 'imagined' emotions, such anticipations were made more vivid through actual, embodied consumption activities: 'Every time I do something else towards it ... like this week I've been looking at bridesmaid's shoes ... I want it to be tomorrow. I can't wait for it to come' (Beverley); 'It's just a nice party to look forward to and also it's given us something to *think about* and *do* for us' (Jessica, my emphasis); 'When we were organizing the food for Sumner House we went over with my parents and they did us this four course meal and we all had a different meal to decide what sort of food we'd like. We made sort of events out of choosing things' (Jessica). These examples alert us to the extent to which a Romantic ethic and the type of consumption it promotes is enacted and negotiated through certain kinds of bodily ritual and performance.

Armed with her supposedly superior creative powers and embodied 'autonomous' (as she perceives it) imagination, the way is cleared therefore for the bride's authorial voice to be assumed over most wedding consumption matters. To this extent, the voice of the groom (quite literally) becomes somewhat passive or subordinated in relation:

Sharon: Are those colours reflected in the groom's dress?
John: Yeah, go on. I can't remember.
Louise: Yours is black pinstripe trousers, just a short jacket because of his height. He didn't want tails or anything. So just a short black jacket, white shirt and it's called a Tudor gold cravat.

Jessica: On every decision *we* make *I've* got very specific ideas on what *I* think is nice and what *I* think isn't. (my emphasis)

Here, as Radner (1995, p. 178) reminds us, we can detect the changing nature of women's roles as consumers – roles in which many become 'actively rather than passively engaged in the process of her own constitution as subject', and indeed the constitution of her husband as a reflection of her.

The female consumer role, however, returning to focus upon the bride, is one that remains constructed (partially at least) by the wedding industry (think, for example, of the opportunities for self-construction offered to the 'superbride'), as well as one which does not exist independently from the gendered dynamics between herself and her groom. Whilst we may be able to detect changes to the female consumer role occurring alongside and in relation to those already mentioned concerning the 'new' wedding occasion itself and the 'ideal' (super)bridal identity, these changes do not necessarily lead to unrestricted 'freedoms' for women in the marketplace of new weddings. On the contrary, as the issue of cost is now so central to the wedding preparations, there is much evidence of brides' 'emotions' being a source of concern for their grooms – the implication being that purchases governed by emotional drives (whether 'natural' or induced) are not necessarily concerned with the 'rational' or financial dimensions of the transaction (for example, whether the product/service is value for money or justified in its inclusion).

This concern became most clearly articulated as part of the division of labour (which includes consumption duties) between husbands and wives or any other couple in a long-term, heterosexual partnership – that is to say, whilst wives may hold authority over the 'stylistic' decisions associated with consumption (and its embodied 'feminine' shopping activities), husbands remain largely in control of the consumption budget. As one couple put it:

Mark: Well, Beverley is really doing all the wedding.
Beverley: And then he says whether we can afford it or not.
Mark: I'm happy to fall in with whatever she wants, as long as it doesn't go over the top, like costwise.

This duality of roles when consuming, underpinned as it is by a gendered reason/emotion dichotomy, did not appear however to be regarded by brides as a restriction upon their efforts to create a perfect, fantasy day. Rather, the assumed 'rational' consuming role of the groom was accepted and even welcomed as a necessary 'check' to the bride's own (self-recognized) tendency towards emotionally-driven purchases. In this sense, brides felt that they could be more mentalistic and fantasize about their weddings if they knew someone else would control their recklessness. This shows how dependent the traditional wedding fantasy is on heterosexual gender relations, not just individual gendered psyche.

It may be that brides purposely 'split' the division of labour this way so that they can enjoy the mental fantasy of the wedding with more freedom – that is, they are freed somewhat from making the 'hard' decisions to say no to this or that particular fantasy and the material consumption required to realize it. One bride seemed to want her groom to exert more control over her consumption activity in this respect: 'William's so easy-going on that front, maybe he should just be a bit more firmer' (Dawn). Here, then, we can perhaps detect further influence of the wedding industry defining, shaping and, in the process, gendering the activities of wedding consumption. As the last chapter illustrated, the wedding industry 'trains' brides to strike a correct balance between the rational and emotional dimensions of their own disposition when consuming – rationally channelling and managing their emotions, that is, into the business of wedding consumption. In light of the interview data, though, it is possible now to extend this argument to suggest that brides are also able to negotiate a similar dualism by setting up and maintaining a particular division of labour between themselves and their grooms. In doing so, the corresponding 'emotional' and 'rational' consuming roles of the couple are viewed as both constitutive of and productive to the successful construction of the big day rather than as a source of restriction or conflict.

Conclusion

So, to conclude, this chapter has begun to identify and contextualize the significance of wedding consumption for the sampled brides and grooms. In doing so, I have argued that the new commercial world of weddings has given couples the opportunity to create an occasion felt appropriate to their relationship and reflective of their style, taste and values. Wedding consumption, however, has not simply become a matter of stylistic choices but remains closely tied to the personal requirements of the couple as well as their social structural location. The changing status of the wedding has in turn provoked certain anxieties and ambivalence, most often voiced in relation to the issue of escalating costs, the limits on consumer behaviour that arise from this, and the 'take over' of financial concerns in the preparation of a wedding. I then chose to analyse the gendered dimensions of wedding consumption and its associated shopping activity. This enabled me to explore whether the new world of weddings helped to construct new consuming roles for brides and grooms.

The discussion in this chapter has extended and developed the earlier theoretical engagement with Campbell's Romantic ethic to consider its operation in the activities of consuming for a wedding. As Chapter 3 argued, in promoting the wedding as a constructable 'experience' (and indeed in providing the information, strategies and opportunities to create such an event), the wedding industry itself helps to set up suitable conditions for acts of Romantic consumption to occur. Certainly, the interview data suggest that brides were much more likely to engage in and describe forms of Romantic consumption than grooms were. Moreover, in discussing wedding-related shopping activities and the bride's emphasis upon her own physicality when consuming, I have highlighted the extent to which any Romantic ethic is enacted and negotiated through certain kinds of bodily ritual and performance.

The evidence presented in this chapter returned us once again to the issue of the Romantic ethic thesis being premised upon a 'hybrid' model of reason and emotion relations, whereby the former manages and controls the latter when people consume (either materially or imaginatively). Whilst the wedding industry urges brides to reconcile the rational and emotional aspects of their own personalities into the business of wedding consumption, we have also seen how the consuming roles of men and women are conceptualized and distributed along similar lines – that is, to repeat, the 'rational' groom retaining the 'final say' in financial matters, with the 'emotional' bride, although assuming authority over stylistic matters, welcoming this 'check' over her behaviour. In other words, en route to marriage and in the context of consumption, the genders become regarded as interdependent in that women's fantasizing (along with the pleasures and 'freedoms' it brings) depends partly on allocating the 'rational' role to their partners.

The next step in piecing together this case for the operation of a more embodied and socially embedded Romantic ethic (than Campbell's thesis recognizes) within wedding consumers is to examine the emotional and imaginative experiences of marrying couples in the immediate pre-wedding build-up and on the 'big day' itself. It is to these issues, amongst others, I now turn.

5
The Wedding Fantasy: Consuming Emotions on the Big Day

This chapter takes as its focus the immediate pre-wedding build-up through to and including the 'big day' itself. To begin, I briefly sketch what I take to be the typical wedding narrative, following the chronology of events related to me by brides and grooms. Formative stages here, as we shall see, include the last few days and hours of preparation, the wedding morning, the final transformation into the bride, the ceremony and the reception speech.

Having done so, I then move on to consider these events in relation to three key issues. First, I ask what the experiences of marrying couples *qua* 'emotional consumers' of their wedding day can tell us about the relationship between consumption and emotion in this context. Second, leading on from examining how wedding consumption is conceptualized in emotional terms, I explore how the wedding is constructed and experienced as a fantasy, fairy-tale occasion. In particular I chart how (a number of) women feel themselves to be transformed, objectified and finally 're-enchanted' as they progress through their wedding experience. We shall see how some brides, in imitation of 'superbrides', consume and work hard on their bodies in order to embody a successful bridal identity.

These discussions in turn lead me to address a third issue – the romanticism surrounding the wedding day. It is my intention here to distinguish which elements of the wedding are categorized as 'romantic' by brides and grooms and, correspondingly, those which are not. Underpinning this analysis is the issue of where exactly 'romance' is located. Is it a quality couples feel to be already inherent in their relationships, which is celebrated and displayed openly in the wedding context? Or is it to be found in commodities with particular symbolic value, items like the dress or the ring that are marketed primarily as the material embodiments of romantic sentiment? The answers to such questions, to be sure, do not have to fall into one camp or the other, instead they further problematize any notion of 'authentic', unmediated emotion standing theoretically opposed to the emotions that are potentiated or enhanced through consumption. In fact, as I shall go on to argue, the evocation of 'authentic', spontaneous emotion which pre-exists consumption is itself part of the romantic narrative which continues to structure the wedding occasion. As a final point, I identify the relevance of these discussions to the ongoing critical appraisal of Campbell's Romantic ethic thesis. This chapter concludes with a summary of the main issues and arguments raised.

En route to marriage: the couples' narrative

During the last weeks leading up to the wedding day, brides' and grooms' activities reached fever pitch. This period of pre-wedding hustle and bustle, which typically ran from a fortnight before to the wedding morning, culminated in a flurry of last-minute decisions and a concentration of consuming duties. Even at this late stage on their road to marriage, most of the brides in the study still spoke of the active wedding preparations as their sole responsibility: 'I think I was more stressed than anything, what with having to arrange it all myself' (Louise). Traditional rituals or occasions reinforced the imminence of the wedding further and provided some sort of structure to the pre-wedding period. Such rituals – hen nights, stag nights, rehearsals, wedding preparation classes, for example – enabled the preparations of certain couples to retain a developmental, processual feel to them in the midst of an otherwise seemingly chaotic and panicked environment. The last days of preparation were spoken about with a strong sense of finality as the impending reality of what had up to then remained a fantasy drew ever closer: 'Twenty-one months of planning and at last the week before here it is, it's just coming to an end now' (Sarah).

The night before the big day, pre-wedding behaviour was segregated by gender. Grooms were banished to their friends' or mothers' houses, going out to socialize armed with strict instructions not to take any form of risk that could endanger the perfection of the following wedding day: 'I just went out with my mates, but I was a good boy and I was in before midnight' (John). Brides, on the other hand, stayed in the relative safety and security of their own or their mother's house. Key female members of the wedding party were invited to stay over in order to add to the sense of occasion and to fuel the bride's emotion: 'My chief bridesmaid, Carly, she stayed over and we just had like a girlies' night in' (Louise); 'My best friend was with me as well and she was going "Oh this is really good, this is so exciting"' (Hayley).

This gendered segregation of pre-wedding behaviour intensified on the morning of the wedding, producing very different accounts of the actions and feelings of brides and grooms. The following extracts from one couple, Fiona and Leon, were typical in this respect. Grooms' activities were not directly wedding-oriented. Instead, they centred on typical masculine leisure activities like watching television (especially music or sports programmes) and socializing in pubs with their friends. As Leon recalled:

> Me and the best man, we were all right. We went to McDonald's for our breakfast. Came back and we'd got all the suits hung up like, and we were sort of like sitting down. We just didn't know what to do with ourselves because we were just fairly normal. And I just said, 'I'm getting married in a couple of hours, we should be jumping around or something'. We just sat there watching MTV till the time we changed. Had a couple of whiskeys and then went, got in the car.

By contrast, brides' accounts of their wedding morning rituals centred on the careful and co-ordinated transformation of both self and surroundings in anticipation of living out their fantasy day. Putting on the wedding dress was nearly always referred to as the start of the wedding day proper – it was, to all intents and purposes, the defining moment in the transformation of the bride:

> It only hit me ... I went upstairs to get dressed, came down the stairs and my brothers were both there, and my Dad, and that's when I burst into tears ... No, nerves didn't hit me till I'd actually got the dress, the veil and everything on. (Fiona)

From this point onwards, the events of the day seemed to unfold with great momentum. Both the ceremony and the reception were spoken about as highly emotional occasions, with brides focusing primarily on the former and grooms on the latter. Whilst some couples were able to recall distinct and vivid memories of most aspects of their big day, others either struggled to formulate mental images or could not articulate their experience into words. Brides, in particular, stressed the unreality of the whole experience, and the certain amount of unease they felt from being centre of attention: 'Just having everyone looking at you all day, I didn't really like that part of it ... but you accept it really' (Hayley). As the wedding day progressed, the role of the groom, hitherto foreshadowed by the bride's, grew in significance, structured around responsibility for ensuring the smooth running of the day and culminating in the reception speech:

> You don't have chance to even have a drink because then the photographer turns up. Then you're waiting for the registrar to turn up and get the details from them and then you're having to greet your guests that are turning up. These brides have it easy! [*laughs*] (John).

Consumption and emotion: a mixed bag of possibilities

Whilst we saw in the previous chapter that shopping was the most obvious and important aspect of wedding consumption in its initial stages, the immediate pre-wedding build-up and the day itself revolve around other forms of consumption and other activities which are consumption-related. There are in fact different types of consumption and different types of emotion that interweave and intersect at different points in the wedding narrative. We shall also see in the examples that follow how gender becomes an important structuring factor in the relationship between consumption and emotion. The following section has been organized around three specific themes which illuminate the different ways consumption and emotion interact: these are control, knowledge and identity.

(i) Control

Consumption offered brides a way of controlling their emotions in the immediate days and hours before the ceremony. It also functioned as a means of negotiating, or passing back and forth, control over the wedding between the bride and groom. Although brides often conceived of the intensely active pre-wedding period as 'stressful', 'rushed' yet still 'exciting', these feelings, as Sarah's account reminds us, were not regarded as 'emotional states':

> I think myself I ... I didn't have time to have an emotional state as such. We were so busy. It was very hectic, I was very rushed, I was very excited, a lot of adrenaline. We had people flying in from all over the place, dresses to pick up.

Sarah saw any feelings she may have had as inevitable or unavoidable reactions to external pressures rather than emotions that had been allowed to form seemingly independently and autonomously at their own pace. Brides, in fact, spoke about the emotional anticipation of their weddings as a luxury or indulgence that they could hardly afford to pursue. This claim was premised upon the belief – a belief clearly articulated in bridal magazines – that at this crucial concluding part of the wedding preparations the bride must strive even more to control and postpone her emotions in order to remain rational and clear-headed for as long as possible.

Some brides justified this enforced rationality by conceptualizing those around them as dependants, in need of guidance or instruction in their wedding duties. Homes, in effect, at this stage became makeshift wedding headquarters, with brides positioning themselves as the indispensable nerve centre of the operation:

> I was taking an average of eight calls a day in the week leading up to the wedding and an average of ... in that week we had approximately thirty-five e-mails from, like, the caterers wanted final instructions, the people who were doing our seating plan wanted final instructions, the top hat and tails people, they'd basically got our order wrong and we had to sort that out at the last minute. (Sarah)

> *Louise*: I mean I boxed everything up, I did all my own favours and scrolls and everything. So we boxed everything up and everything had a label on it, what it was and what was to be done with it. And I wrote a list as well. The guy at Pipers Hotel, where we had the reception, he thought it was all very organized actually, didn't he?
> *John*: Yes, it was foolproof.

In fact, purposely retaining primary responsibility of such matters and not sharing any of the associated worries or tasks with their partners could be seen as a conscious attempt to keep their minds sufficiently occupied, thus preventing thoughts turning to the fast approaching wedding day. The organization of consumer goods and people, in this sense, functioned to control emotion, or at least dull the existence of any nerves or possible doubts about the wedding occasion.

It is interesting to note here the emphasis of brides on their total control over the impending wedding when, historically, marriage was about handling over autonomy and control to one's husband.

Certainly, notions of bridal control did seem to be somewhat fragile and fleeting. For example, the bride's emotional anticipation of the wedding day might begin to turn to feelings of dread, nervousness or sheer panic. If this became the case, grooms pointed to the inappropriateness of such emotional overspilling:

> *James*:   She was getting a bit ratty with me.
> *Tina*:   Yeah, I got a bit ratty with him. He told me off a couple of times, like 'calm down'.

When a subtle, cautionary reminder did not prove effective, a number of grooms felt it necessary to step in and oversee the final, yet all-important fine details. These roles, conceived almost as backstage directors, emphasized an emotionally detached and calm, controlled authority over the activities that surrounded them. Some grooms described their wedding at this point in business-like terms – a type of 'work', once again, instead of leisure: 'The horse and carriage was at Marchand Hall at 10 a.m. They were the first contractors to actually arrive on site' (Robert). This allowed their own status as newly appointed supervisors of the wedding production to follow:

> And I was down to this sort of level, you know, having an itinerary [*groom shows me a timetable of how he expected the wedding day to run*] that I had to run through for the guy, which I did because he needed it. Then I could like chase him up and make sure everything was like working out. (Matthew)

> You have to keep chasing everybody and having a contingency plan. (Robert)

The steady male hand and head of reason were required, in effect, to step in to rescue the wedding preparations from the hands of the increasingly emotional, irrational and hence, incapable, bride.

(ii) Knowledge

Foreknowledge of the affective potential of consumer goods enabled couples to construct and manage some of the emotion of the wedding day. Robert and Sarah's explanation for achieving (but, interestingly, not exceeding) what they wanted for their wedding revolved around accumulating extensive knowledge of the consumption required to realize their fantasy day. Most importantly, they already reassuringly 'knew' the emotions that their consumption was going to evoke from their several 'trial runs' and their extensive programme of consumer testing:

> I think by and large our expectations were met because everything we did we checked out first. Everything we'd actually seen so we knew what we were getting. We sampled everything, so we weren't taking risks on that. (Robert)

Such a rationalistic pursuit of risk-elimination through consumption secured satisfaction well in advance of the event for which it was intended. Excluding the possibility of disappointment through the acquisition of high levels of consumer knowledge, and the subsequent risk-elimination it facilitated, points to the fact that consumers themselves realize how 'disappointment' and 'disillusionment' can often be part and parcel of the usual cycle of consumption and have now become (on this most important of occasions) sophisticated enough as trained consumers to plan how to evade it.

Perhaps predictably, however, despite the apparent shared opinion of Robert and Sarah, the role consumption played in this sense (that is, foreknowledge of its affective potential) typically differed for brides and grooms. Most brides said they simply 'knew' they were going to have the day they wanted, yet still felt an incredible sense of achievement when beholding their creation in its totality. Grooms, on the other hand, who had not been involved in pre-wedding consumption, either through choice or through the control and dominance of their partner, often expressed a genuine amazement at the visual impact of the reception room – an impact that was duly credited to the careful consumption of the bride and the industry professionals she employed:

> But the layout of the room when you walked in and saw it ... you could never imagine ... I mean that can't be planned. I mean the woman who did the flowers, she was spot on. She explained what she was going to do, but you couldn't visualize it until it was all in there. So that was a gasp when you walked in. (John)

> With the reception the most vivid memory I've got is when I went into the room, because you have in your mind a picture of what it is going to look like and it was so much better than I imagined. (Nick)

The implication here is that due to their limited knowledge of and involvement in the wedding preparation, grooms had little information or material with which to construct an accurate mental picture of the event. This allowed 'real life' to easily surpass what had been imagined or expected.

(iii) Identity

I have addressed the role both consumption and emotion play in the construction of bridal identity at several points in this book, and indeed go on to explore this topic further later in this chapter with respect to brides' attitudes towards romance. It is important, however, also to highlight how consumption and emotion interact to construct and reinforce the identity of the groom. All grooms who took part in this study (except those marrying abroad – although they did often allude to a type of reception or party on arrival back home) considered the reception to be the focal point of their wedding experience. Whilst during the wedding preparation and the ceremony grooms can be said to play a supporting role to their bride, they clearly reposition themselves as equal partners or, in some cases, as the dominant 'Master of Ceremonies' when the reception commences. Understanding how grooms negotiate their identity in the reception reveals how their opinions on both consumption and emotion seemed to change somewhat in this context. Grooms felt their own role was placed under the spotlight for the first real time in the reception. The symbolic importance of the reception to the groom can be said to centre on the traditional masculine identity of 'provider'. Food rituals, especially the collective consumption of food, function as a basis of social meaning and serve a very important specific function in legitimizing the authority and identity of the patriarchal figure (Douglas, 1982). The hospitality of the groom and his ability to facilitate sociability between his guests through collective consumption can be connected to his invention of a new self in the next part of his lifecourse – to establish himself, in other words, in his new role of husband and to be seen to be embodying all the traditional masculine qualities that are associated with it (provider, protector, host, for instance).

Although not a direct form of consuming in itself, the groom's reception speech (along with that of the best man) is usually regarded as the pinnacle of that particular consumption occasion. Grooms seemed to view their speech as an opportunity for being openly emotional in front of the wedding party in much the same way as the bride expected to display her emotionality during the ceremony. Matthew, for instance, told me how much his reception speech meant to him:

I mean, I suppose it's difficult to talk about really, but when I was giving my speech as well I was saying some things about Kate at various stages at which one point my voice was going ... and then Kate was on that side sitting there and Kate's mom was sitting on the other and she sort of put her hand on my arm sort of thing ... I had a few people come up to me in the evening and say, 'What you said was really nice, I wish my husband had said something along those lines'. For some reason the mentality of some of them was to sort of say, 'Well, all I did was to get up and take the piss out of her. I didn't even say how nice she was'. So perhaps from my point of view, I wanted to stand up and say what I want to say from the heart or whatever you want to call it. As far as I'm concerned it's sort of like a platform to stand up and get people to laugh and to cry and all the rest of it.

As we have seen, grooms do not appear to invest much emotional energy in pre-wedding consumption activities. Yet the speech, one might argue, its apprehension, content and delivery, along with all the hopes and fears it signified as well as its required discipline (typically in relation to restricting alcohol), do appear to be somewhat comparable to the more directly consumption-based preoccupations of the bride, especially in terms of the emotional and imaginative anticipation it causes.

The wedding fantasy: transformation/objectification/re-enchantment

We have seen, then, several ways in which consumption and emotion interact. However, much of this interaction is a product of the wedding experience itself, especially its construction as a magical, fairy-tale occasion. To explore this further, in this section I focus on how brides and grooms (but brides in particular) emotionally consume the wedding fantasy. Central to my discussion is the way a number of brides describe being transformed, objectified and re-enchanted through their wedding experience.

Bridal transformations required extensive labour and discipline. There is evidence here to support Winship's (1987) idea of the 'work' of consumption being a distinctly female activity. First, brides recalled the domestic labour that was required of them in order to ensure nothing impinged or intruded upon their later emergence out of the house and into the public gaze as a bride:

On the day of the wedding, I mean we got up about eight o'clock and we started off by sweeping the front yards for when we walked out, putting bags over the gateposts so we didn't get our dresses mucky. (Louise)

Domestic labour, on this occasion, was a necessary form of consumption-related work, one that eliminated risks before the final assemblance of the bridal identity could proceed and be displayed to others.

The construction of bridal appearance through appropriate hairstyling and the application of make-up, along with wearing the dress and other accessories, was also referred to as a type of work or production that depended now upon the skills and proficiencies of industry professionals. Whilst brides had earlier described the months of effort put into pre-wedding dieting and beautification, control over the bridal appearance at this penultimate stage was willingly delegated to other, more experienced, parties (hairdressers, beauticians, make-up artists). Relinquishing a certain amount of control over the finished product of the bridal identity was strongly tied to the belief that after the work of consumption had been completed brides have to 'let go' somewhat in order to achieve and experience a full transformation. Such transformations, typically into a Cinderella-like princess (see also Tseëlon, 1995; Schouten, 1991), were thought to be both more achievable and more perfected if conducted by a qualified professional. However, as we shall see, this process of objectifying or commodifying herself as 'the bride', which, in certain respects, intensified when the bride's own labour into this endeavour was replaced by that of an industry worker, came to play an important role in her sense of self as the day progressed.

As we saw in the case of Fiona, putting on the wedding dress was the defining moment in the transformation of the bride. It brought with it unprecedented levels of emotion, conveyed as an intense and sudden moment of realization. Until this definitive moment of getting into costume it seems that the bridal identity primarily centred on and limited itself to two closely connected roles, that of 'consumer' and 'worker'. The wedding dress, however, seemed to trigger in brides a fuller, and more full-bodied, emotional realization of what being a bride signified; the dress of course being a key wedding symbol long before the current commercial explosion of wedding consumption.

Perhaps not surprisingly, whilst the wedding dress was regarded as the most 'sacred' artifact in the bridal ensemble (Otnes and Lowrey, 1993) it equally holds the power to evoke considerable feelings of disappointment or unease in its wearer. Louise's comments highlight the fragility of the fantasy she is trying to live out:

> I came in here and sat watching Cinderella on video ... As soon as I went to put the dress on, I don't know where the time went and that's when I had problems. I started crying because my dress when I'd been trying it on, because my shoulders tend to be a bit slopey, if you know what I mean, and erm, with the dress, I kept saying 'The shoulders are too big for me' and the woman in the shop kept pulling it down and saying 'That's fine'. But then when I'd got it on obviously in the morning, yeah you'd pull it down and it was fine, but I was walking about and it was rising up and I think that's what got me in tears. My brother gave me away. He was here ... bridesmaids and that just left me and it was my brother that helped me and I was all miserable going 'I may as well of just had you, not had a bridesmaid!' Because he actually helped me more than they did. (Louise)

The dissatisfaction felt by Louise during what should have been her full transformation into the bride prevented her feelings from being conceptualized beyond the discourse of consumption – that is to say, consumption is only perceived to be perfect when it is transcended. The wedding dress, in this case, remained a substandard commodity. The false assurances of the bridal shop sales assistant along with the imperfections of the dress itself, which were at the same time ironically juxtaposed to the perfect fantasy of the Cinderella fairy-tale currently playing on the video in the background, functioned to dispossess Louise's dress of its own magical, transformatory powers.[1] This, in turn, provoked an emotional outburst that needed to be tempered by a male figure.

The consumption-based construction of the bride as a fantasy 'object' for the wedding party, and also for herself, to admire, caused a continued self-consciousness of her position as the unequivocal centre of attention for the whole day. This self-consciousness was never felt more intensely than in the early stages of the wedding ceremony, an occasion which marked the first close public scrutiny of the bride. Whilst the wedding is, for most of us, a visually familiar ritual, for those actually marrying this familiarity seemed to contradict the strangeness of their own participation as the central actors in the proceedings:

> *Fiona*: You knew it was happening, but it didn't feel like it was happening to you. Do you know what I mean?

Leon: Like I say, you go to that many weddings it just felt a bit funny because it was you up there this time.

A few couples, however, managed to reconcile any feelings of estrangement or disconnection from their own wedding by conceptualizing the day as a purposely extraordinary, spectacular and, hence, unfamiliar experience. The wedding day, typically spoken about using theatrical analogies – the 'final curtain' (Patricia), the 'main event' (James), a 'big play' (Harriet) – was a stage upon which the bride and groom took the starring roles in performing their new identities to a captive audience. Sarah's description of arriving at her wedding, for instance, tellingly reveals her self-dramatization as making a movie-star entrance:

We had the carriage arriving, twenty people sort of stood outside the front of the house taking photographs. The whole vision of it coming true 'OK, here we go, camera rolling, lights, action'. I'll never forget that.

Robert, her groom, also commented on the photographer describing their wedding as being 'like a film set'. This was taken as a compliment in both Robert and Sarah's minds that it was not just themselves who felt the unreality and enchanted, elaborate spectacle of the occasion, and that the day was therefore not just in their own imaginations.

The unreality of the wedding was emphasized further through the seeming disjuncture between the bride and groom's sense of time passing on the day and the 'real time' chronology of the event. On the one hand, brides, especially, often had little recollection of certain aspects of the day, snapping their fingers to relate in disbelief how their wedding had came and gone in a bewitching instant – '... and it just went like that' (Fiona snaps her fingers). This is further evidence of the bride viewing her wedding as a magical, fantasy occasion – a spellbinding experience almost, or twenty-four hours in the land of make-believe. Yet, at the same time, certain aspects of the wedding were experienced as if in cinematic slow motion:

Sarah: When I actually got out of the carriage at Marchand Hall and then started to walk down the stairs after that it was like I was in a dream sequence. I just … we had approximately 180 photographs took that day and I can't remember being stood in half of them. I felt like it was a complete dream sequence and then you wake up at the end of the dream ten hours later.

Sharon: So it's like a fairy tale?

Sarah: Absolutely, yes. Floating around on some unique drug or something, I don't know.

We have encountered the notion of brides trying to 'let go' in order to experience their weddings in a more intense emotionally embodied manner before, most recently in the context of allowing others to assist in perfecting the bridal identity. For most brides in the research, the wedding facilitated a daylong re-enchantment of their selves, which was synonymous with experiencing their immediate surroundings in a kind of child-like wonder and bewilderment:

> I just smiled all day. I woke up smiling and I was just ... it was like ... the only way I can describe it was like all my Christmases and birthdays as a child ... that excited feeling but multiplied ... and I was just like that all day long. It was just fantastic. I was worn out from adrenaline by the end of the day ... You don't have it as an adult. Birthdays and Christmas have lost their sort of excitement, haven't they, by the time you've got to twenty or so ... But I didn't realize the buzz I'd get from it. I thought I'd just be like, oh yeah false smile 'thanks for coming', all that, but no it was just a complete adrenaline rush the whole day long. (Tina)

The emotions brides experienced on their wedding day, despite being portrayed as authentic and overwhelming, were equally regarded as an inevitable and expected part of the occasion – explained as 'just the emotion of getting married' (Natalie). Whilst brides like Tina may not have predicted the intensity or depth of feeling they would experience, most assumed it would be themselves along with other female members of the wedding party who were most likely to 'get emotional' (Beverley). Crying, even under the gaze of the congregation, was seen as normal bridal and, by implication, female behaviour. This left some brides (unintentionally) coming close to caricaturing themselves as emotionally uncontrollable women in floods of tears even before the wedding ceremony had officially begun: 'I cried all the way down the aisle. I was crying at the bottom of the church. He daredn't look at me because he could hear me sobbing' (Fiona). The emotionality of brides appeared to be at least partially separate from their feelings for the men that they were about to marry. Rather, emotion seemed to be triggered by a sensory, aesthetic experience of the wedding at a more symbolic, fantasy level. The way consumption and emotion become intertwined in the wedding fantasy is also further related to if and how brides and grooms conceptualize the experience as 'romantic'. It is to this issue I now turn.

Romance: the most important guest at the wedding?

In this final section, I discuss the surrounding romanticism of the wedding day and explore in what sense a traditional romantic narrative continues to structure the occasion. Before doing so, however, I take a brief look at some of the connections social scientists have made between romance, marriage and the wedding.

Much has been written by feminists about the institution of marriage.[2] Although the many insights and arguments gleaned from this pool of literature will not be rehearsed again here, it is worth at least extracting a few of the main issues. Brook (2002) usefully distinguishes between critiques arguing that marriage is a sexist institution and those regarding it as a institution of patriarchy. The former, it seems, concentrates on exposing how, through limited opportunities and choice, the consequences of marriage disadvantage women. These arguments infer that a radical reform of marriage is needed to address the unequal power relationship between husbands and wives. The latter cluster of critiques – those arguing that marriage is a patriarchal institution – see marriage as structurally and necessarily oppressive to women. Brook goes on to list a catalogue of examples which illustrate the relations of economic and emotional dependency organized through marriage. These include the exploitation of women's domestic labour, men's (hetero)sexual rights, sexual domestic violence and the household/family economics of dependency and subordination.

Ingraham (1999), in particular, has widened such critiques to expose broader links between marriage, economics and politics, all of which serve to reinforce further male dominance and female subordination. It is argued that weddings can offer certain advantages in the workplace:

> When used in professional settings, for example, weddings work as a form of ideological control to signal membership in relations of ruling as well as to signify that the couple is normal, moral, productive, family-centred, upstanding, and, most importantly, appropriately gendered. Consider the ways weddings are used by

coworkers in line for promotions or to marginalize and exceptional-
ize single or non married employees. For example, two employees
are competing for a promotion. One is single, the other engaged to
marry. The engaged worker invites all members of the office, including the hiring committee, to the wedding. Because of the heterosexual imaginary, weddings are viewed as innocuous, fun-loving, and
as signalling membership in dominant culture. As such, they give
people significant advantage in the workplace and are anything but
benign. (Ingraham, 1999, p. 18)

So too, weddings can be subject to political usage (Ingraham, 1999).
This is evident in two main ways. On the one hand, certain right-wing
groups might seek to discredit (both legally and ideologically) those
who do not subscribe to the dominant heterosexual arrangement (for
instance, lesbians, gays, single mothers, domestic partners or transgen-
dered people), thereby reaffirming and naturalizing the institution of
marriage as an 'ideal' model of normality. On the other hand, an
increase in the number of weddings may be prescribed as a solution to
socio-economic problems. Ingraham argues, in this respect, that certain
state policy proposals in the US recommend that women and children
who have become reliant on state benefits must do the responsible
thing and get married, thus aiding recovery from welfare dependency
and from a national deficit.

Feminist research has therefore long sought to expose heterosexual,
romantic ideology as a fabrication or type of fiction used strategically to
subordinate and exploit women. As Hollway (1984, p. 228) puts it, 'heterosexual relations are the primary site where gender difference is repro-
duced'. Rites of passage, ceremonial occasions and consumables which
seem to embody and reinforce this ideology, and in turn create and nor-
malize particular gendered positions (via the taken-for-grantedness of
heterosexuality) have been critiqued (Leonard, 1980; Hollway, 1984;
Ingraham 1999; Langford 1999). The catalogue of criticism on romantic
fiction has, for example, highlighted several points of interest in this
respect. Through their representations of female characters as fantasy
objects of male desire, romance texts perpetuate the passive looked-
at-ness of women (Pawlowicz, 1995); romances offer an illusory escape
from the dissatisfactions of real life and can be regarded therefore as
compensatory rather than liberatory texts (Radway, 1984); romantic
fiction endorses the dominant ideological discourses of 'race', class,
gender and sexuality, thereby increasing their consumers' acceptance of
them (Cranny-Francis, 1994); romances, through strategies of reader-

character identification, coerce and stereotype women into subordinates, distorting female subjectivity in the process (Light, 1984).

Whilst the concept of romance and the ways in which we experience and express romantic emotion may be subject to social and cultural contextualization, it is also claimed that our orientation towards love is rooted in our biology. Walsh (1996), for example, discusses how evolution exerted different selection pressures on the males and females of our species, arguing that, alongside culture and individual experience, our evolutionary legacy plays some part in determining the different ways men and women love. To state it simply, males on the whole prefer younger women because of their reproductive fitness, whereas women prefer older and more mature men who have better prospects as a provider and protector for her and her family.[3] The process of 'falling in love' with a mate who more or less readily fits our inbuilt or programmed 'ideal' is consequently demystified as a kind of 'biological revolution':

> 'Falling in love' is most often preceded by a steady build-up of acts, thoughts, gestures, imaginations and delicious fantasies. We meet someone, and somehow his or her unique characteristics begin to have an anabolic effect on what scientists unromantically call our hypothalamic-pituitary-gonadal axis ... Romantic love, then, is an intense emotional state precipitated by the stimuli presented to us by the love object. (Walsh, 1996, pp. 186–7)

We have seen then, albeit briefly, how romance is produced and consumed via gender relations – relations which cannot stand apart from social and biological influences (in varying degrees). To this end, love and romantic emotion, throughout history, have been open to negotiation and appropriation by the sexes. This is well illustrated in the Romantic period itself which enforced strong gender boundaries between literary forms (Mellor, 1988). The literary canon of Romanticism was divided into a 'higher' male genre of epic poetry (including romances), heroic tragedies, odes and satires, leaving the domestic novel as the main territory of the feminine 'lower' sphere. Since male Romantic artists were succeeding in a vocation which demanded and valorized conventional feminine traits – self-expression, sensitivity, emotionality – constant struggles arose to prevent total absorption into the feminine. Traditional female characteristics were therefore appropriated and used as a means of gendering male poetic practise. 'The categories of gender,' Ross (1988, p. 28) states, 'both in their lives and in their work, help the Romantics establish rites of passage toward poetic identity and toward masculine empowerment'.[4]

The dominant definition of love in contemporary culture is feminized, being primarily associated with women and with qualities seen as feminine (Cancian, 1990). This can easily lead to the assumption that women are not only more skilled than men at love, but that women *require* love *and* marriage in order to achieve a sense of well-being. Yet this need not imply that women have an overtly romantic orientation towards relationships. In fact, some evidence points to the contrary. As Cancian notes, the usual sociological explanation for men's romanticism is that women are more dependent on men for money and status and consequently are responsible for more of the 'emotion work'[5] in the relationship.[6] Men, on the other hand, according to Cancian, see love as 'magically and perfectly present or absent' (1990, p. 77).

The conceptualization and experience of romance by men and women may be further complicated as gender roles and interpersonal relations become redefined. For example, drawing on the work of Duncombe and Marsden (1993), Langford (1999) repeats the point that gender differences in emotionality may be highlighted and intensified by the shift from marriage as an 'institution' to the ideal of fulfilment within personal relationships. It may also be the case that the advances of feminism alongside the recent popular emphasis on 'girl power' have meant that younger women in particular now express 'romantic' views of *independence* over and above *coupledom*[7] – or at least argue that whilst they want weddings, they are reluctant to become 'wives' (Spender, 1994). Equally, though, it might appear to be more 'romantic' to get married in an era of high divorce rates and associated cynicism, striving against the odds to live happily ever after as husband and wife.

As a way of entering a discussion on the ways romance was conceptualized by the sampled brides and grooms in reference to their own weddings, I reproduce a substantial post-wedding interview extract with one couple. It identifies the themes and issues typically raised when couples were asked whether or not their wedding was 'romantic' and, depending upon their response, what factors did or did not make it so?

Sharon: Would you say your wedding was romantic?
Sarah: Yes I would. A hundred and ten per cent.
Sharon: And what made it so?

Robert: Fairy-tale.

Sarah: Fairytale. Cinderella. That's the first thing you think of, you think of the castle in Cinderella, you think of ... I suppose maybe it's an incorrect thing to say, but it's like a person that's like a little girl that's growing up and has had ... not an easy life, I haven't, and then she meets her handsome prince and she has the fairy-tale wedding and that's what she represents to me because I've always had to work quite hard in life for things. I've had to wait a long time for various things, like I've had to wait for this for a fairly long time, for the wedding that I've always wanted, and it was very romantic. I think Robert is very romantic and for me it is ... I don't know, I can't explain.

Robert: Yes, but you just look at the period, the 1700-style house and the traditional dress of that period, you could argue that that is the Romantic period. I may say traditional instead, but it may mean the same thing.

Sarah: Traditional, yes, but it was very romantic. The dress is ... I mean somebody described it as a 'dream creation'. That's what somebody described it as.

Robert: I'm thinking more *Pride and Prejudice* ... for other reasons. Again, there was a romantic theme there, wasn't it? The woman's main objective in life was to find herself a rich husband. That's the truth of the matter and it fits in with that.

Sharon: What factors do you think influence how romantic a wedding is?

Sarah: Romantic music I think most certainly, and it has to be a string quartet because they can play some wonderful romantic music and things. We had very romantic music at our wedding, didn't we? And the dress, I mean the dress has to be something that has stepped out of a Cinderella scrapbook. It's got to be something with beautiful detail, big flowing train and everything like that and cute little bridesmaids. That to me is romanticism. And also the very elegant surroundings. The horse-drawn carriage, I mean Rolls Royces to me don't have the romanticism of a horse-drawn carriage. I mean, they can't possibly can they? And again it's like Cinderella arrived in a coach and she had this beautiful dress on and everything and the orchestra started playing and the heavens opened up, you know, it's all those sort of things to me.

Robert: I think you might say from the male point of view, in our particular wedding, it's playing the Darcy of this world. You could argue that, couldn't you? Projecting yourself into that if you like. That's reasonable. Lord of the Manor ... That's quite reasonable, right? Playing out your fantasies in certain respects.

The above interview highlights several points of interest. Most explicitly perhaps, both Robert and Sarah equated the romanticism of their wedding with what they deemed to be its 'fairy-tale' quality. They were not alone in making this connection, with four other couples responding similarly (Jessica and Josh, Beverley and Mark, Hayley and Nick, Fiona and Leon). The Cinderella fantasy, in particular, provided a poignant source of identification for the bride. This is due, as Sarah herself explained, to the fairy-tale's underpinning romantic narrative – one which tells a rags-to-riches story of a young girl escaping the mundane drudgery of ordinary life when she meets, falls in love and eventually marries a handsome prince – which she felt mirrored, although in a somewhat exaggerated form, her own lifecourse. Whilst Cinderella is a childhood story, it has become symbolic of the marketized romantic image of weddings, not least in the significance of weddings for women as a rite of passage from childhood to adulthood. A well-known storyline with similar underpinning themes, that of the relationship between Mr Darcy and Elizabeth Bennett in Jane Austen's classic romance *Pride and Prejudice*, provides a comparable and complementary source of identification for the groom. Both sources of identification are used by Robert and Sarah to infuse the meanings of their own wedding with those signified by what can be termed the 'traditional romantic fantasy' that structure these and many other popular love stories.

The significance of the traditional romantic fantasy in the wedding narratives of some brides and grooms requires further comment here. Whether frameworked by a fairytale narrative (Cinderella) or historically contextualized within a literary genre (*Pride and Prejudice*),[8] the conventions of the traditional romantic fantasy seem timeless, formulaic and familiar. Its leading characters, at the same time, remain somewhat unspecific (prince/princess, groom/bride, hero/heroine, man/woman), their only real defining feature being the part they play in the construction and completion of the primary storyline. Such characters (as caricatures of people 'in love') create roles or identities in the popular imagination that 'real-life' couples can embody. Some contemporary couples do, as Robert and Sarah amongst others testified, conceptualize their weddings in ways akin to the traditional romantic fantasy, inserting themselves as the main protagonists in the narrative.

The question remains, however, why should brides and grooms feel the need to do this? A series of connected explanations can be suggested. First, it could be argued that the traditional romantic fantasy can be quite easily replicated and controlled. Once couples have effectively 'made it' to the church, or equivalent licensed venue, it is likely that they have already experienced many of the romantic conventions associated with courtship. They now have only to construct and perform the final wedding scene (which has, effectively, already been scripted). In contrast to the impending marriage, therefore, with its indefinable lifespan, its unpredictable scripts and its unknown emotional journeys, the wedding appears to be a more controllable occasion. This is perhaps why some couples are so eager to embrace the traditional romantic fantasy as a structuring framework for their wedding – it has very familiar, obvious and widely understood significations and connotations.

It is also, moreover, thought to be easily achievable through consumption. As Chapter 3 illustrated, the wedding industry has further commodified romance into an extensive array of goods and services for inclusion in the big day. Successfully constructing and then living out the traditional romantic fantasy through consumption would be one sure strategy for avoiding disappointment and disillusionment on the wedding day. This success, relating back to Campbell's 'desire-acquisition-use-disillusionment-renewed desire' cycle is of particular importance to wedding consumers since a 'renewed desire' to have a bigger, better and more fulfilling wedding would be highly undesirable for newly married couples. The traditional romantic fantasy, then, through its familiarity and accessibility through consumption, provides an 'ideal' model towards which wedding consumers can be directed.

The idea of couples 'performing' or 'staging' romance, however, in imitation of the final scene of the traditional romantic fantasy, need not imply that such practices be inauthentic or void of any deep emotional significance. Rather, through photographs and videos, couples were concerned to capture tangible evidence of their present romantic feelings – possibly, one might suppose, to provide an emotional trigger in case such feelings were to fade once married:

I think the photos ... this is a good album because it shows you the whole day. Yes, it's like a story. That's why we want to get so many because it's like a story and it does portray a fairy-tale wedding. (Nick)

Capturing images of the perfect romantic wedding did, however, often involve a willing suspension of disbelief: 'I met my brother at the church because he had to pretend he'd come in this car with us for the photographs' (Beverley). By striving to replicate and experience their own weddings as romantic, some brides and grooms, in effect, sought to transform 'real life' as it was being lived out into another form of imaginary.

The traditional romantic wedding fantasy, with the bride as a Cinderella/princess figure is still promoted by the wedding industry as the 'ideal' (and easiest) narrative to replicate or realize through consumption. An additional reason for this has been suggested by the research. As this traditional bridal role is symbolized by virginal whiteness and its connotations of purity and innocence, the traditional romantic wedding fantasy cannot accommodate (pre-existing) children into it and therefore renders them invisible or, at best, subordinates them in relation to the dominant romantic narrative. However, as many couples already cohabit before marriage and also often are parents, children are now being brought into the traditional romantic wedding narrative without challenging its underlying ideology. This is achieved through appropriate consumption to absorb children into the fabric of the wedding experience. As such, the wedding industry (not one to miss a marketing opportunity) has simultaneously commodified and romanticized the child into either a bride or groom 'in waiting' – that is, dominant wedding fashions for girls are typically fairy or princess costumes, whilst boys can be dressed in replicas of their Dad's (or step-Dad's) suits.[9] Several of the couples in my sample did indeed dress their children in this way.

So far, then, I have emphasized how a number of brides and grooms equated the romanticism of the wedding day with its fairy-tale quality. I argued that such a quality refers to the image, storyline and associated emotions of what I term the 'traditional romantic fantasy'. In this sense, romance is celebrated as a timeless essence between those who feel themselves to be in love. It is at once an ethereal and embodied emotion which resonates over and above the specificities of each wedding occasion.

Yet, referring back to the interview extract from Robert and Sarah, whilst their own ideas about romance were articulated at this more generalized, almost abstract level, they, along with all of the other couples in the study who themselves labelled their own weddings as 'romantic' in some sense or replied affirmatively when asked directly whether or not their wedding was a romantic occasion, were able to cite specific examples of romance personal to their own day. These examples fell into two distinct categories – one covering commodities or other tangible objects with obvious romantic connotations, the other documenting the intimate emotional interactions between the bride and groom.

Beginning with commodities, motifs and other material expressions of romance, the following responses can be cited: 'The champagne in the car' (Beverley); 'We had somebody playing the piano' (Harriet); 'He gave me a present ... a white gold heart' (Kate); 'The church' (Mark); 'The photos' (Nick); 'The string quartet' (Sarah); 'The dress' (Sarah); 'The horse-drawn carriage' (Sarah); 'He'd got me a massive bouquet of red roses' (Louise).

Yet, as I have already stated, 'romance' was not only present at the wedding in these material forms. The word seemed, in many more instances, to capture the essence of emotional interactions between the bride and groom, whether those moments were to occur alone or under the gaze of the congregation: 'Little things like holding hands when we did our vows' (Tina); 'The emotions more so than anything else, what you are doing and saying' (Mark); 'Because I did not understand that I would be that emotional. You can't foresee how you are going to feel' (Fiona); 'We got choked up saying our vows' (Beverley); 'Things we did on our own' (Louise); 'Being close to Josh all day' (Jessica); 'Speaking our vows in front of everyone so everyone knows we are committing to each other' (Josh); 'Quite a lot of tears' (Sarah); 'When I walked up the aisle ... the little look he gave me' (Tina); 'The speech' (Kate); 'Little bits, like your first dance' (John). In addition to these responses, two interviewees directly associated the romantic nature of their wedding with their own authorial control over the event: 'Just because it was our decision' (James); 'Doing it the way we wanted to' (Jessica).

At this point, however, it is worth comparing which elements of the wedding were felt to be 'unromantic'. These responses, although few and far between, appeared to have a unifying theme. This can be described as the more public roles, responsibilities and duties brides and grooms had as hosts of their own wedding – the associated discipline of which only allowed spontaneous romantic interactions to occur sporadically throughout the day. As John explained:

I wouldn't say that you can have an actual whole day when you got married where all day it's romantic not just little bits. It's because you're centre of attention, there's that much going on, that many people there wanting your attention all the time, wanting to talk to you, you talking to them.

These public roles became even more demanding and antithetical to sharing intimate, romantic moments together if couples also still had to assume a parental role towards their (often young) children. Matthew, for instance, a father of two toddlers who were present at the wedding, told me he was 'used to being on the edge of his seat with everything' and subsequently described the day as more 'stressful' than anything else.

In fact, this point leads on to a more general issue concerning the personal circumstances and social context of each couple and how this may influence their opinions on romance or indeed whether they planned a typically romantic wedding occasion in the first place. Certainly, several examples can be cited which show opinions on romance were linked to gender, age and class. Leon, for instance, expressed a gender-based discomfort with using the adjective 'romantic' to describe his wedding: 'I just don't use that word. Men don't say "romantic"'. Beverley, on the other hand, rejected having a harpist at her wedding since its overtly romantic connotations seemed inappropriate at their age:

We don't want any music there like a harpist in the corner because we're not sort of in the first throes of love and romance. It would look a bit silly.

Also, referring back again to the earlier extract from Robert and Sarah, one can identify a distinct class element to their conceptualizations of romance – many of which made literary and historical references to the original Romantic period and can be said to demonstrate the couple's cultural capital.

There appears, therefore, to be no simple or straightforward way to theorize the relationship between, in this case, 'romantic' emotion and consumption, partly because of its constructed nature and partly because of the mixed bag of possibilities which opens up when these two experiences interact. As I argued in Chapter 2, theories of Romantic consumption like Campbell's (1987) are lacking in the attention they give to romance. Yet, the discussions of this chapter have highlighted how, in the wedding occasion at least, the role of romance is important to our understanding (as well as the understandings of brides and grooms) of the intimate, complex connections between consumption and emotion. Romance and its associated emotions, it seems, have not been totally commodified, yet neither do they remain wholly resistant to commodification. Nor can we confine romance and its associated emotions to a particular location – whether in the hearts, minds, bodies or purchases of wedding consumers. The identities of the bride and the groom, balanced between the social pressure of discipline and the private pleasure of hedonism, nevertheless are marketed, constructed and experienced as thoroughly romantic in nature. Equally, as we have seen, the experiencing of intense, 'heart-felt', spontaneous emotion, one that pre-exists consumption, is itself a longstanding element of romantic ideology. The concept of romance therefore continues to structure the wedding narrative and, as such, provides a means for brides and grooms to emotionally consume their weddings as 'authentic'.

Conclusion

This chapter has raised and developed several arguments about the emotional aspects of wedding consumption. Along the way, I have documented what can be termed the 'mental functioning' or 'logic' of consumers as well as their more full-bodied emotional experiences or realizations at key stages en route to marriage – namely, the last few weeks and days of preparation, the wedding morning, the final transformation (especially of the bride), beholding the wedding in its totality on arrival at the chosen venue, the ceremony itself and the reception speech. Consumption, I argued, offered brides throughout their wedding a way of controlling or redirecting their emotion. It also functioned as a means of negotiating, or passing back and forth, control over the wedding between the bride and groom – periodically reinforcing the interdependence of the genders perhaps, despite the overall dominance of bride.

This chapter highlighted, however, several instances of brides wanting or needing to 'let go' and lose control somewhat in order to achieve a fuller, emotionally embodied transformation. This periodic release from the shackles of their (self-) enforced rationality combined with the later delegation of some of their consumption 'work' facilitated a day-long 're-enchantment' of their selves on their wedding day. This in turn reinforced conceptions of the day as a magical, fantasy occasion. These examples, amongst others related in this chapter, can been used to argue that wedding consumers appear to recognize the tense yet constitutive union between reason and emotion.

To develop my ongoing critical appraisal of Campbell's thesis, I also chose in this chapter to explore what brides and grooms considered to be the 'romantic' and 'unromantic' elements of their wedding day. The research findings revealed romance on the wedding day being described simultaneously in several ways which were not exclusive of each other – in an *ethereal* sense, as a timeless essence between those who feel themselves to be in love; in an *embodied* sense, as a deeply felt, spontaneous and overwhelming emotion that surfaced periodically between brides and grooms; and in a *material* sense, as the symbolic or sign value of certain commodities or tangible objects. I related these opinions on romance to what exists in the popular imagination as the 'traditional romantic fantasy' and, moreover, to the reason/emotion and discipline/hedonism dualisms that we have seen to be inherent in so many facets of wedding consumption. In doing so, I argued that because of its familiarity, controllability, replicability and accessibility through consumption, the 'traditional romantic fantasy', particularly its final fairy-tale wedding scene, provides an 'ideal' model towards which the rationalizing imperatives of consumers (that is, heterosexual consumers with sufficient disposable income) can be directed. The issues raised in this discussion further problematized the notion of authentic, unmediated emotion being superior, or at least (ontologically) different to those 'emotions', romantic or otherwise, that can be facilitated and enhanced through consumption. In this sense, to repeat, theories of Romantic consumption like Campbell's can be said to have seriously underestimated the important role romance plays in the relationship between Romanticism, consumerism and emotion.

6

A Never Ending Story? The Aftermath of Wedding Consumption

In this chapter I focus on the aftermath of wedding consumption. By and large, the later ramifications of any consumer behaviour remain an oversight in the literature, as few sociologists trek beyond the actual moment of consumption and few marketeers care about the consumer once she or he has consumed. And yet the effects and affects of consuming for a wedding exert a strong, continuing influence over the bride and groom long after the curtain has drawn on their own big day. This chapter therefore explores how the wedding and its associated consumption are evaluated in hindsight. In doing so, I argue that the wedding aftermath is a period of highly reflexive mentalistic exercise in which a Romantic ethic still appears to have some relevance. Yet, as we shall see, in no sense are such *post*-consumption experiences dislocated from commercial pressure, social structure and the dynamics of interpersonal relationships.

I begin by considering why the later ramifications of consumption have never been a research priority. Certain aspects of the wedding (videos, photos) in fact imply from the outset that the occasion will never come to a definitive closure. As we shall see, through both physical and mental *re*-interactions with its associated consumption matters, the wedding continues to be the overriding preoccupation of newly-weds. I argue that this preoccupation has tremendous significance, revealing as it does the various *consumption-related strategies* used by brides and grooms to reformulate themselves as 'a married couple' – that is to say, a successful, joint decision-making and consuming unit. Reflections upon the wedding industry and their own consumer behaviour (as well as that of other couples) in relation to it are heavily implicated here as a backdrop to articulations of this new 'married couple' identity. The arguments and evidence presented in this chapter in turn build a case for extending and developing ideas of Romantic consumers to include their post-consumption activity.

Ramifications of the consumption experience

> Every weekend, every day we were living and breathing it. The wedding was the focus and now it *seems* to have gone, but we still haven't gotten away from it, have we? (Robert, original emphasis)

Despite the considerable attention paid to consumption in sociology as a whole, there has been insufficient research undertaken on the later ramifications of the consumption experience. This oversight may in part be due to the relocation of consumption (via postmodern preoccupations) into the symbolic realm of the hyperreal, or to the rush to extend the labels of 'consumption' and 'consumer' to more and more diverse people, services and situations[1] leaving the study of patterns of interaction and use with actual material products underdeveloped. Moreover, whilst sociologists have thought through consumption as a discursive domain in which consumers articulate personal identity, it has not necessarily been considered how far consumers think through their own consumption *in its aftermath* as a means of individual identity construction, or in the case of the wedding, as a means of reformulating the couple's relationship.

Profiles of the Romantic and hedonistic consumer, in particular, seem to end abruptly at the moment of actual consumption, and an apparently 'disappointing' moment at that (Campbell, 1987). This is hardly surprising since accounts of Romantic or hedonistic consumption are typically 'forward-looking' in their central theoretical focus upon emotional and imaginative anticipation in the pre-acquisition phase of consuming and consequently neglect to study the subsequent reminiscing of consumers. Hirschman and Holbrook (1982, p. 95), for instance, emphasize only two ways emotion is important to hedonistic consumption: (i) the role emotion plays in the selection of products, and (ii) measures of emotional arousal during actual acts of product consumption. In a similar vein, Bagnall stresses the circularity of physical, emotional and imaginary responses as they 'feed in and out of each other *during* consumption' (1996, p. 240, my emphasis). Considerations of the consumer's *post hoc* emotions therefore remain few and far between.

As well as pointing out the oversights of Romantic or hedonistic consumption theorists, we can equally critique those who emphasize the ritual dimensions of consumption for failing to scrutinize sufficiently the aftermath of the experience. Rook (1985) has argued that ritual experiences (commodified or otherwise) conventionally have a clear-cut beginning, middle and end, moving episodically from one phase to the next. Yet this assumption imposes a somewhat artificial temporal framework upon 'the ritual'. The assumption of a definitive 'closure' to the ritual disregards the possibility of a more 'open-ended' experience whereby participants continue to interact with or linger on particular aspects of the ritual (either physically or mentally, or both) for a long time to come. As McCracken (1990, p. 85) has indeed shown, ritualized behaviour can extend far beyond the actual moment of consumption (or whatever the climax of the ritual might be), through, for instance, 'possession rituals' which involve 'cleaning, discussing, comparing, reflecting, showing off and even photographing' new possessions.

Of course, the wedding occasion has a distinctive aftermath. The time frame of the wedding is somewhat open-ended by intent, as couples expect to have the rest of their lives together to recollect and reflect upon their big day. It should also be recognized that the attitudes of brides and grooms to wedding consumption expressed after it is over depend to a certain extent upon the particular kind of consumption experience or commodified ritual that the 'new' commercial wedding now offers – one involving the interplay of tangible and intangible products and services, perishable goods, and people as commodified versions of their fantasy selves. Leading on from this, it becomes necessary to consider how far the mental imagining of the wedding in its aftermath is open to modification and distortion (for instance, in relation to a couple's future marital path, or from continued exposure to wedding imagery in the media). Developing these and associated issues, I now begin to consider the temporal and psychological framing of the aftermath of wedding consumption, and, by inference, the identity of the newly married couple.

Closure and continuance of the wedding

Perhaps the first point to be made here is that when I returned to interview couples after their weddings there was little evidence of them achieving or indeed desiring a definitive 'closure' to their wedding experience. Although a few brides said in passing that they felt 'upset' when the wedding day had come to an end, only one expressed this sentiment to any extent:

In fact, it started on the Sunday, the day after the wedding. All I wanted to do was come home and relive my day again. I did. If I could have gone back to Marchand Hall and turn the clock back twenty-four hours and do it all again, I would. You feel low, you feel depressed. I don't know, you feel as though somebody's ripped your heart out. That's how I felt, definitely. You feel like you're sinking into quicksand. That's how I felt. It was hard to give up and I can remember being at the front of the minibus and ... I felt quite tearful. I didn't cry or anything like that, but I felt quite tearful. Goodbye marquee. *My* marquee, *my* marquee, *my* venue. (Sarah, original emphasis)

It was far more frequently the case, however, that even weeks after the final curtain had drawn on the big day, the wedding continued to occupy couples' thoughts to much the same extent as it had done for the past months and years – a preoccupation no doubt heightened by the imminent return interview. Their responses exemplified how wedding consumption and organization were a strongly mentalistic exercise. For example, we can detect here how brides and grooms found it difficult to shake off this consumer mentality:

The first week we got back it was a case of 'I should be organizing something, I should be checking on something.' (Tina)

When we came from Bath it was a bit like 'Oh god, now what do we do?' We had like four or five months of just having always something to organize or get on with. There was a lull definitely afterwards. (Kate)

I've been so used to rushing around and organizing things and getting excited about it and I think I did go a little bit down. (Beverley)

Even if you put it out of your mind, it's in your mind, even if you didn't do anything that week. (James)

You've spent all that time organizing such a big day and it's just gone. Even if you're not actively organizing it, it's always on your mind. It's the same as anything ... when I did my degree it was ... it does, it rules your life. (Harriet)

You're totally overpowered and you don't realize you're overpowered. You don't realize how much it dominates your life, how much you

talk about it. We'd spent twelve months arguing backwards and for-
wards … constantly the conversation … I mean we only have one day
off together and that was always, for twelve months, always used up,
either one way or the other, with sorting things out. (Patricia)

The wedding also had a direct and continuing influence over the
couple's future consumption patterns – evidence not just of the mentalistic or emotional legacies of the big day, but of the economic ones
too. As one couple said:

Matthew: We'd got a load of vouchers and cash and then, well,
           most of the furniture in here has come from Ikea, but we
           managed to spend double that, although we had like four
           hundred pounds to spend in Ikea regardless.
Kate: That's nothing to do with the wedding though, is it?
Matthew: No it's not. Well it *is* in a respect, because it's still coming
           out of it. In other words, we had the wedding and we got
           a load of presents for it, we accept that we got a load of
           cash to spend so we went to Ikea but then we ended up
           spending double that. If we hadn't had the wedding …
           you know, it's one of those chicken and egg things.
Kate: If we hadn't had the wedding, though, we'd have had a
           few grand to spend on things like furniture so …

In fact, when couples were asked how they felt towards each other now
the wedding was over, or to speak about their own sense of themselves
as 'newly-weds', their current economic situation was immediately
stressed. The tone of such responses was typically negative given their
recent extensive financial outlay for the wedding. Nick and Hayley, for
instance, replied that they felt 'the same but poorer', whilst Louise and
John were able to sum up their newly-wedded status using just one
adjective – 'skint!'

We have seen, then, that the brides and grooms in this study made
two clear, initial associations back to their wedding consumption when
asked about how they were feeling at the start of married life. The first
of these was to the continuance of the wedding as a primary mental
preoccupation despite, and perhaps in contention with, acute feelings
of its loss. The second association, more often alluded to in relation to
their new identity as a 'married couple', was to the economic legacies
of the wedding and its (negative) influence upon future consumption
patterns.

In addition to these two associations, and as I shall go on to argue, undoubtedly connected to them, was the emphasis brides and grooms placed on not 'feeling' married, and the corresponding sense of ambivalence or awkwardness that accompanied this feeling. Most significant, in this respect, was the unease and embarrassment conveyed when using what Hobson (2000) calls a new 'language' of couplehood. According to Hobson (2000, p. 247), 'Becoming "a couple" is in part achieved through the acquisition of a "language" with which to "do" intimacy'. Yet as the following responses show, even if couples had been together for some time, this new 'language' of marriage did not come at all 'naturally' – an outcome, one could suppose, of the primary 'language' between some brides and grooms over the past months and sometimes years of wedding build-up being one of *consumption* rather than couplehood:

I still can't believe we're married. It seems strange because people phone up and say 'Is Mrs Thompson there?' and I go ... [*pause*] ... 'Yes!' I feel like going to say 'Mom!' ... It's strange. And to a couple of people I've said, 'Oh Harriet my girl ... oh wife'. It sounds a bit tacky 'Me and my wife'. I don't like that, I just say 'Harriet', 'The Mrs'. But not 'My wife'. (Alex)

I find it more when, like, people come to me and say 'Oh hello Mrs. Wright', and the other day I just got the giggles when I said, 'Oh John, my husband' and I just cracked up [*laughs*]. (Louise)

When I was in the taxi, and I said 'My girlfriend' and then said 'Oh she's not my girlfriend, she's my wife', and they just laughed, because everyone knows we've got married and all that, and they say 'How's you're wife?' and I think 'Oh yeah!' (Peter)

Taking all of the above observations into account, it could be suggested that the aftermath of the new commercial wedding can pose several problems for newly weds. For example, past consuming tensions or conflicts might resurface. So, too, the tight financial budgets couples find themselves on as a direct consequence of wedding expenditure prevents, or at best restricts, subsequent joint purchases which might establish them as a single consuming unit. Equally, one might suppose that the dominance of wedding consumption and its associated hopes and fears did on many occasions serve to overshadow the time and importance devoted to the development of the bride and groom's personal relationship – that is, the more *emotional* preparations for marriage and married life as opposed to the *economic*, consumption-based preparations for the wedding. This resulted in the couple's own sense of themselves as 'newly-weds' and the language they used to articulate this identity seeming somewhat strained or unnatural. The influence consumption has upon notions of couplehood in the wedding aftermath is further problematized when one takes into account the role it may have already played when the decision was made to cohabit.

Wedding consumption and the construction of couplehood

Whilst the initial reactions of couples may be to the loss of both the wedding and the functions of their associated consuming behaviour, wedding consumption continues to serve particular functions long after the occasion. On closer inspection, a more complex relationship between wedding consumption and the construction of a particular type of couplehood in its aftermath emerges – an aftermath in which brides and grooms think through their past consuming behaviour and begin to associate their new status as a 'married couple' with their successes as a joint, 'conjugal' decision-making and consuming unit (Young and Willmott, 1975). This behaviour in turn helps us to understand in other less obvious ways why the wedding event is so important to the new identity of the married couple and why the increasing levels of consumption involved in it are of equal importance in this respect. For example, as we shall see shortly, the conscious, cognitive reframing of the wedding and of the consumption matters that accompanied it involves a high level of mentalistic exercise and offers a new 'language' with which to articulate and synthesize together the experiences of both consumption and couplehood.

It is also important to flag up at this point the downplaying or, in some cases, total absence, of two factors that may traditionally have aided the transitions of brides and grooms into the identity of a married couple after their wedding. These earlier factors were: (i) the wedding list, which through the joint choice and acceptance of gifts, provides not only a concrete materialization of the new 'union' but anticipates the probability of an expanding family/household unit, and (ii) first-time cohabitation, whereby couples can begin to negotiate their new identity through the spatialized and routinized aspects of living together. Yet, with all but one couple in the sample already cohabiting before the wedding,[2] and no couples attaching any real significance to the wedding list,[3] the extent to which these two factors help to constitute the bride and groom as a married couple seems minimal. These points might further explain why couples are so active in constructing new discursive strategies to emphasize the long-term significance of their wedding consumption.

The following extract from Louise and John's second interview illustrates how the couple rewrite the script of their past consuming behaviour to emphasize the apparent 'jointness' of control over their wedding. This new emphasis functions to cover up a previous division of labour. Here we can see that the groom begins by recollecting the disparate 'authorities' of himself and his bride in their pre-wedding consuming and decision-making:

Sharon: So, if you could give one piece of advice to a bride and a groom getting married soon, what would you say to them?

John: Basically, if you're a groom just shut up and let the bride do what she wants anyway, because grooms know nothing. Because they'll get their own way.

Louise: That's not fair.

John: Excuse me, one of the biggest arguments we used to have was 'I've had these, what do you think?', 'Not really keen', 'What do you know anyway?', so we got them anyway. Just go with the flow. Just enjoy it basically.

Louise: Do what you want to do at the end of the day, that's basically it.

John: Don't try and please everybody.

Louise: You can't, you never will. You wouldn't notice it anyway. Don't worry about people not having a good time. Just you enjoy it.

John: Just you enjoy it. It's their problem if they don't want to enjoy it. That was like our attitude. Just enjoy it all, don't get ... I'd say too bogged down with too many details and traditions.

Louise: Don't be ... I suppose some people would be fretting all the time worrying, 'Are you having a good time?' You can see if they are. If they aren't, it's their own tough luck. You've invited them and paid for a meal for them, if they want to sit there and be miserable that's their problem. But nobody was like that at ours, were they? We were worried about it.

John: Yeah, you don't want them all sitting there looking miserable, you know.

Louise: But they didn't.

John: They all mixed; well most of them.

Despite both John and Louise's acknowledgement of their unequal participation in the consumption decision-making, the couple nevertheless come round to a sense of jointly providing a day for their guests. Previous points of tension or inequality are effectively silenced through a re-emphasis upon the bride and groom as a single, decision-making unit (an 'us') whose consumption choices cannot possibly hope to please the whole wedding party (the 'them').

In a similar vein, taking several brief examples from Sarah and Robert's post-wedding interview, the responsibilities of themselves *as a couple* over *their own* wedding consumption were continually reaffirmed:

> Because you're putting it on yourself, nobody's going to interfere with it. You can do it *your* way. When you get somebody else paying for it they want to put their oar in. So we actually had total control over that. Nobody actually interfered at all. They weren't allowed to, because we were paying for everything ourselves. (Robert, original emphasis)

> At the end of the day the only people who know what their tastes are, are the couple. (Sarah)
> Yeah, and you're in control, you're in control. (Robert)

> A couple of our friends have actually said because their parents are actually paying for their wedding, it was a case of it wasn't their day it was their parents' day and it's very unfortunate really. But, no, I think we knew exactly what we wanted and nobody was going to influence our decisions. (Sarah)

> It is a reflection of us as a couple. (Sarah)

The emphasis of brides and grooms on themselves as holding joint responsibility for their wedding decisions was also articulated in relation to the avoidance of typical wedding problems. What seemed to occur here, in effect, was a mutual patting each other on the back for retaining joint responsibility for and control over the wedding and, as such, for avoiding the conflicts and debts that other less successful couples incurred:

> *James:*   I think from a man's point of view you've got to do it as a joint effort. A lot of men just let the wife get on with it all,

or the wife-to-be get on with it all, let her family get on
with it ... we discussed everything, we made our decisions
equally ... you can imagine the resentment there could be
after the wedding, after the honeymoon's finished, the
wedding's finished, lots of things. Like the wife might be
saying 'We've got a five thousand pound loan' or whatever
it is and he'd be saying 'Well that's because you wanted
that, you wanted this' and she'd be thinking 'Well I did it
for us, I didn't do it for me, but you wouldn't listen', you
know, 'If you'd have took any part in it you'd have known
how much I was spending' and all that type of thing. I can
imagine that's just what it's like and I have no sympathy
for the bloke at all because you should have listened to
what she was saying.

Tina: And get involved.

James: 'Did you want that, did you what this' and he'd probably
say 'Well ... '.

Tina: 'I wasn't bothered'.

James: 'I wasn't bothered' but all of a sudden you *are* bothered
because you've got to pay for it.

Nick: So, yes, we splashed out on a really good honeymoon. It's
once in a lifetime. Not got into debt like, you know, some
people. Like 'Yeah, let's go on a fantastic honeymoon'.

Hayley: And pay it off for the next five years!

Nick: Yeah, because I expect if anyone had debts to get married
when they come back and it's all over as soon as the credit
card bill comes in they must feel really bad and think ... .

Hayley: 'Was it really worth it?'.

This brings me to the point that the financial implications of wedding
consumption are so important to each couple's subsequent construction of themselves as a joint decision-making and consuming unit.
Whilst talking about, reconstructing and remembering the wedding is
indeed a highly symbolic activity, it is also the actual, material fact of
being jointly responsible for the acquired wedding bills that makes
them aware of their dependence on the other's decisions. For couples
already living together, the wedding especially offers a means of reconciling and combining their separate incomes.

Besides economic factors, the construction of couplehood in the
wedding aftermath is also tied to the wider social network of the brides

and grooms. When discussing reactions to their wedding consumption, couples proudly recalled the positive feedback they had received from friends and family who attended. Such affirmations of wedding success, often praising the ambience of the whole occasion as well as specific consumption choices, were significant as 'objective' evaluations of the day which in turn reinforced the couple's own subjective interpretations:

> Everybody said to us to be honest it was one of the best weddings they'd been to, erm, because it looked absolutely ... flowers and everything and candles, it looked absolutely gorgeous. (Louise)

> People are still talking about how perfect everything was. (Peter)

> Guests that we've spoken to since have said that it was just a really nice day. (Patricia)

> A lot of friends said to us afterwards it was a really good wedding because it was a really relaxed atmosphere. (Tina)

> And people were still talking about it weeks after, 'Oh I wish we were at the wedding again, at Sarah and Robert's wedding'. (Sarah)

Brides and grooms used accolades like these to rate and locate their own wedding success (in terms of style, cost, impact, enjoyment, atmosphere, for instance) in relation to other weddings they had attended or expected to attend in the near future. As two couples discussing it with each other said:

Kate: This girl I work with spent two grand on her wedding dress and things like that don't add up to us. Even if I had all that money I don't really feel that I could justify it. I'd never wear that dress again. Certainly, I think you are under scrutiny, everyone had been married before, we'd been to nearly everybody's wedding in that room, so we'd made judgements. So, I suppose in a way we were lucky because if we hadn't been to all those weddings we might not have enjoyed our wedding so much because we used all of them as a benchmark, 'Oh I liked that about their wedding, but I didn't like that'.

Matthew: There were some friends in Leeds and I remember nothing about the day, well obviously I remember something but not anything there that was useful. I don't remember his speech at all.

Kate: Yeah, it was very unmemorable.

Matthew: It was all like if you look at this, this is how you do your wedding and opened a book, that's what would be in it.

Kate: Yeah, they didn't have anything to ...

Matthew: They had morning suits on and that was fine, but so what?

Kate: Bland really, I suppose is the word. There wasn't anything in the day that made it memorable. But I think we achieved the kind of day we wanted. Everything went really well.

Sarah: There was also erm ... Jim and Samantha who are having a big church wedding, very beautiful, and Samantha came up to me at the end of the day and she said 'This will take some beating'.

Robert: The only worry is that ... our family was there and they'll be at the next wedding, is not putting pressure on that couple.

Sarah: That they've got to live up to that.

Robert: Expectations. But everybody's taste is different.

Sarah: But she did say to me that this wedding will take some living up to. And I feel really touched by that. And the letters and things we've got, it's as though people have to pour their hearts out to you.

Whilst couples explicitly positioned their own wedding consumption in relation to that of the other couples they knew, this process can equally be interpreted as an active positioning of themselves *as a couple* (again, in terms of their style, taste, values, finances) within their wider kinship and friendship networks. This reveals how a wedding, and the social products or commodities used in this ritual, impacts not only on the self-identity of the male and female (as a couple) but also on how they are viewed by others. The reformulation of couplehood in this respect centres on a type of *'relational* identity construction' in which consumption, once more, is strongly implicated in the method and language used to express this new, joint identity. Here we can therefore echo and extend an argument made earlier in this book – even if, in this case, the *aftermath* of consumer behaviour entails a high level of mentalistic activity and

organization it is not autonomous from the surrounding social structural and interpersonal relations of the consumer.

Criticisms and celebrations of the wedding industry

> A wedding's become like a commodity like a house or a car, you
> know, you're supposed to have the biggest and the best and the most.
> I mean you can have the biggest or the flashiest or the fastest or what-
> ever it is, but if it's not you you're just like a fish out of water. Erm ...
> and it's like ... we're quite proud that our wedding cost what it cost
> because it was better than we expected it to be and it didn't cost us
> ten grand. And I look and think there's a hell of a lot of people, there
> must be, who will say 'Mine cost ten' and then someone else will say
> 'Mine cost twelve' and you think 'Well big deal'. (James)

So far in this chapter I have examined how couples evaluate wedding
consumption as they begin married life. In doing so, I have argued that
wedding consumption has important functions in the aftermath of the
occasion. Thinking back through their whole wedding experience,
couples now began to stress their new identity as a joint decision-making
and consuming unit, effectively equalizing the division of labour and disparate involvement between themselves that typically characterized the
pre-wedding preparations. Equally, brides and grooms recalled the positive and affirming 'objective' feedback that had been received from their
wedding guests. These views help to construct an agreed evaluation of the
wedding's success (especially in terms of its style, cost, impact, enjoyment
and atmosphere), which in turn was used by brides and grooms to rate
and locate their own wedding consumption, and, by inference, identity
as a couple, within their social network.

There is, however, a very significant dimension to all of these points
which up to now has remained implicit in the evidence presented –
reflections upon the wedding industry and the influence it was deemed
to have upon themselves, as well as upon other brides and grooms and
the occasion as a whole. In raising this issue I wish to argue that, to a
certain extent, the responses of couples when thinking through their
own wedding in its aftermath have resulted from structural features in
the marketplace – namely, the increasing commercialization of the
event. Certainly, in this respect, brides and grooms in this study voiced
positive and negative opinions towards the wedding industry, generating both a catalogue of criticism about the wedding industry (if somewhat partial or shallow) and a simultaneous celebration of what it had

to offer. Most importantly, the process of expressing an opinion on the wedding industry offered brides and grooms an additional means of articulating and confirming they were 'of the same mind' in such consuming matters.

For instance, the following extract from Anne and Geoff's return interview illustrates well their generally 'negative' perspective on the wedding industry:

Sharon: Do you think weddings in general are becoming more commercial?

Anne: Oh yes, undoubtedly.

Sharon: And what would you consider evidence of this to be?

Anne: Well, there's a classic in the local paper at the moment – *a wedding fayre*. A great big event so everyone can go and see what's on offer. Photographs and dresses and god knows what. I mean it's ridiculous. Actually I noticed in British Home Stores yesterday for the first time ever they've got a section on wedding clothes, all these satin shoes and what not. I thought, 'This is ridiculous'.

Geoff: I mean also the fact that tour operators are getting in on it. You know, having special wedding packages to St. Lucia or Puerto Rico or wherever.

Sharon: And what, in your opinion, are the causes of this commercialization?

Anne: Moneymaking. That's the cause of all things nowadays. That's all it's about. Making money for somebody.

Geoff: It's just a natural extension of what business has been doing for the past twenty years or so.

Anne: Well, since the rise of Thatcherism.

Geoff: I think it's been driven by business. And I think they are just feeding on the fact that people have got more money than sense. There are some professionals that are so highly paid, you know like the people in the IT industry. Their salaries are so ridiculous that they've got more money than they know what to do with. And of course that has a knock-on effect when you go down the chain, you know, somebody in IT did this so let's see what we can do similar. And that goes down even further, and it gets to the point of people who can't really afford it.

Sharon: Can you understand why people choose to spend thirty, forty thousand on one day?

Anne: It would be completely alien to me, but I can understand
        why if your peers all do it. We know only too well that
        people are terribly influenced by what their peers do. So if
        you're twenty-three and your mate has just got married last
        year and had a splendid bash I dare say you think you ought
        to do the same ... And what sort of baffles me is that they
        don't actually seem to realize that that's just the technicality
        and it won't make any difference to the rest of their lives just
        because they've spent forty thousand. They might have just
        as well of spent forty quid because it won't help them.

Geoff: I think some of it has been driven by celebrity as well. In
        the sense of people seeing pictures of David Beckham and
        Posh Spice and they see that they've spent a million
        pounds on their wedding. Great, well ...

Anne: If they've got a million to spend.

Geoff: And it's probably all tax-deductible anyway. People don't
        seem to realize that people like that ... money's nothing,
        money's totally incomprehensible to them. So everyone
        thinks 'Well they spent a million so we'll spend forty thou-
        sand pounds'. I still find it baffling.

To these criticisms of the wedding industry, and of the people who
succumb to it, expressed here at length by Anne and Geoff, we may
add numerous examples from other return interviews: 'I think that
the minute you mention it is a wedding the price doubles. I think
you're ... in a sense ... ripped off' (Patricia); 'Just making loads of
money, that's all they're interested in' (Nick); 'You can't hide the fact
that it's all a big rip-off really' (Leon); 'We are still at the beginning of
the industry really surging because as more venues become available
people can make more off them' (Tina); 'They know you want your
day to be right, so you *do* pay top price and you pay top price because
you don't want something that's not going to make it perfect'
(Beverley, original emphasis); 'I think people are just cowboys when
it comes to weddings. They just put the price up that much because
they know that you've got to have it' (Harriet); 'They all jump on the
bandwagon, don't they? Money to be made' (Alex); 'If you do see
these glamorous weddings it can actually put people under pressure
to spend more than they can actually afford' (Sarah); 'I think if the
mother-in-law, the bride's mother, is heavily involved as is often the
case, I think they tend to want "the show". They want to show everybody "Look what spread we've put on for our daughter". So I think

that's going to be a big target for the salespeople' (Tina); 'They do work on the fact that your wedding's got to be better than the last one you went to definitely ... there's a lot more competition with women getting married' (John).

In fact, every single couple returned to for a post-wedding interview had something 'negative' to say about the wedding industry, the only variances in this sense being how much criticism they voiced and how far they now considered themselves to have been under its influence. Their criticisms, as we have seen, centre on a number of themes.

First, there was an acute awareness of the extent of the wedding industry and the likelihood of its increasing in both scale and influence in forthcoming years. Evidence of this increasing commercialization was deemed to be found in the spiralling amount of goods and services that were being 'tied into' the occasion. It was assumed that the motive behind the wedding industry was to make money rather than to supply brides and grooms with value-for-money purchases. Second, couples commented on the ways they thought the wedding industry worked. This was conceptualized as a type of 'emotional blackmail', with the wedding industry exploiting the emotional significance of the event and the desires of couples to 'get it just right', more or less regardless of cost. Third, the wedding industry was criticized for promoting perfected, 'ideal' weddings which led to consuming for the purposes of social or celebrity emulation. The economic consequences of this process were stressed. This type of 'Veblen effect', however, was typically recognized in relation to the consumer behaviour of other couples as opposed to their own consumption. Finally, and leading on from this last point, the commercialization of the wedding was claimed to foster unnecessary competition between families. Such competition had a strong gender bias and was thought by both women and men to be most evident amongst brides and brides' mothers.

Most importantly, the existence of an ever-present wedding industry offered couples a way of asserting their own roles in relation to it. Here one might suggest that the wedding industry existed not only as something to struggle against, oppose or resist, but as a useful backdrop for couples in hindsight to construct particular self or joint conceptions – usually as authoritative, autonomous decision makers on their own wedding consumption. In this respect, Cronin's (2000) theory that contemporary consumer culture promotes a form of 'compulsory individuality', whereby the ideals of individuality and identity *through free choice* provide the imperative to consume, seems to have relevance for some couples in the study. Robert and Sarah, for example, reinforce the notion of *making* an *active choice* from one of the many opportunities on offer to the wedding consumer:

Sharon: There seems to be a thriving wedding industry nowadays, the magazines, the Internet sites, the shops. Did you see your roles as you were preparing your wedding as wedding consumers?

Robert: No.

Sarah: Not really, no, no. We just sort of went out really and looked for ... whatever we were looking for and like I say we are quite discerning customers and we weren't influenced at all by what anybody else has had. It was a case of we wanted something very romantic, like I said, but *we also wanted something that was very individual to our tastes and nobody else's.* [my emphasis]

Sharon: Why don't you see this role as being a consumer? You've said instead that you were customers, are you implying there is a difference between the two?

Robert: Yeah, because consumer implies you're manipulated by the industry, you know, you have that because they want you to have it.

Sarah: It's like a sort of brainwashing.

Robert: Brainwashing marketing, and you could very easily fall into that because you'd sort of see your friend had this venue, that dress designer or gone to your local dress shop and I'm afraid that's not it because we travel more than most people. So when Sarah came to look for a dress, she knows what Italian dresses, American, German, French look like, not just UK. So she knows a lot more ...

Sarah: ... than the average bride.

Robert: Than the average bride.

Sharon: Maybe you see yourselves as examples of consumer empowerment?

Sarah: Very true. Very much so because I looked around Banbury, for example. There was nothing wedding-wise, dresses or venues that impressed me. So I thought 'Right I'm going to have to go further afield'

Robert: It does take a lot of looking, to find something you want.

It must be made clear, however, in Robert and Sarah's responses, as with several other couples in this study, emphasis was exclusively placed upon their choice from *one of the choices* on offer, rather than their choice of *whether or not* to consume.

What might be termed 'positive' responses to the wedding industry can be grouped thematically. First, some brides and grooms applauded the increasing choices, opportunities and ideas on offer: 'I think the wedding industry doesn't do a bad job because if you look at the magazines, for example, they do put quite a wide range of things in there' (Robert); 'The choice is nice' (Natalie); 'I think on the positive side I would always say shop around. There are a lot of opportunities' (Patricia); 'I think it's nice that you can have your options' (Nick); 'You can make your wedding whatever you want it to be now really, can't you?' (Louise); 'Well you go to the right people and they've done it so many times before and they know exactly what you want and they can do it really good' (Nick); 'The photographer, we felt he was there to help us and the people at the reception were there to help us and people at the registry office they were so nice, remembering your name and personal identities, "Oh, nice to see you again"' (Hayley); 'I'd rather pay the extra to have a contractor that's more expensive who's got the quality and the reputation who you know you're not taking a risk with. I'd rather pay the extra money and not take a risk. That's the trade off at the end of the day' (Robert). Second, following on from this, brides and grooms seemed even more positive about how these options could be put to use. In particular, weddings could become more personalized, communicating the couple's own taste and style to their guests: 'You can make it more personal' (Sarah); 'It gave us the day that we wanted and we had piece of mind knowing that everything was going to be OK' (Beverley). Ultimately, therefore, whether largely 'for' or 'against' the impact of the wedding industry on the changing nature of the occasion, formulating an agreed opinion of their own wedding consumption in relation to it became a significant part of the wedding aftermath for couples.

Theorizing the aftermath of romantic consumption

We have seen, then, various ways couples try to 'make sense' of their wedding experience, and especially its associated consumption, in the aftermath of the occasion. Above all, this chapter has suggested that the aftermath of wedding consumption is a period of highly reflexive, mentalistic exercise. It is a period, moreover, in which brides and grooms reinforce the meaningful nature of the wedding, rationally defend their own consumer behaviour and articulate themselves as a 'new' consuming unit. This final section will draw together the main threads of the arguments and evidence presented and show their significance to our ongoing exploration of the workings of a Romantic ethic in wedding consumers.

Responses generated in the wedding aftermath can be connected to the specificities of self-illusory hedonism and the type of consumption it underpins (Campbell, 1987). To be sure, this type of consumption, as I have illustrated throughout this book, is characterized by the close and constitutive relationships between Romanticism, fantasy and rationality. My argument here, though, is in no way meant to deny that these very same characteristics are themselves closely related to the structural features of the marketplace already recognized in this and in earlier chapters.

Whilst the aftermath of the Romantic or hedonistic consumption experience may be insufficiently theorized at present, one can draw from and, in turn, develop a number of useful arguments made in the literature on related topics. Braun (1999), for example, has discussed how consumers learn from experiential consumption. Conceptualizing wedding consumption in this way (that is, as a learning experience), it would be reasonable to propose that in this context consumers above all learn about the relationship between consumption and emotion – the *affective potential*, in effect, of commodities, and their own status as 'emotional consumers'. It is also important to Braun to consider *when* such consumer learning occurs. As she herself puts it, although the information from experiential consumption is learnt fast, 'this type of information is also the most fragile, context-dependent, and subject to distortion' (1999, p. 319). This perhaps implies that Romantic or hedonistic consumption experiences are in fact the most likely to be rationalized or 'emotionally managed' in their aftermath. It is also highly significant that the wedding aftermath involves the couple returning to their 'real selves' as opposed to the 'fantasy selves' they temporarily embodied as part of the traditional romantic wedding narrative – their 'real selves', in this sense, having a greater capacity to rationalize the whole experience. Furthermore, as Braun argues, advertising can exert a strong influence on the reconstructive memory process. Indirect and continuing exposure to the wedding industry, its imagery and ideology, long after the couple's own big day, may therefore serve to modify and distort subsequent mentalistic activity towards a more favourable re-interpretation of events.

This leads me to propose that wedding consumers have just as much of an 'imagined' relationship to their past (their recollections of the wedding in its aftermath) as they appeared to have had with their future (their anticipations of the wedding in its build-up). Indeed, Bagnall (1996, p. 239) rightly argues that, in general, consumers 'now have a greater capacity for imagining because they are continually bombarded with images and, frequently, images of the past'. In particular, implicitly following the logics of Campbell's Romantic ethic, she goes on to suggest that since nostalgia is a largely self-referential emotion, it has a continuing capacity to stimulate the imagination. As the previous chapter has shown, brides and grooms certainly gave special significance to their wedding photographs and videos as evidence of a romantic perfection that could be drawn upon at a later date to rekindle these feelings. Moreover, returning to this chapter, the failure of brides and grooms to make or recall any real, substantive critiques of the wedding (either from themselves or from others), alongside their active and rational construction of new discursive strategies to emphasize the ongoing significance of their wedding consumption, implies that, in its aftermath, the wedding can be *rationalized* into even more of a *romanticized* version of events. One might also argue here that the wedding is *fantasized* as even more romantic.

In this respect, it appears that brides and grooms can derive a high level of pleasure from remembering their wedding and its associated consumption. This reinforces my argument that accounts of Romantic or hedonistic consumption, through their prioritization of the emotional and imaginative anticipation of an experience, have in turn neglected to recognize the equally Romantic dimensions of its aftermath. Le Bel and Dubé provide further supporting evidence for this claim, concluding from their own study of daily hedonistic experiences that:

> The pleasure derived from anticipating and reminiscing about an event accounts for the fact that the pleasure from the actual experience *per se* can be much smaller than the *total* pleasure associated with that experience. (1998, p. 177, original emphasis)

This seems to echo Campbell's idea of the central importance of Romantic consumption being the *potential* something (for example, a product, event, service, person) has for emotional and imaginative interaction rather than the *actual* qualities it may possess – the argument here, of course, being that Romantic consumption is primarily a mentalistic, self-directed and creative activity rather than a materialistic, mundane one.

An additional point to be made here is the continuance of the consumers' projection of themselves as a 'Romantic hero' (or, as in the case of the now 'equally' consuming bride and groom, as a partnership of 'Romantic heroes'). For instance, in Vander Veen's (1994, p. 333) deciphering of the script of the consuming 'hero' in his or her post-consumption phase, 'sharing' is the final scene – the complete heroic consumption experience being *'dream-do-rationalize-share'*. Certainly, the keenness of couples to 'pass on' the conclusions they had drawn from their own first-hand experience of wedding consumption reinforces this argument: 'Erm, what can I recommend on here?' pondered Robert, 'I think the thing is to be certain in your own minds on how you want to do it.' Besides the supporting data from my own interviews, one can also detect high levels of post-wedding consumption sharing more generally in the wedding industry and growing wedding culture, apparent, for instance, in the chat rooms of wedding web-sites and the letter pages of bridal magazines. These points further problematize the temporal framing of wedding consumption and blur the boundaries between the past, present and future effects and affects of the experience.

My research, then, has shown that the aftermath of wedding consumption entails a complex *re*-imagining of the occasion itself and of the build-up to it. Yet this process does not occur within an autonomous, independent, unmediated, socially and culturally disembodied and disembedded consumer. The mentalistic activity undertaken by brides and grooms in their wedding aftermath, as described in this chapter, tells a different story – one in which their primary objective is to reformulate themselves into a 'married couple', where their consumption is evaluated and positioned in relation to their wider circle of friends and family, and one which may be continually stimulated with full-bodied re-interactions with associated material items, attendance at other weddings and media imagery. Therefore, if, as I propose, my account of the wedding aftermath can help to extend theorizations of the Romantic consumer far beyond the actual moment of consumption, it also testifies to the extent to which such consumers and their consumption remain influenced by commercial ideology, social structure and their own interpersonal relations.

Conclusion

In this chapter I have focused on the attitudes to wedding consumption expressed once the big day is over. I have been especially concerned to show how *post*-consumption experiences include high levels of remembering, imagining and thinking in which a Romantic ethic still appears to have relevance. The findings of this chapter have raised several points with respect to this issue. First, the wedding aftermath has been characterized as a period of intense, active and rational, cognitive activity, in which imagination and emotion play pivotal roles. This period can be said to equal the pre-acquisition phase of consuming for a wedding in having 'Romantic' dimensions. Second, whilst such Romantic consumption has been regarded by Campbell (1987) amongst others as an individualistic or masculine phenomenon, or as a synthesis of the two,[4] this type of consumption equally lends itself to the reformulation of two consuming individuals into 'a married couple' in its aftermath.

In fact, bringing me to my third and most important claim, it is precisely *because* wedding consumption involves a strong and continuing Romantic dimension (infused as it is with popular ideas about romance) that newly-weds can articulate their new couple identity and go on to periodically revisit and reinforce this identity and its emotional associations throughout the duration of their married life. The specificities of self-illusory hedonism and the type of Romantic consumption it is said to foster were argued here to be vital to this process in a number of ways. These, to repeat, present further evidence of the ongoing negotiations between reason and emotion throughout the wedding experience and its associated consumption. Whilst such consumption involves heightened, intense and speedily learnt consumer information (especially concerning the relationships between consumption and emotion), it seems that the very nature of the information learnt leaves it open to rationalization, management, and distortion in hindsight.

7
Conclusions

This book has provided the first and only full-length study of wedding consumption in Britain since the 1994 Marriage Act. It is also the first empirical study of wedding consumption to engage fully with sociological consumer culture literature, providing data on the beliefs and actions of brides and grooms as well as exposing and analysing the commonsenses constructed and circulated in contemporary popular culture that give further meaning to the whole wedding experience. I have sought to document and understand the emotional dimensions of wedding consumption and, in the process, have begun to integrate the phenomenon of the new commercial wedding into sociological theory. More specifically, this book has offered an insight into the workings of a Romantic ethic within both the market-led images of ideal weddings and the actual experiences of wedding consumers. In doing so, I have analysed the gendered and mediated nature of such an ethic (or alternatively, a Romantic 'habitus' or 'disposition') as well as the socially embedded and embodied consuming actors to which it is inextricably tied. This has enabled, in ways I will go on to summarize in these final reflections, some interesting observations to be made about consumption, emotion and the interpersonal and social relations in which consuming for a wedding takes place. To put it simply, wedding consumption affects and is affected by a combination of external and internal constraints and expectations. Wedding consumption provides an avenue for couples to think through and enact what the whole occasion means to them. Gender ideology is central to the whole wedding experience, influencing brides' and grooms' attitudes to the occasion and their behaviour as consumers.

Wedding consumption: insights and limitations

We must of course bear in mind how far the wedding experience, and indeed the experiences of those couples upon which this book draws, provides a generalizable case study for researching the relationship between consumption, emotion and a Romantic ethic. Certainly, as I discussed in Chapter 2, theorists of Romantic consumption do not claim that the practice of self-illusory hedonism is universal, but can be most explicitly identified in forms of non-utilitarian consumption which involve new, exciting commodities with affective potential. Since the wedding is widely recognized as a 'romantic' occasion already – whether or nor its surrounding romanticism is highly commercialized – it is logical to assume that the experiences of its consumers would have more affinity with existing theories of Romantic consumption than, say, a study of mundane, domestic shopping would do.

Although analysis of the interview data sought to convey the emotional and imaginative experiences of wedding consumption, I have sought neither to exaggerate the similarities between couples' accounts nor downplay differences between idiosyncratic or highly personalized responses within the sample. The experiences of the sample may not be representative of those of the marrying population as a whole however, simply because of the emphasis (explicit or otherwise) placed upon emotion and consumption matters in the interview situation and the consequent influence this may have had upon the couple's behaviour. Yet, given this disclaimer, the findings generated from the sample are probably fairly typical, in varying degrees, of the experiences of most couples who engage with the new commercial world of weddings. Having said this, all of the interviewees I did recruit regarded themselves as having 'a wedding'. There must, of course, be couples who decide to marry without planning an 'occasion' at all, therefore eliminating consumption almost entirely from their concerns. Whilst it is perhaps understandable that such couples were unable to be recruited for this research, their views on the contemporary wedding and the expanding wedding industry would certainly be interesting.

The above point raises important questions regarding wedding consumers who did not participate in this study and might in turn be targeted for recruitment in future research of a similar nature. Two groups, in this respect, stand out – ethnic minorities and gay couples. Such research would highlight how groups marginalized by the mainstream wedding industry regard the issue of consumer choice, and how they formulate their beliefs and negotiate their dealings with the wedding industry alongside other values (such as religion or political commitments). What factors structure their wedding fantasies and what means are available to realize them? Moreover, do they even articulate 'a wedding fantasy' as such, since, as Ingraham (1999) has so correctly argued, the 'perfect' wedding fantasy is perceived not only to be *white*, but exclusively *heterosexual* in nature. These kind of questions would also uncover the various perspectives from which 'romance' is viewed, promoting further discussion of the specificities of Romantic consumption.

Some of the experiences of consumption, emotion and romance articulated by brides and grooms in this book have certainly resulted from structural features in the marketplace of commercial weddings. In fact, I have highlighted the complexity of the relationship between 'ideology' transmitted by the wedding industry (that is, the ideas characteristic of many dimensions/fractions that play a part in the production of a commercial wedding – bridal magazines, web-sites, exhibitions, and so on), alongside and integrated with commonplace assumptions about gender and the nature of romantic relationships, and the self-illusory, autonomous aspects of consuming. As I mentioned in Chapter 2, O'Guinn has already suggested that Romantic consumption is in part a *'learned* interpretive orientation' (1996, p. 85, my emphasis), one which is shaped by the concerns and values of the particular consumer culture in which it comes into play. Yet although the wedding may be an exaggerated forum for the expression of emotion through consumption (which in turn positions its central actors as 'emotional consumers'), it would be hard to research a romantic, interpersonal relationship without considering the meaning and function of commodities, since, by its very nature, romance is a construct equally defined by its 'authentic' emotion as by its commodification.

It is the consumer's obsession with 'living out' or 'realizing' the imagination (and his or her own imagined emotions) which most strikingly illustrates how critical the Romantic ethic thesis is to our understanding of brides and grooms as consumers and as emotional managers of their own 'big day'. The book has also illuminated how a Romantic ethic comes into play in the negotiation of consumption matters at an interpersonal level, most explicitly in the dualistic, gendered allocation of consuming duties that I shall go on to summarize shortly. The body, itself now a key sociological issue, becomes an emblem of the self (or couplehood) and a site of discipline, fantasy and release in consumption, with brides working hard on their bodies in order to embody the (super)bridal identity as promoted by the wedding industry. The wedding industry indeed functions as a key shaper of the experience and expression of Romantic consumption through blurring together popular understandings of historical, literary Romanticism with more modern consumption-led definitions of romance.

Focusing upon the connections between Romantic consumption and emotion management, a central argument running throughout this book in this respect is that the conceptualization of consumption, in scholarly approaches to the topic, is often considered in dualistic terms – whether these be the dualisms of reason/emotion, mind/body, manipulation/autonomy, discipline/hedonism or many others we can cite – a conceptualization that may well impede and distort the study of many 'real-life' experiences of consumption. For instance, these underpinning dualisms, as I demonstrated in Chapter 2, are well illustrated through a focus on Campbell's Romantic ethic in which a 'hybrid' model of reason/emotion relations is put forward – the former (de)controlling and managing the latter in the mentalistic 'rational passion' of consuming – producing a relation of 'calculation' or 'cultivation', as it can be termed.

To be sure, reason and emotion, coupled with a definite emphasis upon 'romance', are key facets in the wedding industry's marketing of the occasion as a fantasy-laden, cultural event that is dependent upon consumption. But, *contra* Campbell, I emphasize the conceptualization of a *productive union* of reason and emotion within the bridal identity. Bridal magazines, for instance, were found to continually reinforce the point that consumer rationality was needed to enable or live out a later fairy-tale romantic fantasy. They reassure their readers that their own exercise of reason and direction would not spoil the wedding fantasy but ensure its realization. This is evident in the depiction of the split personality of the 'superbride' – that is, to repeat, the 'rational' project manager existing alongside the 'emotional', childish fantasizer, yet managing to negotiate successfully these aspects of her personality into the important business of wedding consumption.

The analysis of interview data also demonstrates that a unified, productive relation between reason and emotion is a key theme in the lived experiences of marrying couples. Gender ideology is central to the exercise of reason and emotion. Much of the interview evidence supports the argument that men and women view wedding consumption in very different ways. Gendered differences pre-exist the wedding fantasy, but romantic and consumer discourses are also partly constitutive of them. Since the wedding occasion appears to heighten these differences at the same time as it proceeds to join two people, such differences are 'naturalized' by the couple and the industry. Consuming for a wedding not only prescribes emotional expression, it also promotes stereotypical forms of gendered behaviour which in turn reinforce hegemonic forms of masculinity and femininity and their relation to each other.

We have seen evidence of this in Chapter 5 in which the duality of roles when consuming (underpinned as they are by a gendered reason/emotion dualism) were clearly articulated as part of the 'normal' division of labour between heterosexual couples. In many cases, it seemed, the 'rational' consuming role projected by the groom was perceived by the bride to be a necessary control or 'check' on her own self-recognized propensity for emotion- and desire-driven consumption. This enabled the corresponding 'emotional' and 'rational' consuming roles of the couple to become viewed as both constitutive of and productive to the successful construction of the wedding, rather than being an unresolveable source of conflict. Then, in Chapter 6, we saw how brides used consumption as a means not just of controlling their own emotion, but as a means of negotiating, or passing back and forth, control over the wedding between themselves and their grooms. This functioned to periodically reinforce the interdependence of the couple, or, more precisely, the constitutive harmony between supposedly masculine and feminine orientations towards consuming.

The implications of this are clear – the relationship between reason and emotion in consumption, as elsewhere, is not simply oppositional or even that tensionful, but one in which the 'marriage' between them is both constituted and consummated in more or less happy, harmonious ways, and in the case of the wedding, becomes productive to the successful construction of the 'big day'. The outcome of this conclusion, returning to Campbell and ongoing debates surrounding consumption, is that equating the emotional components of the consumption experience with imaginative hedonism and the rational (de)control of affect, results in a somewhat partial account of what is a far more complex process – one which incorporates, quite literally, a more full-bodied and socially embedded, non-dualistic understanding of emotions both in rationality and consumption alike.

If Campbell's Romantic ethic thesis results in a somewhat partial account of emotions and a less than full-bodied approach to consumption, then the 'desire-acquisition-use-disillusionment-renewed desire' cycle upon which it rests is equally open to criticism, particularly with respect to the disillusionment part of the equation. Whilst disillusionment may indeed be an important if not characteristic feature of consumption, other responses are nonetheless possible, thereby countering the largely 'anti-climactic' experience at the point of actual consumption, where consumers' attempts to realize their fantasies and desires in this or that commodity are more or less doomed to failure.

On the contrary, though, whilst this research attests to the fact that wedding consumption throughout all stages is highly reflexive and mentalistic in nature, it has equally shown that consumers themselves realize that disappointment is part of the usual cycle of consumption and have become sophisticated enough as trained consumers to plan how to evade it or negotiate around it in this important and supposedly unrepeatable case. Certainly, such heightened consumer reflexivity and advanced consumer sophistication can in part be credited to the various modes of learning how to be a successful wedding consumer provided by the industry. This is not meant to imply that contemporary brides and grooms are manipulated to such an extent that they revel in the pleasures of their own successfully constructed fantasy and are thus insensitive to the 'loss' of the wedding which follows. It is, however, to suggest a somewhat more complex picture of 'mixed possibilities', however fleeting, in which disillusionment is not the only response to the realization of desire in actual patterns of consumption, nor perhaps the guaranteed kick-start to the renewal of desire in this or that product, or the rationally (de)controlled pleasures with which they are imaginatively imbued.

Contemporary consumer culture: an integrated analysis

However, wedding consumption tells us much more about contemporary consumer culture and the motivations of contemporary consumers over and above those 'romantic' dimensions already outlined. This research has contributed to a clearer understanding of the continuously changing consumer environment, shedding light on the processes and relations of contemporary consumers in a relatively new context and providing insight into how new consumer cultures are produced and promoted. In the introduction to this book, I toured through other themes and issues that have guided consumption studies – identifying dominant perspectives as 'Veblenesque', 'manipulationist', 'postmodern', 'social relations' and 'feminist'. I am now, in this conclusion, able to offer a series of reflections in this respect.

Our starting point here is the significance of the Veblenesque perspective as an explanation of wedding consumption. On the whole, the couples in my study did not consume to emulate their 'betters' in the traditional class-based sense. Yet, having said this, we might assume that since more lavish weddings are now available to 'ordinary' consumers, not just the upper classes, the decision to have a particular 'wedding experience' could serve to communicate a relatively high level of disposable income. It was more often the case, however, that, guided by the wedding industry, some couples (either directly or indirectly) wished to imitate the precedents for wedding styles and fashions set by 'classy' celebrities, in turn displaying and communicating their own status as sophisticated, discriminating wedding consumers.

Turning more centrally to issues of consumer manipulation, given the linkage between a form of conspicuous consumption and the portrayal of certain weddings deemed worthy of emulation, we have seen how the wedding industry commodifies the big day and its central actors in imitation of the traditional romantic wedding fantasy. Rather than turning away from the new commercial world of weddings, though, the sampled couples (the brides much more than the grooms) repeatedly commit themselves to it in a series of encounters with differing fractions of the wedding industry – most notably, bridal magazines and face-to-face dealings with specific wedding professionals. Even if the resulting consuming 'needs' are recognized as 'false' or constructed in nature, they can still be incorporated into the wedding fantasy as extra factors to long for and desire. It is in this sense, as theorists of Romantic consumption argue, that some consumers become implicated in their own manipulation, a manipulation which, through further fuelling the imagination, itself produces pleasure.

Taking a postmodernist approach to wedding consumption, it could be argued that through their wedding choices brides and grooms are active and reflexive composers of their own identities, as well as their new joint identity as a married couple. Hence it is the stylistic, symbolic nature of consumption that serves as an important, emblematic marker of identity (or simulator of a particular ambience like 'romanticism'), rather than the material qualities or economic value of commodities *per se*. For example, as Chapter 5 discussed, the construction of a perfected wedding fantasy and the stylistic coherence this necessitates were highly significant in the motivations of wedding consumers. Yet we might well wonder how wedding consumption can open up new worlds of experience for some couples, releasing fantasy and the imagination in an act of self-fashioning, whilst remaining somewhat artificial for others.

The key to understanding this lies in the relative social importance of consumption to each wedding consumer. As I suggested in the book's introduction, what I take to be the 'social relations' perspective on consumption allows us to study how consumption is structured through our social (encompassing our interpersonal and romantic) relationships or context as well as through socio-cultural understandings of what, in this case, wedding consumption is for. My continued emphasis on the 'social relations' of consumption has, moreover, brought out the economic dimensions of wedding decisions which coexist alongside, and interact with, stylistic choices. Wedding consumption in this new era of highly commercialized weddings, as we have seen, is centred on notions of free or unlimited choice in the marketplace – in other words, it is deemed justifiable to consume whatever it takes to construct and live out each bride's own particular wedding fantasy. In 'real life', the wedding industry's rhetoric is one influence on brides and grooms who regard themselves as being able to have the event they want, an event appropriate and relevant to them, and expressive of their current personal or social situation should they so desire (or alternatively, to escape somewhat from mundane reality into a Cinderella-like romantic fantasy). In short, wedding consumption provides an avenue for couples to think through and enact what the whole occasion means to them. Set in the context of theories of the so-called postmodern lifecourse (Featherstone and Hepworth, 1991) – one where marked, age-specific identities or role transitions are collapsed into a more flexible and fluid form, spliced together with notions of the 'consumable' life – it seems that the wedding consumption of brides and grooms in this study is more traditionally put to use to differentiate and legitimate marriage as a (chosen) stage of the lifecourse.

Finally, drawing things to a close, but simultaneously raising additional points for future discussion, we return to the issue of gender and the illumination that a feminist perspective brings to wedding consumption and its gendered dynamics. Taking a positive stance, it could be suggested that wedding consumption offers certain advantages and opportunities to women as the primary consumers of the occasion, whilst subordinating male consumers to them in the process. Although wedding consumption is unquestionably assumed to be 'women's work', an extension of their domestic role, it nevertheless appears to be 'work' willingly and happily undertaken by most brides (which, worryingly, from a feminist perspective, remains unquestioned). Indeed, the wedding experience would not take place without some consumption of a sort. It is, moreover, a 'work', often simultaneously pleasurable and frustrating, which temporarily confers the bride with a particular identity that she experiences as powerful – that of a consumer with agency, knowledge and discriminating taste, combined with an active and authorial presence over the organization of the event. Moreover, the contemporary, commercial wedding (as shaped by the wedding industry) demands and in turn celebrates the typical 'feminine' disposition of the female consumer, one thought to be centred on emotion, expressiveness, imagination, heterosexuality and an overall propensity to 'romanticism' and fantasy.

It is at this point, however, given the direction of the above argument, that, analysing the situation from a feminist perspective, we may begin to question and critique the construction of male and female subjectivity in the wedding experience and expose the power held by superbrides as illusory. This book indeed has argued that 'reason' and 'emotion' are harnessed during wedding consumption, unifying the couples' consuming roles as complementary, interdependent and productive. Yet whilst this evidence may signify a progressive and more sophisticated way of viewing emotion and rationality in consumption (as elsewhere), it appears, at one and the same time, somewhat regressive in its stereotypical representation of the genders and their interpersonal negotiations. As we have seen, consuming for a wedding, however much playful pleasure the construction and performance of the bridal identity may afford, in no sense signifies either the creative escape from, or ironic imitation of, the binds of fixed gender scripts. The behaviour and experience of both genders throughout the wedding experience are in fact highly circumscribed as stereotypically masculine or feminine, with little or no room for manoeuvre or resistance – patterns of behaviour that may well extend into and structure married life. We are also left in little doubt that, despite their apparent dominance over wedding consumption matters, the majority of women remain objectified and manipulated within the new commercial world of weddings, regardless or not of whether this is fully realized or deemed pleasurable.

Yet, whilst traditional gender divisions are exaggerated during much wedding consumption, they are also periodically diminished. Although the conventional gendered relationship between reason and emotion is maintained in the wedding build-up and on the day itself, after the wedding gender difference recedes somewhat from view. Instead, couples come together in presenting a particular view of themselves as wedding consumers which disguises earlier differences between them. In Chapter 6, for example, we saw the important function wedding consumption played in its aftermath, in terms of the active and rational construction of new discursive strategies by brides and grooms to emphasize the ongoing significance of their past consuming behaviour. In particular, couples were found to articulate themselves as newlyweds primarily in terms of a joint decision making and consuming unit. This effectively equalized the division of labour and disparate consuming roles that prevailed in the pre-wedding preparations, paving the way for a harmonious entry into married life. The question remains, however, how long will it all last?

Appendix A: A Summary of How the Research was Conducted

The interview research

The empirical research design of this study is a qualitatively oriented one. There are several ways that my use of the Romantic ethic thesis as a theoretical framework had an impact on the design of the interview research. In order to engage with Campbell's theory I needed to conduct interviews both before and after the wedding. First, I needed to understand if, when and how brides and grooms began to imaginatively anticipate their big day. Did they only begin to get a mental picture of their wedding day after important consumption decisions had been made, during the making of such decisions or, indeed, were the consumption decisions themselves being used to fulfil a wedding fantasy that had been imagined since childhood? Was the wedding day itself longed for as a means of living out this ultimate fantasy or was its approach filled with apprehension and dread? Or did some brides and grooms have more prosaic, instrumental attitudes to the whole affair? Thus, I had to schedule the first interviews some months before the actual wedding, to coincide with when couples might be beginning to script and construct the big day, both in their imaginations and in 'real life'.

Second, following on from the first point, my interviews would need to be sufficiently informal, loosely structured and 'safe' occasions so that brides and grooms felt comfortable sharing with me the emotional aspects of their wedding experience. I wanted couples to feel able to relate to me their wedding fantasies and desires as well as any frustrations and fears that they might have. And third, since a key premise of Campbell's theory is that actual material consumption always turns out to be a disappointing, dissatisfying affair in comparison to the perfected fantasy individuals have constructed and mentally consumed, I needed to include a return visit to my couples some time after the wedding day to try to establish whether such a 'letdown' had occurred. In other words, how far was it felt that the wedding day lived up to, exceeded or fell short of their expectations, either individually or as a couple, and what were the reasons offered for this?

Having chosen to conduct semi-structured, qualitative interviews, further practical decisions then had to be made. In contrast to Mansfield and Collard's (1988) methodology, I reasoned that it would be more advantageous to interview brides and grooms together in order to witness interactions between the two respondents. I also anticipated that some grooms might be reluctant to engage in 'wedding talk' in a one-to-one situation with a female researcher and would feel more comfortable, and therefore somewhat more responsive, in an interview situation where they were likely to be naturally brought into the conversation by their fiancées. However, having said this, conducting interviews with the couple together is somewhat problematic in the sense that it makes it difficult for them to express negative feelings, such as disappointments associated with their wedding or anger at how much money was spent, and consequently may skew any conclusions in this area.

The research process began by disseminating awareness of the forthcoming study at a local level in the winter months of 1999. This was done by a range of methods, including advertising my research in several local newspapers and in the waiting room of a registry office, and visiting local vicars to gain access to their lists of couples due to marry. I also tried to contact couples who had announced their forthcoming big day on a British wedding web-site. In addition to these methods of generating a sample, a few couples were contacted through kinship and friendship networks. Whilst I recruited a reasonable sample of people having commercialized weddings, my research sample is not necessarily representative of all marrying couples and in no way claims to be representative of the cultural plurality of weddings in Britain today. Despite the multiple methods I used to generate a sample, I was unable to obtain any respondents from ethnic minorities. In an attempt to rectify this situation I tried a more direct method of reaching such couples. The decision was taken to write down the details of marrying couples who had Asian-sounding names from the public notice board in a local registry office. Although these notices are not displayed for this purpose, when I sought to gain permission from a registry office worker I was told that since marriage notices were public information no one could really prevent me from doing what I wanted with the information. Yet, despite such efforts, only white British-born people responded to my invitations to participate in the research.

My final sample of fifteen couples were all Midlands-based. Just two of the couples were not living together before they married (Anne and Geoff, Lucy and Stuart). Two of the couples (Dawn and William, Heather and Darren) asked to have a joint interview since the brides, who were close friends as well as work colleagues, had a significant amount of influence upon each other's wedding preparations. All interviews were completed between November 1999 and November 2000, with the pre-wedding interview scheduled approximately 3–6 months before the big day and the return interview occurring 2–3 months after it. It should be made clear that the names of respondents along with the place and venue names have been changed throughout this book for the sake of confidentiality.

With regards to the representativeness of the sample in relation to the wider population of marrying couples, drawing from the evidence of the tables below, a number of points can be made. First, as I expand upon in Chapter 3, the average expenditure on weddings in Britain has been estimated as approximately £14,000–15,000 (figures from *You and Your Wedding* magazine quoted in the *Guardian*, 18 May 2000). The average expenditure of my sample was somewhat below this estimate, averaging £8,000–9,000 with a range from £500 to £30,000. On a related note, the average active wedding planning and preparation time for the fifteen sampled couples was eleven months, with a range between six weeks and twenty-one months.

It is significant that all brides in the sample were marrying for the first time, although three grooms had previously been married. This is a bias in the sample perhaps due to first-time brides feeling more excited about the day and wanting to talk about it. The average age of the sampled brides was 30, ranging from 20 to 51 years. This figure stands slightly higher than the average age of first-time brides marrying in England and Wales in 1999 (age 27, *Social Trends 2001*). With regard to venue, one third of my sample were marrying in approved premises licensed by the 1994 Marriage Act. By 1999, as *Social Trends 2001* illustrates, almost a quarter of civil marriages in England and Wales occurred on such premises, constituting a significant alternative to the registry office or church.

Table 1: Variations in wedding details

Couple	Wedding venue	Wedding costs	Planning time
Patricia and Peter	Registry Office	£4,500	9 months
Anne and Geoff	Registry Office	£500	6 weeks
Tina and James	Stately Home	£4,000	8 months
Natalie and Daniel	Church	£4,000–5,000	11 months
Harriet and Alex	Church	£10,000–11,000 *	9 months
Lucy and Stuart	Abroad	£3,000–4,000	3–4 months
Hayley and Nick	Registry Office	£6,000	11 months
Jessica and Josh	Hotel	£13,000	18 months
Sarah and Robert	Stately Home	£30,000	21 months
Dawn and William	Hotel	£18,000	21 months
Heather and Darren	Abroad	£5,000–6,000	15 months
Kate and Matthew	Registry Office	£3,000	8 months
Beverley and Mark	Church	£7,000	5 months
Fiona and Leon	Church	£12,000 *	12 months
Louise and John	Hotel	£5,000	15 months

*Full wedding costs were shared equally by the bride's and groom's parents.

Table 2: Range of personal characteristics

Couple	Age (bride/groom)	Previous marriage	Children
Patricia and Peter	33/41	No	No
Anne and Geoff	51/46	No	No
Tina and James	33/34	Yes, groom	Yes, one. Bride's from previous relationship
Natalie and Daniel	29/33	No	Yes, two children together
Harriet and Alex	26/26	No	No
Lucy and Stuart	29/29	No	No
Hayley and Nick	25/26	No	No
Jessica and Josh	24/27	No	No
Sarah and Robert	32/46	No	No
Dawn and William	33/37	Yes, groom	No
Heather and Darren	26/26	No	No
Kate and Matthew	30/34	No	Yes, two children together
Beverley and Mark	43/48	Yes, groom	Yes, one together. Groom has two other children
Fiona and Leon	20/23	No	No
Louise and John	22/34	No	No

Table 3: Range of social characteristics

Couple	Occupation (bride/groom)	Highest education (bride/groom)*	Joint income (p.a.)
Patricia and Peter	P/T Bar staff/ Taxi driver	GCSE/GCSE	£17,000
Anne and Geoff	School inspector/ Scientist	MA/MSc	£45,000
Tina and James	Computer officer/ Financial adviser	MSc/A-level	£50,000
Natalie and Daniel	Student nurse/ Mechanic	GCSE/GCSE	£27,000
Harriet and Alex	Nurse/ Engineer	BSc/GCSE	£31,000
Lucy and Stuart	Dental nurse/ Electrician	GCSE/GCSE	£38,000
Hayley and Nick	Environmental officer/ Software engineer	BA/BA	£40,000
Jessica and Josh	Car designer/ Computer programmer	GCSE/BA	£57,000
Sarah and Robert	Medical secretary/ Electrician	GCSE/MA	'above average'
Dawn and William	Accountant/ Manufacturing manager	GCSE/GCSE	£68,000
Heather and Darren	Personnel officer/ Pattern-maker	BA/GCSE	£49,000
Kate and Matthew	Nurse/ Teacher	GCSE/BA	£38,000
Beverley and Mark	P/T office work/ Bank official	GCSE/GCSE	£39,000
Fiona and Leon	Office clerk/ Office clerk	GCSE/GCSE	£20,000
Louise and John	Office clerk/ Groundsman	GCSE/GCSE	£25,000

* Refers to formal school or university education rather than professional qualifications. 'O-level' recorded as GCSE.

One third of the respondents had a University degree (five brides, five grooms), locating my sample as above-average in relation to current national statistics (16 per cent of white men and 13 per cent of white women in Great Britain have a degree or equivalent: *Social Trends 2001*). The joint income of the couples in this study (excluding Robert and Sarah who did not give an exact figure) averaged £39,000, with a range of £17,000 to £68,000. According to the *New Earnings Survey 2000*, the gross average income of individuals in the West

Midlands stood at approximately £20,000 (in line with the national gross average of £21,000, with males averaging £24,000 and females £17,500; *New Earnings Survey 2000*). These statistics, along with a bias towards non-manual employment, therefore helps to define my sample as broadly lower middle class.

The first interview was designed to cover topics like the cost of the wedding, the length of planning time thought necessary for the big day, and who was paying for it, for example, which could then be used for comparative purposes, whilst remaining sufficiently open-ended and unstructured to reveal the more emotional and imaginative dimensions of their wedding, its preparation and its anticipation. The second interview, however, did include more direct questions about the nature and purpose of wedding consumption and the conceptualization of the event as 'romantic'. Each informant was also asked to provide information for a data sheet on socio-demographic variables at the outset of the interview. Moreover, as most interviews were conducted at the home of one or both of the informants (or, on one occasion, at the bride's parents' home), an assessment of an interviewee's socio-economic status could be supplemented by my own observations, in particular observations on the residential situation (such as the area the interviewee lived in, and the type of residence occupied).

Example of first interview question and prompts

1. Can you start by telling me what sort of wedding you are having, and why you decided to have that sort of wedding?
2. Can you tell me a little about the specific elements of your wedding, and how you came to choose these?

Prompts
Timing
Venue
Ceremony
Bridesmaids/Guests
Flowers/Music
Dress (and men's)
Reception
Wedding list
Honeymoon

3. What would you say your main priorities and considerations in your wedding preparations are?

Prompts
Cost
Family and friends
Your own wishes
A sense of want you don't want

4. Are there any types of wedding that you would never consider?

Prompts
Abroad/beach
Themed
Church
Registry Office
Why/Why not?

5. How long have you been planning your wedding?
6. Where, do you think, help, inspiration, ideas, about your wedding come from?

Prompts
Magazines
Exhibitions
Internet sites
Shops
Other

7. Could you estimate how much your wedding will cost in total (including the honeymoon). May I ask who is paying for the wedding as a whole, or specific parts of it? And why is that?
8. Who has responsibility for planning/organizing the wedding?
9. The prevailing attitude to wedding is that it is 'the bride's day'. Do you agree?
10. Could you describe some of the problems you have encountered in your wedding preparations?
11. What relationship do you feel that the wedding has to the marriage? Or, alternatively, what is your reason for having a wedding?
12. If you won a million pounds on the lottery last year would you have had a different type of wedding?
13. Looking ahead to the wedding day, do you think it will live up to your expectations? Do you have a strong sense in your imagination of what the day will be like? What do you think your emotional state will be as the day approaches?
14. Are there any other details/issues that you think need we need to cover?

Example of second interview question and prompts

1. Can you tell me a little about how you were both feeling the week before the wedding?

Prompts
Emotions
Stress
Nerves
Panic
Relaxed
Controlled

2. What about the day itself? What did it feel like to be a bride/groom?
3. Looking back, what is your single most vivid memory of the day?
4. Were there any problems, unforeseen circumstances or surprises on the day?
5. Did the day live up to, exceed or fall short of your expectations?
6. Overall, what did your wedding say about you?
7. In hindsight would you have done anything differently, either at the preparation stage or on the day itself?
8. If I asked you to give one piece of advice to a couple planning to marry soon, what would you say to them?
9. How did you feel after the wedding was over?
10. Do you feel married? Why/Why not?
11. Was your wedding romantic? What made it so? What factors affect how romantic a wedding is?
12. Do you think weddings have changed in the past few years? In what ways?
13. Did you see your role leading up the wedding as 'consumers'? What are your opinions on the wedding industry?
14. Was your wedding value for money?

Example of biographical checklist

	Bride	*Groom*
Name		
Date of birth		
Occupation		
Highest education		
Annual income		
Previous marriages		
Children		
Religion		
'Race'/Ethnicity		

Wedding date		
Venue		
Type of marriage service		
Approximate wedding attendance		
Bride taking husband's name		
Date of first interview		
Date of second interview		

I conducted all the interviews myself. Given the certain amount of apprehension that accompanies participation in any sort of interview, the face-to-face conversations I had with brides and grooms succeeded in being fairly informal and relaxed. This atmosphere was aided by the fact that most interviews took place in the living room of either the bride's or the groom's home, or more typically, the house they shared together. Each interview was tape-recorded and transcribed verbatim, within several days where possible. I also made note of any non-verbal communication that may have been missed in the later audio transcription. Brides, especially, seemed to relish having the opportunity to talk to somebody who genuinely wanted to hear about their wedding plans, expressing disappointment that their close family and friends and, increasingly, their grooms, had grown tired of hearing about it. Certainly, I feel that access to the more intimate emotional and imaginative aspects of their wedding was premised upon the female-to-female rapport established between the brides and myself, an experience long documented by feminist researchers (see Ribbens and Edwards, 1998). Furthermore, given my status as an academic researcher, I was assumed to have prior knowledge of most aspects of the wedding occasion including everything from current bridal fashions to the legal aspects of marriage and was sometimes asked for my opinion or advice on a particular problem that had emerged.

The interview seemed to provide an occasion for each couple to assess how much progress had been made so far in their own wedding preparations. Often, brides brought their wedding folders with them to the interview. These contained important wedding information and receipts as well as lists of things still left to organize. In this respect, I often became a primary witness to the decision-making processes of the couple as they negotiated impending or existing problems together and used my presence as an objective 'third party' who was qualified to evaluate their proposed solutions. Robert and Sarah, in this respect, responding to my query about how they might justify such high wedding costs, directly asked for my opinion on the matter before proceeding to calculate their remaining expenditure:

Sharon: Some people may ask whether £30,000 was justifiable just for one day. What would you tell them?

Sarah: I'd tell them to mind their own business! That's what I would say, because you can waste money on so many things in life. And again we've had the years together to be able to save up. What's your opinion?

Sharon: I think it is up to each individual couple.

Robert: It's relative, yes. It's a various thing.

Sharon: So, are you splitting the wedding costs between you?

Sarah: Yes we are. What's happening is with my dress my father's giving me £1,000, Robert's mother has given me £500, I've paid £1,700 on my dress so I've still got ... well I'm almost there, aren't I? The bridesmaids' dresses I've paid £1,000 on already, so I've only got £400 to go. They're £1,400 together. And all the other bits and bobs and whatever, the other £5,000 goes on that. But it's worth it. It really is.

In a similar vein, Jessica and Josh were keen for me to visually appreciate and confirm the beauty of their wedding venue and, for the bride, her intended wedding dress, and to sympathize with their disappointments:

Sharon: Have you had any major problems yet?

Josh: There's a major problem, yes.

Jessica: Oh, Sumner House. We had to go and sit down with the owner of Sumner House and complain. Let me just bring down my wedding file.

[*tape turned off for about two minutes whilst bride gets wedding file and groom gets refreshments – bride returns first, tape turned back on – bride secretly shows me a photo of a wedding dress in a magazine*]

That's a bit like what my wedding dress is going to be like, but don't mention it [*Jessica, pointing to a photo of a wedding dress*]

[*groom walks back in*]

Right let me show you the venue so you know what we're talking about. So it's a big conservatory down the side. It is actually huge in there. There's all lakes around it, it's actually set in acres and acres of land. But they are meant to be the premier wedding venue around here and that's their main business – weddings. They're very good. They have sixteen bedrooms and behind there [*points to photo*] they were going to build an additional eighty bedrooms, it's a new building. They said it was going to be complete in March.

Josh: Easter 2000, yes.

Jessica: And then we turned up and we found instead they're building it there [*points again to photo*] and it's got scaffolding up still and it's not going to be ready. And we were not informed about this at all.

Congratulation cards were sent to each of the couples on their wedding day offering my best wishes. It was hoped that these cards would also act as a reminder to brides and grooms that I would be contacting them again shortly to schedule our return interview. Several brides took the lead in re-establishing further contact with me after the wedding by informing me of any changes of address (both actual and e-mail) and saying how much they were looking forward to re-living the wedding day with me when I returned to speak to them.

The return interviews were even more of a social occasion. Brides and grooms seemed noticeably calmer and more reflective, looking back with hindsight over their many months of wedding preparation. Understandably, they were also more at ease with the interview procedure and remarked that they were not at all anxious about what I might ask them. As one bride put it:

Hayley: I'm a lot less nervous this time around than the first time.

Sharon: Oh, you didn't seem it.

Hayley: Yes, I don't know why, maybe it's the combination of having a tape recorder and just suddenly having to think of all the wedding things you're planning for at once, and you suddenly start to think 'Oh I haven't done that yet'. Now it's all over you can't possibly make us nervous about anything.

As expected, during a number of the return interviews, I was invited to watch the wedding video and to look at wedding photographs. A number of brides were eager to show me their dresses and other parts of their bridal outfit (shoes, tiara) so that I could appreciate them 'in real life'. In a similar situation to one documented by Mansfield and Collard (1988), one couple who had relocated since our first meeting took the opportunity in the return interview to show me the survey plans for the impending house renovations and to give me a guided tour of their new property. Moreover, in the return interview some couples were forthcoming with momentos of their wedding (photos, invitations) for me to keep and add to the all the wedding-related items I had collected in the course of my research.

The media and magazine research

As preparation for the interviews, I collected materials containing wedding imagery and advice that were available to the general public. I hoped that this process would make me a more informed, knowledgeable interviewer and enable me to understand and develop a genuine interest in the preoccupations and decisions of brides and grooms. I also intended to structure a proportion of my interviews around the themes that had emerged from the media's conceptualization of wedding consumption. My research at this stage, then, included finding and subscribing to useful Internet wedding sites, purchasing bridal magazines, collecting wedding-related articles in the local and national presses, attending wedding fayres and exhibitions, and visiting several newly licensed venues for civil marriages to get their promotional materials.

The most widespread and easily accessible form of such materials to me, and therefore I assumed to most brides, was certainly the bridal magazine. I located thirteen bridal magazines in total. Of the thirteen publications, seven can be described as 'non-specialist', offering a comprehensive spread of wedding-related topics (*Brides and Setting up Home, You and Your Wedding, Bride and Groom, Bliss for Brides, Wedding and Home, Wedding Day, For the Bride*) with the remaining six effectively constituting a subgenre within the bridal magazine market which specializes in just one or two aspects of the wedding (*Wedding Hair and Make-Up, Wedding Flowers, Wedding Cakes, Wedding Dresses, Wedding Venues and Services, Asian Weddings*). The magazines selected for the final analysis were: *Wedding and Home* (June/July 1999), *Bliss for Brides* (June/July 1999), *Bride and Groom* (Spring 1999), *Brides and Setting up Home* (May/June 1999), *You and Your Wedding* (May/June 1999), *Wedding Day* (millennium issue, November 1999).

In order to help me situate the bridal magazine in the broader genre of women's magazines and in relation to wedding imagery in the popular press, I also began an informal review of other relevant material. Primarily, these textual materials spilt into three categories – mainstream 'glossy' women's magazines, which I deemed to be pitched at a similar market segment as the bridal magazine (*Elle, She*), celebrity magazines, which frequently carried wedding exclusives (*Hello! OK! Now*) and local and national press articles on wedding-related subjects. Of particular interest were two high-profile weddings in 1999, both appearing to receive more coverage than others – celebrity couple Victoria Adams and David Beckham and the winners of Britain's first blind-date wedding competition, Carla Germaine and Greg Cordell. I wanted to know which weddings were important to national media and in looking at these two cases I concluded that such occasions had become newsworthy, spectacular media events primarily because of their highly commercial and public nature.

The bridal magazine analysis was designed as a combined semiological and content analysis to describe and deconstruct the prevalent themes and images that give meanings to the wedding and, especially, the bridal identity. My main objective here in doing so was two-fold – to expose the strategies employed by advertisers and journalists to mobilize positive consumer action in relation to the big day; and to discover what about the wedding was hidden, unspoken or denied.

Content analysis is a popular tool for media researchers and is based on the systematic identification and enumeration of overt, recurrent content features, usually generating quantitative data (Holsti, 1969). Content analysis can provide a useful basis for developing other types of media analysis (e.g. semiotic deconstruction, psychoanalytical approaches, audience research) which are concerned more with exploring unstated intentions and effects achieved by the content features of a particular media site, since what is intended and achieved may not be overtly stated and so might be missed out of a content analysis. The key advantage of content analysis is its effectiveness in measurement. Typically, researchers devise a checklist to guard against inaccuracies in data recording and to limit the influence of researcher expectations. In this respect, content analysis is often credited as being a fairly objective, value-free, reliable and consistent method for media researchers. After calculating that my sample of six British bridal magazines totalled 1,194 pages (including front and back covers) I felt that my study would need to begin with some form of content analysis before developing into a more in-depth, qualitative method.

Content analysis is therefore a useful first step but, as Leiss *et al.* (1990) state, by breaking down written or visual material into discrete categories for data collection, the meaning of an article or advertisement and its connection to the ideological thrust of the magazine as a whole are lost. Furthermore, the construction of a checklist is in itself an 'active' process and is rarely in practice completely free from bias, as researchers may operationalize certain concepts whilst downplaying or even omitting others. Problems are also likely to occur at the data collection stage if there is little flexibility for recording content features that do not seem to 'fit' into the pre-devised categories. As Leiss *et al.* (1990, p. 218) summarize, 'content analysis can do little more than "unpack" the surface meaning of an ad in a rather obvious way'. However, if only for this purpose, the content analysis method proves to be a valuable tool for media researchers.

Semiotic analysis is a deconstructive method used and applied to texts by media researchers. It is most often used in the study of advertisements to analyse the entanglement of the product with the implicit and explicit meanings (en)coded in it. Semiology is based on the study of a system of 'signs'. Commodities, people and other 'material vehicles' (Leiss *et al.*, 1990, p. 200) signify, connote or stand for more elaborate social discourses. Advertisements, for example, are regarded as discursive sites (en)coded with both deliberate, connotative meanings as well as more subtle, multiple denotative meanings. These codes or signs are then actively shaped and given meaning by their audience. These meanings appear natural and commonsensical to the reader, although the anticipated subtext of an advertisement is constructed and manipulated by media and market forces (McCracken, 1993). The more complex advertisement requires its audience to 'perform semiotic work' (McCracken 1993, p. 80), requiring them, in other words, to attach or transfer meaning from other referents, including those not present in the text, in order to understand it.

Certainly, the semiotic method has its weaknesses. Classic examples of the semiotic analysis of advertisements (Goffman, 1979; and Williamson, 1993) can be critiqued for their failure to provide easily generalizable findings. Semiology can be a highly selective method with researchers using idiosyncratic and there-fore unrepresentative advertisements to support their arguments – that is to say, the reading of a specific advertisement cannot be extended and applied to others. Developing this critique, Leiss *et al.* (1990) state that reliance upon the interpretative skills of a single analyst, the lack of quantifiable results and an inability to check the consistency of findings all hinder the exclusive use of semiological analysis in media research.

After reviewing the benefits and pitfalls of each approach it seemed appropri-ate to my research intentions to combine the most useful elements of both research tools, first observing and cataloguing content patterns and characteris-tics before beginning to unravel the discourses, signs and referents drawn upon in the construction and consumption of cultural material – a 'middle-range methodology', as Leiss *et al.* (1990, p. 225) term it, since it fuses both quantitat-ive and qualitative elements into its design.

Appendix B: Couple Profiles and Wedding Details

Couple 1

Patricia, 33, and Peter, 41, married in summer 1999 at a South Midlands registry office and held their reception at a marina clubhouse. They initially wanted to marry in their former local parish church, but were refused permission to do so because they no longer lived in that village. Patricia worked part-time in a restaurant and Peter was a taxi driver. They had a combined annual income of £17,000. Neither had been married before and neither had children. Patricia and Peter expected 45 guests at their wedding and estimated that their big day would cost £4,500 in total. There was no evening function at the wedding and the day was over by 5 pm. Patricia and Peter spent two weeks on honeymoon in Majorca. For them, the wedding represented total commitment to one another forever – 'the final icing on the cake', as the bride put it. They concluded that their consumption was enough to make the day feel like it was special, without being overpowering.

Couple 2

Anne, 51, and Geoff, 46, married in winter 1999 at a registry office in Warwickshire and held their reception at a hotel. Through their hobby, the couple had a wide variety of friends nationwide and decided to keep their wedding secret because of the politics and expense of constructing the guest list. At the post-wedding interview, though, I was told that by sheer coincidence a family friend spied the public announcement of their wedding on the wall of the registry office and leaked the information to others. Anne was a schools inspector and Geoff a scientist. They had a combined annual income of £45,000. Neither had been married before and neither had children. Anne and Geoff expected fourteen guests at their wedding and estimated that their wedding would cost about £500 in total. Anne's parents paid for the newlyweds to spend a weekend together in a quiet Gloustershire village and the couple planned to have something more 'honeymoonish' the following year.

Couple 3

Tina, 33, and James, 34, married in spring 2000 at a stately home in the West Midlands. They held a reception for 50 guests at the same venue and then relocated to a local pub to hold an evening disco for up to 100 guests. Tina was as a computer officer and James was a financial adviser. Tina had a young daughter by a previous partner, but had not been married before, whilst James had been married before but had no children. They had a combined annual income of £50,000. Tina and James estimated that their wedding would cost £4,000 in total and went to France for their honeymoon. The couple wanted a vegetarian wedding but were worried that some people would 'make a fuss' and so opted for two menus. The couple felt that the wedding had sealed their relationship and made it stronger.

Couple 4

Natalie, 29, and Daniel, 33, married in spring 2000 at a Methodist church near Coventry and held their reception at a clubhouse. Natalie was a student nurse and Daniel worked as a mechanic. The bride's grandfather used to be a Methodist minister and this exerted a significant influence on their choice of venue. Natalie also commented that she wanted bridesmaids and pageboys and that she felt it inappropriate to have these in a registry office ceremony. The couple had a combined annual income of £27,000 and had two young children together. Natalie spoke about how the wedding was for the children as well, and worried that questions might be asked about why she had a different surname from her children's when they started school. Natalie and Daniel expected 115 guests at their wedding and estimated that their wedding cost between £4,000 and £5,000. The couple had a short honeymoon break in the South of England, leaving their children with relatives.

Couple 5

Harriet, 26, and Alex, 26, married in summer 2000 at a Church of England church in the West Midlands which was visible from their home, and held their reception and an evening event at a local country house. Whilst the bride described herself as not particularly religious she had always wanted to 'walk down the aisle and do the traditional wedding'. Harriet was a nurse and Alex an engineer. They had a combined annual income of £31,000. Neither had been married before, neither had children and they had been dating for seven years prior to their decision to marry. Harriet and Alex expected between 50 and 100 guests at their wedding and up to 200 guests for the evening event. They estimated that their wedding cost between £10,000 and £11,000 and honeymooned in Mauritius. Alex was requested by his bride to leave the first interview for several minutes so she could relate to me secret details about her dress.

Couple 6

Lucy, 29, and Stuart, 29, married in winter 2000 in Barbados and held a reception at a ballroom in the West Midlands when they returned back home. The wedding ceremony took place in a pagoda in the grounds of the hotel where they were staying. Neither the bride nor groom felt they could cope with a traditional English wedding, citing reasons such as its formality, its costs and its solemnity. Alternatively, marrying abroad was described as living out a fantasy. They did not invite any guests to attend the ceremony but expected about 100 people to attend the reception. Lucy was a dental nurse and Stuart was an electrician. They had a combined annual income of £38,000. Neither had been married before and neither had children. They had been engaged for seven years but had never cohabited. Lucy and Stuart estimated that their wedding cost between £3,000 and £4,000.

Couple 7

Hayley, 25, and Nick, 26, married in summer 2000 at a registry office and held their reception at a pub. Hayley was an environmental officer and Nicholas was a software engineer. They had a combined annual income of £40,000. Neither had been married before and neither had children. They chose to marry at a venue in Devon as the groom's large family were based there. The local council had acquired a mansion house to use as a registry office and so the couple commented that this venue was extremely more picturesque than the average 'pebble-dashed' council premises. Hayley and Nick expected 30 guests at their wedding and estimated that their big day cost £6,000 in total. They chose a lakes and mountains honeymoon in Italy.

Couple 8

Jessica, 24, and Josh, 27, married in summer 2000 at a hotel in Warwickshire and held a reception at the same place. The bride described the venue as an old-fashioned manor with a huge Victorian conservatory, lakes and peacocks. Jessica was a car designer and Josh worked as a computer programmer. They had a combined annual income of £57,000. Neither had been married before and neither had children. Jessica and Josh expected 85 guests at their wedding and up to 180 guests later in the day. The major point of tension in their wedding preparations (although the couple were in full agreement on the matter) seemed to be their decision to ban children from the ceremony and reception. This was for financial reasons and for the 'pandemonium' that might ensue. Jessica and Josh estimated their wedding costs at £13,000 in total.

Couple 9

Sarah, 32, and Robert, 46, married in summer 2000 at a Worcestershire stately home owned by the National Trust and held a reception at the same place. Their wedding was traditional – top hat and tails for the groom, a traditional dress for the bride, horse and carriage, a formal reception in a marquee on the lawns of the home, fireworks in the evening, a string quartet and a disco. Sarah was as a medical secretary and Robert was an electrician. They described their annual income as 'above average'. Neither had been married before and neither had children. Sarah and Robert expected 75 guests at their wedding and up to 110 guests later in the day. They estimated that their wedding cost £30,000 in total. The couple had a two-centre honeymoon beginning in Monte Carlo and ending in Venice.

Couple 10

Dawn, 33, and William, 37, married in autumn 2000 at a hotel in Somerset. The bride wanted to marry abroad but the groom did not, so they compromised and married in a hotel in this country which was far enough from their home to provide an element of 'going away'. They were recent lottery winners and held a wedding weekend for 40 guests. The couple seemed in agreement that the least important thing in their wedding weekend was the actual ceremony and that they were far more interested in the nice meals, everybody having a 'good laugh' and seeing all the people they liked together for several days. Dawn was a senior accountant and William was a manufacturing manager. They had a combined annual income of £68,000. Dawn had not been married before but William had. Neither had children. They estimated that their wedding cost £18,000 in total.

Couple 11

Heather, 26, and Darren, 26, married in winter 2001 in Sri Lanka and had a reception in the West Midlands when they returned back home. Eighteen family members and friends went to Sri Lanka with them. The couple had a calypso band playing at the wedding and left the ceremony riding elephants. The bride remarked that her parents' separation made it awkward with regards to inviting them to a traditional wedding, and that played a major part in the decision to marry abroad. Heather was a personnel officer and Darren was a pattern maker. They had a combined annual income of £49,000. Neither had been married before and neither had children. They estimated that their wedding cost between £5,000 and £6,000 in total.

Couple 12

Kate, 30, and Matthew, 34, married in summer 2000 at a registry office in Warwickshire and held their reception at a sports pavilion. Kate was a nurse, Matthew was a teacher, and they had two young children together, one of which was born just weeks before the wedding. The couple had a combined annual income of £38,000. Kate and Matthew expected 40 guests at their wedding and over 60 guests for the evening event. They estimated that their wedding cost £3,000 in total. The couple had been together for eight years and, given their two children, mortgage (and cat!), regarded the wedding as a day to celebrate their continuing commitment to each other.

Couple 13

Beverley, 43, and Mark, 48, married in summer 2000 at a Methodist church in the West Midlands and held their reception at a hotel. The bride made a particular comment about their local pastor being a sincere woman, someone who would make them feel comfortable on their wedding day. The couple had a midweek wedding because of the pressure on reception venues during the summer of the millennium year. Beverley worked part-time for the local authority and Mark worked in a bank. They had a combined annual income of £39,000. Beverley had not been married before, but Mark had. Mark had two children from his previous marriage and had a young child with Beverley. They expected about 100 guests at their wedding and gave estimated costs at £7,000.

Couple 14

Fiona, 20, and Leon, 23, married in summer 2000 at a St John the Baptist church in Derbyshire after being engaged for three years. They held their reception at a hotel. The church was not selected for its religious significance but because it was 'old, traditional and nice' and could accommodate a large number of guests. Fiona and Leon both worked as office clerks. The couple had a combined annual income of £20,000. Neither had been married before and neither had children. Fiona and Leon expected nearly 200 guests at their wedding and estimated that their wedding would cost £12,000 in total. The couple honeymooned in Greece – a gift from the bride's brothers.

Couple 15

Louise, 22, and John, 34, married in autumn 2000 at a hotel in Derbyshire. Although Louise had tried several times to arrange a wedding in her local church, she received no response. Alternatively, the couple chose a local hotel because of the service and value for money they offered. Louise was an office clerk and John was a groundsman. They had a combined annual income of £25,000. Neither had been married before and neither had children. Louise and John expected 50 guests at their wedding and up to 150 guests later in the day. They gave estimated wedding costs at £5,000 in total. The couple honeymooned in Portugal for a week.

Notes

Chapter 1

1 Quotation extracted from the House of Commons Hansard Debates for 15 July 1994. See http://www. parliament.the-stationary-office99394/ cmhansrd/1994-07-15/Debate-5.htlm.
2 Gérard (1974, p. 260), for instance, lists the most common themes Romanticism has been attacked for, including its sentimentality, escapism and deification of the self.
3 Marriages in approved premises continue to be popular, with more than one in four of civil marriages (and one in six of all marriages) solemnized in this manner in 2000. Moreover, in the millennium year, the number of marriages increased for the first time in eight years from 263,515 in 1999 to 267,961 in 2000, a rise of almost 2 per cent. There are currently just over 2,000 approved premises in England and Wales, the most numerous being hotels, followed by sports and leisure venues and then stately homes. Haskey's 1998 and 2002 reports contain fuller information about the impact of the 1994 Marriage Act.
4 As Pahl (1989, p. 21) documents, The Married Women's Property Act of 1882 gave married women the same rights over property as men and unmarried women.
5 Pahl (1989, pp. 67–77) identifies three other systems of money management, these are: 1) the *wife management* or the *whole wage system* whereby wives are primarily responsible for managing finances and expenditure; 2) the *allowance system* in which wives are given responsibility over a set amount of money to cover household expenditure, while the rest of the money remains in the control of husbands and they pay for other items; and 3) the *independent management system* whereby both partners have an income, nether has access to all the household funds, and the principle of separate control over income and separate responsibility for expenditure is maintained.
6 Critics, however, have suggested that Giddens pays far too little attention to the continuing practical and material impediments to the development of 'pure relationships'. See Jamieson (1999).
7 See the House of Commons Hansard Debates for 15 July 1994 at http://www. parliament.the-stationary-office99394/cmhansrd/1994-07-15/Debate-5.htlm.
8 It is unclear at this stage whether and to what extent any future modernization of marriage law will address the civil partnership rights of same-sex couples and unmarried couples of the opposite sex.
9 Approximately 64 per cent of couples cohabit before their first marriage according to *Population Trends*, autumn 2000.
10 Haskey's (1996) article, for example, shows that 28.8 per cent of marriages that started in 1978 had ended in divorce within 15 years. He goes on to

     predict that about 2 in 5 marriages starting in 1993/4 will eventually end in divorce.

11   Two-fifths of marriages in 1999 were remarriages for either or both partners according to *Social Trends* 2001.

12   Other factors that may contribute to the sense of marriage as an evolving social practise include the invention of 'National Marriage Week' and the dissemination of 250,000 free booklets, 'Married Life: A Rough Guide for Couples', part-funded by the British government.

Chapter 2

1   To be sure, in subsequent articles Campbell teases out the complex relations of Romanticism, emotion and consumption, stating emphatically along the way that he is definitely not concerned with 'romantic aspects of consumption' or with 'Romanticism as an ingredient in or accompaniment to consumer behaviour' (1996, pp. 99–100). Campbell goes on to clarify his intention of theorizing the 'distinctly modern' ingredient of consumerism – that is, the 'spirit' of autonomous hedonism – and not endorsing the Romantic ethic as an explanation of *all* consumer behaviour. 'I do not believe that "Romanticism" is a term that successfully characterizes either all aspects of consumption or all consumers' he adds (1996, p. 98). In fact, in another related paper, the historically and culturally bound requirements for modern, self-illusory hedonism are explicitly acknowledged: 'This kind of hedonism requires advanced psychic skills and is dependent on the development of literacy, privacy and the development of a modern conception of the self' (1992, p. 61).

     Campbell (1993) has also further developed the interesting idea of a 'character-action' approach to consumption, thus effectively safeguarding against other researchers universally and indiscriminately applying the Romantic ethic thesis to every aspect of consumer culture. He argues that individuals consciously strive to monitor and adjust their conduct in accordance with one of several possible 'character ideals' they subscribe to and will themselves to create. As Campbell's discussion of character-confirming conduct is historically contextualized, it limits itself to identifying the four most prevalent character types of the eighteenth century – the ideal of sensibility, the aristocratic ideal of character, the dandies and the Romantic ideal of character. Consumption is theorized as a strategy for conforming to the chosen ideal. It then follows that those committed to the Romantic character ideal (whether Romantic contemporaries or present-day consumers), with its primary emphasis upon imaginative creativity and self-expression, are most predisposed to self-illusory hedonism, and ultimately, to a particular type of consumption. Once again, the Romantic ideal of character is argued both to 'stimulate' and 'legitimate' the spirit of modern consumerism (Campbell, 1993, p. 54).

2   But also see Chapter 5 for a discussion of feminist critiques of heterosexual, romantic ideology.

3   I recognize, of course, that the very notion of authenticity is itself a contested issue. My use of the term in this context is simply to flag up the pos-

sibility of more or less spontaneous forms of emotional experience and expression, devoid of calculability or commercial manipulation.

4 For example, one of Brown's respondents, a 20-year-old female, describes the pleasures of shopping thus: 'Then like a vision from heaven I see it, hanging high on a rail. The glow from its warm colour engulfs me. I bound over to where the burnt orange suit is hanging and search like a madwoman for my size. Yes, it's here. Happy days, I want to shout out loud. I hug the suit close to me, like a child with a teddy that someone is trying to take away' (1998, p. 168).

5 Holbrook (1993, 1996) argues that Campbell overlooks key elements of the original Romantic tradition that may have come to play an equally significant part in the precedents set for the motivational drives of modern consumers. Campbell, for example, downplays the Romantic's preoccupation with the 'theme of return, of reunion, of reconciliation with the past, of coming home' (Holbrook, 1993, p. 153), and ignores other historical influences upon the construction of Romantic discourse, including 'aspects of the medieval revival', 'disillusionment over the French Revolution' and 'the Eastern influences associated with the so-called Oriental Renaissance' (Holbrook, 1996, p. 25).

Chapter 3

1 Although there are two studies based on American research: Bulcroft *et al.*'s (1997) analysis of the honeymoon narrative in popular press magazine articles, and Otnes and Scott's (1996) study of consumer rituals, which uses examples of advertisements containing wedding symbolism.

2 These figures are taken from *You and Your Wedding* magazine quoted in the *Guardian*, 18 May 2000. Moreover, as reported in the *Independent*, 11 February 2002, the Asian wedding industry in Britain which caters for 'love' marriages as well as 'arranged' marriages is estimated to be worth £300 million. It is not clear whether the value of this industry is taken into account in national figures. Similar information from across the Atlantic shows the US wedding industry to be worth approximately $32 billion, with an average spend of $19,000 on each occasion (Ingraham, 1999).

3 As promoted by *OK!* Issue 170, 16 July 1999, front cover.

4 Reported to be approximately £500,000 in the *Sunday Mirror*, 1 August 1999, p. 2.

5 As reported in the *Sunday Mirror*, 1 August 1999, p.12.

6 Taken from www.lasvegaswedding.com, accessed 31 May 2002. Other themed wedding packages on offer in Las Vegas include: Fairytale, Elvis, Star Trek, Rockabilly, Gangster, Camelot, Rock 'n' Roll, Intergalactic, Beach Party, Gothic, Egyptian, Western, 50s/60s Disco, Harley Davidson, Sports, Phantom of the Opera.

Chapter 4

1 Please refer to Tables 1–3 in Appendix A and the couple profiles in Appendix B for precise details about each bride and groom and their wedding.

2 The overall lack of religious belief amongst the brides and grooms that I interviewed must be noted. Only one bride, Natalie, whose grandfather used to be a minister, described herself as purposely having a church wedding in order to get married 'in the eyes of God'. 'But I mean, don't get me wrong, I don't go to church every week.' She went on to add, 'But I do believe in God, and it's probably no where near a major influence, but it is there. To get married for me is to do it in Church.' The typical response of couples who chose to marry in a church was to acknowledge that, because they did not really believe in God or attend church, their decision was somewhat hypocritical. As Fiona and Leon discussed:

Fiona: Well, there was no particular reason we chose a church, was there?
Leon: I think we chose the church really just because we liked the church itself. It was a nice church.
Fiona: Very nice church.
Leon: It's a local church.
Fiona: We needed a big church for the amount of guests. No real particular reason though.
Leon: The main thing we discussed was that we always liked the church. I mean there's a church around here and it's built like a pyramid, you know, a very modern thing, and I couldn't imagine getting married in something like that.
Sharon: Is the church you chose an old building?
Leon: Yeah, old stone, hundreds of years old.
Sharon: And would you say that was one of the main reasons you chose it?
Fiona: Its look, definitely, because neither of us are religious. We didn't particularly *want* a religious ceremony, but it's just the way it's turned out, hasn't it? Because neither of us are religious it's hypocritical really, but ...
Sharon: And what has been the reaction from the minister? Most ministers like you to make several visits to the church beforehand.
Leon: Yeah.
Fiona: He wanted us to go every Sunday. So far we've been three times! [laughs]
Leon: We turn up every now and again.
Fiona: He's all right really.
Sharon: So you don't feel at all that you need religious confirmation of the vows? Some people might say that they need the feeling of standing up in the presence of God to exchange their vows?
Fiona: No. It's saying it in front of your friends and family, not God, because we don't believe.

For discussions of the changing status of religion in society, see Berger (1990), Bruce (1996) and Davie (1994). Also see an (as yet) unpublished paper by John Walliss, an associate fellow in the Department of Sociology, University of Warwick, which explores the extent to which weddings have been secularized within contemporary Britain at both the societal/institutional (objective) and personal (subjective) levels.

3 An explicit example of such strategies can be found in the behaviour of 'ethical' consumers who may purposely boycott or 'buycott' (Friedman 1996) particular commodities or companies to protest against mass consumer culture and its social and environmental impact. See Shaw and Clarke (1998).

4 See Campbell (1997) for a discussion of 'feminine' and 'masculine' orientations to shopping.

5 The typical image or depiction of the Romantic consumer/hero is of someone with heightened creative, expressive and visionary powers, concerned with self-definition, autonomy and individuality, who inhabits a highly emotive and imaginative inner-world yet longs to realize his or her fantasies in the material realm. Although works from the Romantic period are littered with such (male) characters, the most famous and enduring is the Byronic hero, analysed at length by Thorslev (1962).

Chapter 5

1 We might also suppose that perfected wedding imagery in bridal magazines leads to a certain amount of disappointment in 'real-life' brides when used as a source of comparison. One bride commented to me that she considered bridal magazines to be 'idealistic', adding, 'they [the depicted brides] are ideals ... and all the girls who are getting married are about a size eight' (Natalie).

2 I refer readers to two key texts as a useful introduction to feminist literature on marriage. The first is Carole Pateman's (1988) *The Sexual Contract*, especially Chapter 6 'Feminism and the Marriage Contract' pp. 154–88. Also see Delphy and Leonard's (1992) *Familiar Exploitation: A New Analysis of Marriage in Contemporary Western Societies*.

3 Biological dimensions are also thought to be apparent in the processing of romantic and sexual information. As Walsh (1996, p. 229) states: 'From the data on brain hemisphericity we know that males have brains designed for processing visual information to a greater degree than women. We should not be surprised, then, if these two different but greatly overlapping methods of processing information affect the processing of romantic and sexual information.' Walsh goes on to argue that the male preference for visual pornography and the female preference for romantic novels are evidence of this biological distinction.

4 For example, Lord Byron, a spearhead figure in second-generation Romanticism, constructed his own poetic identity as 'masculine' in three main, interrelated ways: (i) the overt gender politics of the Byronic hero; (ii) attacks on the Lake Poets (Southey, Coleridge, Wordsworth) for their effeminacy and consequent compromising of the poetic role, and; (iii) his frequent belittling of the Bluestockings and other literary salon ladies.

5 See Duncombe and Marsden (1998) for more on 'emotion work'.

6 Gillis (1985) also found that females had a less romantic and a more practical view of marriage and makes an association between this finding and the forced dependency of women on men through socio-structural inequalities such as low wages and poor career prospects.

7   See Langford (1999, p. 29).
8   It is also highly likely that the recent popular television adaptation of *Pride and Prejudice* (1995) starring Colin Firth and Jennifer Ehle, equals the original text as a source of identification for couples in romantic relationships.
9   Commenting on the secondary wedding market in America, Ingraham (1999) discusses how toy manufacturers have produced a wide variety of wedding-related products, including Mattel's 'Bridal Barbies' and Revlon's 'Caboodles Wedding Playset'.

Chapter 6

1   See, for example, Keat *et al.*'s (1994) *The Authority of the Consumer* for discussions on 'consuming' in many spheres including health, education and religion.
2   The significance of cohabitation as a force for societal change, especially with regards to the construction of the couple, must not be underestimated. I therefore refer the reader to other sociological and demographic literature on the changing meaning of cohabitation. See, for example, Morgan (2000), Manting (1996), Haskey (1995), Prinz (1995), McRae (1993), Rindfuss and Vandenheuvel (1990).
3   Most couples typically replied that they had already bought everything they needed and felt the wedding list to be a largely redundant tradition. For example, Harriet told me that, 'The trouble is having a house already we don't really want much. We've got everything. We're going "erm, what can we have?"' In a similar vein John said, 'What we've decided is that ... with us having actually set up home for a couple of years it's like, you know, you've got enough towels and glass so what we'd preferably like is money because we want a new kitchen'.
4   That is, given the theoretical connection to original Romantic ideology – one of its central preoccupations being the misanthropic and often reckless assertions of an independent, autonomous male identity from perceived societal restrictions.

References

Abercrombie, N. 'Authority and Consumer Society', in R. Keat, N. Whiteley and N. Abercrombie (eds.) *The Authority of the Consumer* (London: Routledge, 1994), pp. 43–57.

Adams, C. J. *The Sexual Politics of Meat* (Cambridge: Polity Press, 1990).

Adorno, T. and Horkheimer, M. 'The Culture Industry: Enlightenment as Mass Deception', in J. Curran, M. Gurevitch and J. Woollacott (eds.) *Mass Communication and Society* (London: Edward Arnold, 1977), pp. 349–83.

Albrow, M. *Max Weber's Construction of Social Theory* (London: Macmillan, 1990).

Appleby, J. 'Consumption in Early Modern Social Thought', in J. Brewer and R. Porter (eds.) *Consumption and the World of Goods* (London: Routledge, 1993), pp. 162–73.

Babbes, G. S. and Malter, A. J. 'Embodied Cognition: Towards a More Realistic and Productive Model of Mental Representation', *Advances in Consumer Research*, 24 (1997) 39–40.

Bagnall, G. 'Consuming the Past', in S. Edgell, K. Hetherington and A. Warde (eds.) *Consumption Matters* (Oxford: Blackwell, 1996), pp. 227–47

Barbarlet, J. *Emotion, Social Theory and Social Structure* (Cambridge: Cambridge University Press, 1998).

Barry, J. and Melling, J. 'The Problem of Culture: An Introduction', in J. Melling and J. Barry (eds.) *Culture in History: Production, Consumption and Values in Historical Perspective* (Exeter: University of Exeter Press, 1992), pp. 3–27.

Baudrillard, J. *The Consumer Society* (London: Sage, 1998).

Bauman, Z. *Intimations of Postmodernity* (London: Routledge, 1992).

Beck, U. *Risk Society: Towards a New Modernity* (London: Sage, 1992).

Beck, U. and Beck-Gernsheim, E. *The Normal Chaos of Love* (trans. M. Ritter and J. Wiebel) (Cambridge: Polity Press, 1995).

Belk, R. W. 'In the Arms of the Overcoat: On Luxury, Romanticism and Desire', in S. Brown, A. M. Doherty and B. Clarke (eds.) *Romancing the Market* (London: Routledge, 1998), pp. 41–55.

Belk, R. W., Ger, G. and Askergaard, S. 'Consumer Desire in Three Cultures: Results from Projective Research', *Advances in Consumer Research*, 24 (1997) 24–27.

Belk, R. W., Wallendorf, M. and Sherry, J. F. 'The Sacred and the Profane in Consumer Behaviour: Theodicy on the Odyssey', *Journal of Consumer Research*, 16 (1989) 1–38.

Berger, P. L. *The Sacred Canopy: Elements of a Sociological Theory of Religion* (New York: Anchor Books, 1990).

Bliss for Brides, June/July 1999 London: InLine Publishing Ltd.

Bocock, R. *Consumption* (London: Routledge, 1993).

Boden, S. '"Superbrides": Wedding Consumer Culture and the Construction of Bridal Identity', in *Sociological Research Online*, 6 (1) (2001) <http://www.socresonline.org.uk/6/1/boden.html>.

Boden, S. and Williams, S. J. 'Consumption and Emotion: The *Romantic Ethic* Revisited', *Sociology*, 36 (3) (2002) 493–512.

Bordo, S. '"Material Girl": The Effacements of Postmodern Culture', in C. Scwichtenberg (ed.) *The Madonna Connection: Representational Politics, Subcultural Identities and Cultural Theory* (Boulder: Westview Press, 1993), pp. 265–90.

Bourdieu, P. *Distinction* (London: Routledge and Kegan Paul, 1984).

Bourdieu, P. *The Field of Cultural Production* (Cambridge: Polity Press, 1993).

Bowlby, R. 'Book Review – Colin Campbell's The Romantic Ethic and the Sprit of Modern Consumerism', *Sociology*, 22 (1) (1988) 137–8.

Braun, K. A. 'Postexperience Advertising Effects on Consumer Memory', *Journal of Consumer Research*, 25 (1999) 319–34.

Bride and Groom, Spring 1999, London: You and Your Wedding Publications Ltd.

Brides and Setting up Home, May/June 1999, London: Condé Nast Publications Ltd.

Brook, H. 'Stalemate: Rethinking the Politics of Marriage', *Feminist Theory*, 3 (1) (2002) 45–66.

Brooker, C. *The Neophiliacs* (London: Fontana/Collins, 1970).

Brown, S. 'What's Love got to do with it? : Sex, Shopping and Subjective Personal Introspection', in S. Brown, A. M. Doherty and B. Clarke (eds.) *Romancing the Market* (London: Routledge, 1998), pp. 137–71.

Brown, S. Doherty, A. M. and Clarke, B. 'Stoning the Romance: On Marketing's Mind-Forg'd Manacles', in S. Brown, A. M. Doherty and B. Clarke (eds.) *Romancing the Market* (London: Routledge, 1998), pp. 1–21.

Bruce, S. *Religion in the Modern World: From Cathedrals to Cults* (Oxford: Oxford University Press, 1996).

Bulcroft, K., Bulcroft, R., Smeins, L. and Cranage, M. 'The Social Construction of the North American Honeymoon, 1880–1995', *Journal of Family History*, 22 (4) (1997) 462–90.

Butler, J. *Gender Trouble: Feminism and the Subversion of Identity* (New York: Routledge, 1990).

Campbell, C. *The Romantic Ethic and the Spirit of Modern Consumerism* (Oxford: Blackwell, 1987).

Campbell, C. 'The Desire for the New', in R. Silverstone and E. Hirsch (eds.) *Consuming Technologies* (London: Routledge, 1992), pp. 48–64.

Campbell, C. 'Understanding Traditional and Modern Patterns of Consumption in Eighteenth-Century England', in J. Brewer and R. Porter (eds.) *Consumption and the World of Goods* (London: Routledge, 1993), pp. 40–57.

Campbell, C. 'The Sociology of Consumption', in D. Miller (ed.) *Acknowledging Consumption* (London: Routledge, 1995), pp. 96–119.

Campbell, C. 'Romanticism, Consumption and Introspection: Some Comments on Professor Holbrook's Paper', in R. W. Belk, N. Dholakia and A. Venkatesh (eds.) *Consumption and Marketing: Macro Dimensions* (Ohio: South-Western College, 1996), pp. 96–103.

Campbell, C. 'Shopping, Pleasure and the Sex War', in P. Falk and C. Campbell (eds.) *The Shopping Experience* (London: Sage, 1997), pp. 166–76.

Cancian, F. M. *Love in America: Gender and Self-Development* (Cambridge: Cambridge University Press, 1990).

Charsley, S. R. *Rites of Marrying: The Wedding Industry in Scotland* (Manchester: Manchester University Press, 1991).

Coffey, A. and Atkinson, P. *Making Sense of Qualitative Data* (London: Sage, 1996).

Corner, J. 'Editorial' in *Media, Culture and Society*, 16 (3) (1994) 371–4.

Corrigan, P. *The Sociology of Consumption* (London: Sage, 1997).

Costa, J. A. 'Introduction', in J. A. Costa (ed.) *Gender Issues and Consumer Behavior* (California: Sage, 1994), pp. 1–10.

Craib, I. 'Some Comments on the Sociology of the Emotions', *Sociology*, 29 (1) (1995) 151–8.

Craig, B. 'Interpreting the Historic Scene: The Power of Imagination on Creating a Sense of Historic Place', in D. L. Uzzell (ed.) *Heritage Interpretation: Volume 1 The Natural and Built Environment* (London: Belhaven Press, 1989), pp. 107–22.

Cranny-Francis, A. 'Feminist Romance', in A. Giddens, D. Held, D. Hubert, S. Loyal, D. Seymour and J. Thompson (eds.) *The Polity Reader in Cultural Theory* (Cambridge: Polity Press, 1994), pp. 191–9.

Cronin, A. M. 'Consumerism and Compulsory Individuality', in S. Ahmed, J. Kilby, C. Lury, M. Mcneil and B. Skeggs (eds.) *Transformations: Thinking Through Feminism* (London: Routledge, 2000), pp. 273–87.

Damasio, A. R. *Descartes' Error: Emotion, Reason and the Human Brain* (New York: Putnam, 1996).

Davie, G. *Religion in Britain since 1945: Believing without Belonging* (Oxford: Blackwell, 1994).

Delphy, C. and Leonard, D. *Familiar Exploitation: A New Analysis of Marriage in Contemporary Western Societies* (Cambridge: Polity Press, 1992).

Douglas, M. *In the Active Voice* (London: Routledge and Kegan Paul, 1982).

Duncombe, J. and Marsden, D. '"Stepford Wives" and "Hollow Men"? Doing Emotion Work, Doing Gender and "Authenticity" in Intimate Heterosexual Relationships', in G. Bendelow and S. J. Williams (eds.), *Emotions in Social Life: Critical Themes and Contemporary Issues* (London: Routledge, 1998), pp. 211–27.

Duncombe, J. and Marsden, D. 'Love and Intimacy: The Gender Division of Emotion and "Emotion Work"', *Sociology*, 27 (2) (1993) 221–41.

Dungey, J. 'Where Arts, Imagination and Environment Meet', in D. L. Uzzell (ed.) *Heritage Interpretation: Volume 1 The Natural and Built Environment* (London: Belhaven Press, 1989), pp. 229–31.

Edgell, S. and Hetherington, K. 'Introduction: Consumption Matters', in S. Edgell, K. Hetherington and A. Warde (eds.) *Consumption Matters* (Oxford: Blackwell, 1996), pp. 1–8.

Elias, N. *The Civilizing Process. Vol 1: The History of Manners* (Oxford: Basil Blackwell, 1978 [1939]).

Evans, M. '"Falling in Love with Love is Falling for Make Believe": Ideologies of Romance in Post-Enlightenment Culture', *Theory, Culture and Society*, 15 (3–4) (1998) 265–75.

Ewen, S. *Captains of Consciousness* (New York: McGraw-Hill, 1976).

Falk, P. *The Consuming Body* (London: Sage, 1994).

Falk, P. and Campbell, C. (eds.) *The Shopping Experience* (London: Sage, 1997).

Fay, E. A. *A Feminist Introduction to Romanticism* (Massachusetts: Blackwell, 1998).

Featherstone, M. 'The Body in Consumer Culture', *Theory, Culture and Society*, 1 (1982) 18–33.

Featherstone, M. *Consumer Culture and Postmodernism* (London: Sage, 1991).

Featherstone, M. and Hepworth, M. 'The Mask of Ageing and the Postmodern Lifecourse', in M. Featherstone, M. Hepworth and B. S. Turner (eds.) *The Body: Social Processes and Cultural Theory* (London: Sage, 1991), pp. 371–89.

Finch, J. and Summerfield, P. 'Social Reconstruction and the Emergence of Companionate Marriage, 1945–59', in D. Clark (ed.) *Marriage, Domestic Life and Social Change* (London: Routledge, 1991), pp. 7–32.

Fine, B. and Leopald, E. *The World of Consumption* (London: Routledge, 1993).

Firat, A. F. 'Gender and Consumption: Transcending the Feminine?', in J. A. Costa (ed.) *Gender Issues and Consumer Behavior* (California: Sage, 1994), pp. 205–28.

Fischer, E. and Gainer, B. 'Baby Showers: A Rite of Passage in Transition', *Advances in Consumer Research*, 20 (1993) 320–4.

Foucault, M. *Discipline and Punish* (London: Tavistock, 1977).

Fournier, S. and Guiry, M. 'An Emerald Green Jaguar, A House on Nantucket, and an African Safari: Wish Lists and Consumption Dreams in Materialist Society', *Advances in Consumer Research*, 20 (1993) 352–8.

Friedman, M. 'A Positive Approach to Organized Consumer Action: the "Buycott" as an Alternative to the Boycott', *Journal of Consumer Research*, 19 (1996) 439–51.

Furst, L. R. *Romanticism in Perspective* (London: Macmillan, 1972).

Gabel, T. G., Mansfield, P. and Westbrook, K. 'The Disposal of Consumers: An Exploratory Analysis of Death-Related Consumption', *Advances in Consumer Research*, 23 (1996) 361–7.

Gérard, A. 'On the Logic of Romanticism', in R. F. Gleckner and G. E. Enscoe (eds.) *Romanticism: Points of View* (Detroit: Wayne State University Press, 1974), pp. 258–68.

Giddens, A. *Modernity and Self-Identity* (Cambridge: Polity Press, 1991).

Giddens, A. *The Transformation of Intimacy: Sexuality, Love and Eroticism in Modern Societies* (Cambridge: Polity Press, 1992).

Gillis, J. R. *For Better, For Worse: British Marriages, 1600 to the Present* (Oxford: Oxford University Press, 1985).

Goffman, E. *Gender Advertisements* (London: Macmillan, 1979).

Goldstein-Gidoni, O. 'Packaged Weddings, Packaged Brides: The Japanese Ceremonial Occasions Industry', Unpublished PhD Thesis (University of London, 1993).

Gould, S., Houston, F. and Mundt, J. 'Failing to Try to Consume: A Reversal of the Usual Consumer Research Perspective', *Advances in Consumer Research*, 24 (1997) 211–16.

Gouldner, A. W. *For Sociology* (London: Allen Lane, 1973).

Gregan-Paxton, J. and John, D. R. 'The Emergence of Adaptive Decision Making in Children', *Journal of Consumer Research*, 24 (1997) 43–56.

Gronow, J. *The Sociology of Taste* (London: Routledge, 1997).

Haskey, J. 'Trends in Marriage and Cohabitation: The Decline in Marriage and the Changing Pattern of Living in Partnerships', *Population Trends*, 80 (1995) 5–15.

Haskey, J. 'The Proportion of Married Couples Who Divorce: Past Patterns and Current Prospects', *Population Trends*, 83 (1996) 25–36.

Haskey, J. 'Marriages in Approved Premises in England and Wales: The Impact of the 1994 Marriage Act', *Population Trends*, 93 (1998) 38–52.

Haskey, J. 'Marriages in Approved Premises and Register Offices in England and Wales: The Proportions of Couples Who Marry away from Home', *Population Trends*, 107 (2002) 35–50.

Hirschman, E. C. and Holbrook, M. B. 'Hedonic Consumption: Emerging Concepts, Methods and Propositions', *Journal of Marketing*, 46 (1982) 92–101.

Hobsbawm, E. 'Introduction: Inventing Traditions', in E. Hobsbawm and T. Ranger (eds.) *The Invention of Tradition* (Cambridge: Cambridge University Press, 1983), pp. 1–14.

Hobson, J. 'Non-occasion Greeting Cards and the Commodification of Personal Relationships', in M. Andrews and M. T. Talbot (eds.) *All the World and Her Husband: Women in Twentieth-Century Consumer Culture* (London: Cassell, 2000), pp. 239–52.

Hochschild, A. R. *The Managed Heart: The Commercialization of Human Feeling* (Berkeley, CA: University of California Press, 1983).

Hochschild, A. R. 'The Commercial Spirit of Intimate Life and the Abduction of Feminism: Signs from Women's Advice Books', *Theory, Culture and Society*, 11 (2) (1994) 1–24.

Hogg, M., Bruce, M. and Hill, A. 'Brand Recognition and Young Consumers', in *Advances in Consumer Research*, 26 (1999) 671–4.

Holbrook, M. B. 'Romanticism and Sentimentality in Consumer Behaviour: A Literary Approach to the Joys and Sorrows of Consumption', in M. B. Holbrook and E. C. Hirschman, *The Semiotics of Consumption: Interpreting Symbolic Consumer Behaviour in Popular Culture and Works of Art* (Berlin/New York: Mouton de Gruyter, 1993), pp. 151–228.

Holbrook, M. B. 'Romanticism, Introspection, and the Roots of Experiential Consumption: Morris the Epicurean', in R.W. Belk, N. Dholakia and A. Venkatesh (eds.) *Consumption and Marketing: Macro Dimensions* (Ohio: South-Western College, 1996), pp. 20–82.

Hollway, W. 'Gender Difference and the Production of Subjectivity', in J. Henriques, W. Hollway, C. Urwin, C. Venn and V. Walkerdine, *Changing the Subject* (London: Routledge, 1984), pp. 227–63.

Holsti, O. R. *Content Analysis for the Social Sciences and Humanities* (Reading, Mass.: Addison-Wesley, 1969).

House of Commons Hansard Debates for 15 July 1994. <http://www. parliament.the-stationary-office99394/cmhansrd/1994-07-15/Debate-5.htlm>.

Illouz, E. *Consuming the Romantic Utopia* (Berkeley and Los Angeles: University of California Press, 1997).

Ingraham, C. *White Weddings: Romancing Heterosexuality in Popular Culture* (New York: Routledge, 1999).

Izenberg, G. N. *Impossible Individuality: Romanticism, Revolution and the Origins of Modern Selfhood 1787–1802* (Princeton: Princeton University Press, 1992).

Jackson, S. and Scott, S. 'Gut Reactions to Matters of the Heart: Reflections on Rationality, Irrationality and Sexuality', *Sociological Review*, 45 (4) (1997) 551–75.

Jaggar, A. 'Love and Knowledge: Emotion in Feminist Epistemology', in S. Bordo and A. Jaggar (eds.) *Gender/Body/Knowledge: Feminist Reconstructions of Being and Knowing* (New Brunswick/London: Rutgers University Press, 1989), pp. 145–71.

Jaggar, E. 'Consumer Bodies', in P. Hancock, B. Hughes, E. Jaggar, K. Paterson, R. Russell, E. Tulle-Winton and M. Tyler, *The Body, Culture and Society* (Buckingham: Open University, 2000), pp. 45–63.

Jameson, F. 'Postmodernism and the Consumer Society', in H. Foster (ed.) *Postmodern Culture* (London: Pluto Press, 1985), pp. 111–25.

Jamieson, L. 'Intimacy Transformed? A Critical Look at the "Pure Relationship"', *Sociology*, 33 (3) (1999) 477–94.

Johnson, M. *The Body in the Mind: The Bodily Basis of Meaning, Imagination and Reason* (Chicago: University of Chicago Press, 1987).

Keat, R., Whiteley, N. and Abercrombie, N. (eds.) *The Authority of the Consumer* (London: Routledge, 1994).

Kim, Y-H. 'The Commodification of a Ritual Process: An Ethnography of the Wedding Industry in Las Vegas', Unpublished PhD Thesis (University of Southern California, 1996).

Kroeber, K. *Romantic Fantasy and Science Fiction* (New Haven: Yale University Press, 1988).

Kvale, S. *Interviews* (London: Sage, 1996).

Lakoff, G. *Women, Fire and Dangerous Things* (Chicago: University of Chicago Press, 1987).

Langford, W. *Revolutions of the Heart* (London: Routledge, 1999).

Larmore, C. *The Romantic Legacy* (New York: Columbia University Press, 1996).

Lash, S. and Urry, J. 'Postmodernist Sensibility', in A. Giddens, D. Held, D. Hubert, S. Loyal, D. Seymour and J. Thompson (eds.) *The Polity Reader in Cultural Theory* (Cambridge: Polity Press, 1994), pp. 134–40.

Le Bel, J. and Dubé, L. 'Understanding Pleasures: Sources, Experiences and Remembrances', *Advances in Consumer Research*, 25 (1998) 176–80.

Lee, M. J. *Consumer Culture Reborn* (London: Routledge, 1993).

Leiss, W., Kline, S. and Jhally, S. *Social Communication in Advertising* (Toronto: Methuen, 1990).

Leonard, D. *Sex and Generation* (London: Tavistock, 1980).

Light, A. '"Returning to Manderley": Romance Fiction, Female Sexuality and Class', *Feminist Review*, 16 (1984) 7–25.

Lockridge, L. S. *The Ethics of Romanticism* (Cambridge: Cambridge University Press, 1989).

Loeb, L. A. *Consuming Angels: Advertising and Victorian Women* (Oxford: Oxford University Press, 1994).

Lowrey, T. M. and Otnes, C. 'Construction of a Meaningful Wedding: Differences in the Priorities of Brides and Grooms', in J. A. Costa (ed.) *Gender Issues and Consumer Behaviour* (California: Sage, 1994), pp. 164–83.

Lupton, D. *The Emotional Self* (London: Sage, 1998).

Lury, C. *Consumer Culture* (Cambridge: Polity Press, 1996).

MacDonald, S. 'Count the Cost of the Big Day', *The Times*, 15 February 2001, p. 29.

Mansfield, P. and Collard, J. *The Beginning of the Rest of Your Life* (London: Macmillan, 1988).

Manting, D. 'The Changing Meaning of Cohabitation and Marriage', *European Sociological Review*, 12 (1) (1996) 53–65.

Marcuse, H. *One Dimensional Man* (London: Routledge and Kegan Paul, 1964).

McConnel, F. D. *The Spoken Seen: Film and the Romantic Imagination* (Baltimore: Johns Hopkins University Press, 1975).

McCracken, E. *Decoding Women's Magazines* (London: Macmillan, 1993).

McCracken, G. *Culture and Consumption* (Bloomington: Indiana University Press, 1990).

McRae, S. *Cohabiting Mothers* (London: Policy Studies Institute, 1993).

Mellor, A. (ed.) *Romanticism and Gender* (Bloomington: Indiana University Press, 1988).

Meštrovic, S. G. *Postemotional Society* (London: Sage, 1997).

Miller, D. (ed.) *Unwrapping Christmas* (Oxford: Clarendon Press, 1993).

Miller, D. 'Consumption as the Vanguard of History', in D. Miller (ed.) *Acknowledging Consumption* (London: Routledge, 1995), pp. 1–57.

Miller, D. 'Could Shopping Ever Really Matter', in P. Falk and C. Campbell (eds.) *The Shopping Experience* (London: Sage, 1997), pp. 31–55.

Miller, D. *A Theory of Shopping* (London: Blackwell, 1998).

Moeran, B. and Skov, L. 'Cinderella Christmas: Kitsch, Consumerism and Youth in Japan', in D. Miller (ed.) *Unwrapping Christmas* (Oxford: Clarendon, 1993), pp. 105–33.

Morgan, P. *Marriage-Lite: The Rise of Cohabitation and its Consequences* (London: Institute for the Study of Civil Society, 2000).

Nava, M. *Changing Cultures: Feminism, Youth and Consumer Culture* (London: Sage, 1992).

Nava, M. Blake, A. MacRury, I. Richards, B. (eds.) *Buy This Book: Studies in Advertising and Consumption* (London: Routledge, 1997).

Nenadic, S. 'Romanticism and the Urge to Consume in the First Half of the Nineteenth Century', in M. Berg and H. Clifford (eds.) *Consumers and Luxury: Consumer Culture in Europe 1650–1850* (Manchester: Manchester University Press, 1999), pp. 208–27.

New Earnings Survey (London: Office for National Statistics, 2000).

Newton Dunn, T. 'Posh and Becks Split the Church', *Sunday Mirror*, 1 August 1999, p. 12.

Nisbet, R. *Sociology as an Art Form* (New York: Oxford University Press, 1977).

O' Guinn, T. 'The Romantic Arbiter: A Comment on Holbrook', in R.W. Belk, N. Dholakia and A. Venkatesh (eds.) *Consumption and Marketing: Macro Dimensions* (Cincinnati, Ohio: South-Western College, 1996), pp. 83–6.

OK! Issue 170, 1999. London: Northern and Shell Plc.

Otnes, C. and Lowrey, T. M. ''Til Debt Do Us Part: The Selection and Meaning of Artifacts in the American Wedding', *Advances in Consumer Research*, 20 (1993) 325–9.

Otnes, C. Ruth, J. and Milbourne, C. C. 'The Pleasure and Pain of Being Close: Men's Mixed Feelings about Participation in Valentine's Day Gift Exchange', *Advances in Consumer Research*, 21 (1994) 159–64.

Otnes, C. and Scott, L. 'Something Old, Something New: Exploring the Interaction Between Ritual and Advertising', *Journal of Advertising*, 25 (1996) 33–50.

Otnes, C. Lowrey, T. and Shrum, L. 'Toward an Understanding of Consumer Ambivalence', *Journal of Consumer Research*, 24 (1997) 80–93.

Packard, V. *The Hidden Persuaders* (London: Longmans, 1957).

Pahl, J. *Money and Marriage* (Basingstoke: Macmillan, 1989).

Pateman, C. *The Sexual Contract* (Cambridge: Polity Press, 1988).

Pawlowicz, P. 'Reading Women: Text and Image in Eighteenth-Century England', in A. Bermingham and J. Brewer (eds.) *The Consumption of Culture: Image, Object, Text 1600–1800* (London: Routledge, 1995), pp. 42–53.

Population Trends (London: Office for National Statistics, autumn 2000).

Praz, M. *The Romantic Agony* (London: Fontana Books, 1962 [1933]).

Prinz, C. *Cohabiting , Married or Single: Portraying, Analyzing and Modeling New Living Arrangements in the Changing Societies of Europe* (Aldershot: Avebury, 1995).

Radner, H. *Shopping Around: Feminine Culture and the Pursuit of Pleasure* (London: Routledge, 1995).

Radway, J. A. *Reading the Romance* (Chapel Hill: University of North Carolina Press, 1984).

Ribbens, J. and Edwards, R. (eds.) *Feminist Dilemmas in Qualitative Research* (London: Sage, 1998).

Rich, A. 'Compulsory Heterosexuality and Lesbian Existence', in *Signs*, 5 (1980) 631–60.

Rindfuss, R. R. and Vandenheuvel, A. 'Cohabitation: A Precursor to Marriage or an Alternative to Being Single?' *Population and Development Review*, 16 (4) (1990) 703–26.

Ritzer, G. *The McDonaldization of Society: An Investigation into the Changing Character of Contemporary Social Life* (London: Sage, 1995).

Robins, K. 'Forces of Consumption: From the Symbolic to the Psychotic', *Media, Culture and Society*, 16 (3) (1994) 449–68.

Rook, D. W. 'The Ritual Dimension of Consumer Behaviour', *Journal of Consumer Research*, 12 (1985) 251–64.

Rose, H. *Love, Power and Knowledge: Towards a Feminist Transformation of the Sciences* (Cambridge: Polity Press, 1994).

Ross, M. B. 'Romantic Quest and Conquest: Troping Masculine Power in the Crises of Poetic Identity', in A. Mellor (ed.) *Romanticism and Gender* (Bloomington: Indiana University Press, 1988), pp. 26–51.

Ruth, J., Otnes, C. and Brunel, F. 'Gift Receipt and the Reformulation of Interpersonal Relationships', *Journal of Consumer Research*, 25 (1999) 385–402.

Schenk, H. G. *The Mind of the European Romantics* (London: Constable and Co. Ltd, 1966).

Schouten, J. 'Selves in Transition: Symbolic Consumption in Personal Rites of Passage and Identity Reconstruction', *Journal of Consumer Research*, 17 (1991) 412–25.

Schwichtenberg, C. (ed.) *The Madonna Connection: Representational Politics, Subcultural Identities and Cultural Theory* (Boulder: Westview Press, 1993).

Shaw, D. and Clarke, I. 'Belief Formation in Ethical Consumer Groups: An Exploratory Study', *Marketing Intelligence and Planning*, 17 (2) (1998) 109–19.

She, June 1999. Leicestershire: The National Magazine Company Ltd.

Shideler, M. M. *The Theology of Romantic Love* (New York: Harper and Brothers, 1962).

Silverman, D. 'The Impossible Dreams of Reformism and Romanticism', in J. Gubrium and D. Silverman (eds.) *The Politics of Field Research* (London: Sage, 1989), pp. 30–49.

Social Trends 31 (London: Office for National Statistics, 2001).

Spender, D. (ed.) *Weddings and Wives* (Victoria, Australia: Penguin Books, 1994).

Stern, B. and Holbrook, M. 'Gender and Genre in the Interpretation of Advertising Texts', in J. A. Costa (ed.) *Gender Issues and Consumer Behaviour* (California: Sage, 1994), pp. 11–41.

Stone, L. *The Family, Sex and Marriage in England 1500–1800* (London: Weidenfeld and Nicolson, 1977).

Strinati, D. 'Postmodernism and Popular Culture', in J. Storey (ed.) *Cultural Theory and Popular Culture* (Hemel Hempstead: Harvester Wheatsheaf, 1994), pp. 428–38.

Strong, P. and Dingwall, R. 'Romantics and Stoics', in J. Gubrium and D. Silverman (eds.) *The Politics of Field Research* (London: Sage, 1989), pp. 49–69.

Thorslev, P. L. *The Byronic Hero: Types and Prototypes* (Minneapolis: Minnesota University Press, 1962).

Tims, A. 'How to Survive Your Big Day', *Guardian*, 18 May 2000, p. 4.

Tomlinson, A. 'Introduction: Consumer Culture and the Aura of the Commodity', in A. Tomlinson (ed.) *Consumption, Identity and Style* (London: Routledge, 1991), pp. 1–40.

Tseëlon, E. *The Masque of Femininity* (London: Sage, 1995).

Turner, B. S. *The Body and Society* (Oxford: Blackwell, 1984).

Urry, J. *The Tourist Gaze* (London: Sage, 1991).

Urry, J. *Consuming Places* (London: Routledge, 1995).

Uusitalo, L. 'How to Study Imaginary Aspects of Consumption', in R. W. Belk, N. Dholakia and A. Venkatesh (eds.) *Consumption and Marketing: Macro Dimensions* (Cincinnati, Ohio: South-Western College, 1996), pp. 87–95.

Van Zoonen, L. *Feminist Media Studies* (London: Sage, 1994).

Vander Veen, S. 'The Consumption of Heroes and the Hero Hierarchy of Effects', *Advances in Consumer Research*, 21 (1994) 332–6.

Veblen, T. *The Theory of the Leisure Class: An Economic Study of Institutions* (London: George Allen and Unwin, 1925).

Veldman, M. *Fantasy, the Bomb and the Greening of Britain: Romantic Protest 1945–1980* (Cambridge: Cambridge University Press, 1994).

Walliss, J. '"Loved the Wedding, Invite Me to the Marriage": The Secularization of Weddings in Contemporary Britain' (unpublished paper).

Walsh, A. *The Science of Love: Understanding Love and its Effects on Mind and Body* (New York: Prometheus Books, 1996).

Warde, A. 'Notes on the Relationship between Production and Consumption', in R. Burrows and C. Marsh (eds.) *Consumption and Class* (Basingstoke: Macmillan, 1992), pp. 15–31.

Warde, A. 'Consumption, Identity-Formation, and Uncertainty', *Sociology*, 28 (4) (1994a) 877–98.

Warde, A. 'Consumers, Identity and Belonging: Reflections on Some Theses of Zygmunt Bauman', in R. Keat, N. Whiteley and N. Abercrombie (eds.) *The Authority of the Consumer* (London: Routledge, 1994b), pp. 58–74.

Warde, A. 'Afterword: The Future of the Sociology of Consumption', in S. Edgell, K. Hetherington and A. Warde (eds.) *Consumption Matters* (Oxford: Blackwell, 1996), pp. 302–12.

Weaver, M. 'A Marriage Made in Media Heaven', *Daily Telegraph*, 26 January 1999, p. 3.

Weber, M. *The Protestant Ethic and the Spirit of Capitalism*, (trans. T. Parsons) (London: Unwin University Books, 1974 [1930]).

Wedding and Home, June/July 1999. London: IPC South Bank Publishing Ltd.

Wedding Day, November 1999. London: Parkhill Publishing Ltd.

Werbner, P. *The Migration Process* (New York: Berg, 1990).

Williams, R. *Culture and Society 1780–1950* (London: Chatto and Windus, 1958).

Williams, R. *Keywords: A Vocabulary of Culture and Society* (London: Fontana/ Croom Helm, 1976).

Williams, S. J. *Emotion and Social Theory* (London: Sage, 2001).

Williams, S. J. and Bendelow, G. *The Lived Body: Sociological Themes, Embodied Issues* (London: Routledge, 1998).

Williamson, J. *Decoding Advertisements* (London: Marion Boyars, 1993).

Wilson, E. *Hidden Agendas: Theory, Politics and Experience in the Women's Movement* (London: Tavistock, 1986).

Winship, J. 'Sexuality for Sale', in S. Hall, D. Hobson, A. Lowe and P. Willis (eds.) *Culture, Media, Language* (London: Hutchinson, 1981), pp. 217–23.

Winship, J. *Inside Women's Magazines* (London: Pandora, 1987).

Winship, J. '"Options – For the Way to Live Now", or a Magazine for Superwoman', *Theory, Culture and Society*, 1 (3) (1993) 44–66.

Wolf, N. *The Beauty Myth* (London: Vintage, 1991).

Wolfe, A. 'Realism and Romanticism in Sociology', *Society*, 32 (2) (1995) 56–63.

Woodmansee, M. and Jaszi, P. (eds.) *The Construction of Authorship* (Durham, NC and London: Duke University Press, 1994).

Woods, J. 'Wedding? It's Pure Cabaret', *Daily Telegraph*, 26 February 2002, p. 17.

You and Your Wedding, May/June 1999. London: You and Your Wedding Publications Ltd.

Young, M. and Willmott, P. *The Symmetrical Family* (Harmondsworth: Penguin, 1975).

Index